Footpaths and Bridges

Footpaths & Bridges

Voices from the Native American Women Playwrights Archive

EDITED BY

Shirley A. Huston-Findley

AND Rebecca Howard

THE UNIVERSITY OF MICHIGAN PRESS

ANN ARBOR

To all of the authors who, as women and as Indians, have been silenced or overlooked, within a cultural landscape that strove to strip them of voice and agency, and to those who are willing to join in collaboration to end the silence.

And to Bill Wortman, who has given so much of his time and energy to keeping the archive alive.

All proceeds from the sale of this anthology go to the Native American Women Playwrights Archive in support of the continuation and development of the collection.

Copyright © by the University of Michigan 2008
All rights reserved
Published in the United States of America by
The University of Michigan Press
Manufactured in the United States of America
♾ Printed on acid-free paper

2011   2010   2009   2008   4   3   2   1

A CIP catalog record for this book is available from the British Library.

Library of Congress Cataloging-in-Publication Data

Footpaths and bridges : voices from the Native American Women
    Playwrights Archive / edited by Shirley Huston-Findley and Rebecca
    Howard.
        p.   cm.
    Includes bibliographical references and index.
    ISBN-13: 978-0-472-11613-3 (acid-free paper)
    ISBN-10: 0-472-11613-4 (acid-free paper)
        1. American drama—Indian authors.   2. Canadian drama—Indian
    authors.   3. American drama—Women authors.   4. Canadian drama—
    Women authors.   5. American drama—20th century.   6. Canadian drama—
    20th century.   7. Indians of North America—Drama.   8. Indigenous
    peoples—North America—Drama.   I. Huston-Findley, Shirley.
    II. Howard, Rebecca, 1957–

PS628.I53F66   2008
812'.54080897—dc22   2007031015

Contents

Preface

SHIRLEY A. HUSTON-FINDLEY

Footpaths and Bridges began with a desire to make available to the public a representative sampling of works by Native American playwrights, which are part of the larger collection housed in the Native American Women Playwrights Archive (NAWPA) at Miami University. While every story speaks the truth of the individual writer, certain characteristics emerge that reflect the collection as a whole, including a clear relationship between form and content, a direct influence of culture on structure, and the notion that art invites healing, a noticeable thread woven throughout many of the following stories. Equally telling are the subjects of preservation, resistance, selling out, revisiting the past, generational relationships, forgiving, and taking responsibility.

Following the wishes of many of the playwrights who participated in a roundtable discussion in 1999, this anthology does not intend to compartmentalize, interpret, or, in the words of JudyLee Oliva, "put a stamp on" the dramatic texts from a Western or Aristotelian perspective. Instead, the following introduces the works by drawing from the plays and the artists' own words as they speak about their creations.

Monique Mojica (Kuna/Rappahannock) provides an obvious entrance into the anthology through her piece *ETHNOSTRESS*, originally presented at a panel at the conference Women's Voices in Native American Theatre held at Miami University in 1997. A poignant yet entertaining lecture/performance piece, *ETHNOSTRESS*, also known as postcolonial traumatic stress disorder, is Mojica's intersection of performative art and resistance: resistance to assumed European-influenced traditions held up as the primary models on which all artistic and political creations must be built. For to accept that ideology is to ignore the potential tensions and intersections inherent in cross-cultural creativity.

An actor who tends to write on her feet, Mojica emerges out of the tradition of Spiderwoman Theatre, "a very organic process of having it come from the body, from the image, from the story, from the gesture . . . (Roundtable)" combined with a university education. In bridging those traditions, her lecture/performance piece confronts the reality of colonization and allows her a place for healing.

Dedicated to Cree culture, Jules Arita Koostachin (the Attawapiskat Band of the Cree) shares a story that reveals how an Inninu boy, Ottanafaycaso, and an Inuk girl, Nipisha, overcome their gender and traditional differences as cultural enemies to create "new souls" and a "new home" and a son, Asivak, "a legendary hunter and trapper." Presented here in both English and Cree, *Asivak's Creation Story* reminds us all of the beauty that may come when we embrace new ways of thinking and knowing.

An award-winning poet and short story writer, as well as a playwright, Marcie Rendon (White Earth Anishinabe) comments on generational differences and the power of healing and identity through her children's play *Bring the Children Home*. A parable woven together by spirits of good and bad, *Bring the Children Home* takes us on a journey with Youth, who can only find herself or himself when she or he breaks free of the pull toward Western society and draws on the knowledge gained from the elders, in particular Min-di-way, the crabby grandmother who goes to the forest to die after years of raising several children and serving as leader of her village. Perhaps Youth's dilemma is characterized best by Maigun (the wolf spirit), who tells us that "people now a-days turn their back on their own, attack the guy lives right next door—pow—bullet in the head cause the neighbor's barbecue smoke blowed inta their yard—world gone crazy." In this society of fear and dread, Youth emerges to bring Min-di-way back to life with the help of the strawberry plant, after which Youth (O-day-min-nug, meaning "heart berry") gains her or his identity and finds a place in the world.

Because Rendon often writes instinctually about two worlds, the physical as well as the spiritual, which she describes as "clearly Native," she struggles in having her works produced and/or understood by predominately white audiences. Therefore, her goal, as she sees it, "is to put the tools into the hands of the people" at a very grassroots level. Tired of explaining her creations based on her Native sensibilities, Rendon asks, "Why don't the white people work harder to get it and work harder to bring in Native performers and educate audiences?" (Roundtable) Certainly Rendon's request is neither new nor radical, and many of the playwrights represented here share the same curiosity.

Blended worlds of the spiritual and physical provide the background for our next piece as well, Marie Clements's (Métis) *The Girl Who Swam Forever*. Like the grandmother, Min-di-way in Marcie Rendon's work, Clements's Grandmother/Old One provides half of the generational link. Described by the playwright as, "a one-act play about a young Native girl who runs away from a residential school in the early sixties and falls into her true form, which reshapes time, her dreams, and her future," *The Girl Who Swam Forever* blends the worlds of young and old, Native and white (represented by images of the Catholic Church), and the beauty of the spiritual and the harshness of reality to create a touching story of familial love, destruction due to colonization, and rebirth as survival. Pregnant by a local white boy, Jim, the young girl, Forever, is transformed into a sturgeon, who "sometimes . . . will make itself available to the fisherman," while her brother, Brother Big Eyes, ascends as an owl, providing "spirit power" to "those that wish to take a sturgeon." Filmic in nature, relying heavily on the visual and the aural, *The Girl Who Swam Forever* borrows from the genesis story of the Katzie descendants on Pitt Lake and their relationship to the sturgeon and the owl.

Through the use of blended worlds (present and Dream Time, as well as physical and spiritual), Martha Kreipe de Montaño (Prairie Band Potawatomi) reminds us of the didactic power of theatre in her play *Harvest Ceremony: Beyond the Thanksgiving Myth*. Revised in 1997 with Jennifer Fell Hayes as an interactive performance piece requiring audience participation, *Harvest Ceremony* re-rights the European Thanksgiving myth by taking a teenager, Matt, on a journey led by Spirit from the Past. Stopping off in 1620, 1621, and 1637, Matt, from an intertribal family, discovers that the Thanksgiving celebration enjoyed by millions of European descendants each year serves as a day of mourning for Native people. As de Montaño writes in her introduction, "By witnessing the events from the past and seeing the people from the past as real people, Matt comes to understand why some Wampanoag fast on Thanksgiving." Through demythologizing the American holiday, traditional history, as it is typically told through classroom texts and passed on through the popular practice of turkey, yams and stuffing, is revisioned so that the truth can be passed from one generation to the next.

A creator of short stories, poetry, essays, and screenplays, Denise Mosley (Cherokee) admits that her play, *Letters*, "began, as perhaps all fiction does, based on a true incident." However, what is revealed through the written words of her three different writers reflects the longings and desires apparent in all of us at one time or another throughout our lives. Whether one focuses on the correspondence shared by pen pals Tonya and Tom (Tomasina), the diary entries to God of young Lisa Worthington, or Angel's "love" letter in a bottle floating downstream, the act of writing takes on significance beyond the mere written word and becomes a vehicle through which basic human desires are communicated and revealed. Prayerlike, the letters almost become characters themselves, serving as the medium through which Mosley weaves together the worlds of these three women in search of love.

Victoria Nalani Kneubuhl (Hawai'ian/Samoan) takes on the struggle of responsibility and cultural identity through her work *Ola Nä Iwi (The Bones Live)*. Born in Honolulu of Samoan, Hawai'ian, and Caucasian ancestry, Kneubuhl became the first playwright of part Hawai'ian descent to have her work presented at the Edinburgh Festival, in Washington, D.C., and at the Los Angeles Festival of the Arts. Many of her plays have been produced in Honolulu, primarily by the Kumu Kahua Theatre and the Honolulu Theatre for Youth.

Not surprisingly, Kneubuhl is a winner of the Keeper of the Past Award from the Hawai'i Heritage Center, which honored her for preserving and sharing Hawai'i's unique heritage through drama. *Ola Nä Iwi* is just one example of her many contributions. A beautifully written drama, *Ola Nä Iwi* weaves together historical figures and events with imaginary contemporary personas to shed light on the friction generated as Native traditions rub up against Christianity, science, and modern day development. As Kneubuhl articulates, "I needed to write this play to express my personal feelings about the human right for all those peoples to be buried with decency and respect in their native land and for those resting places to be forever sacred. It is still our individual committed action to do right for ourselves and our people that makes a difference."

Vera Manuel (Shuswap-Kootenai) is a playwright, poet, and cofounder of the Storyteller Theatre, a company consisting of talented native actors committed to healing and addressing issues of concern to Native people. The eldest sister in a family of four sisters and five brothers, Manuel is a 1988 graduate of the University of British Columbia. She worked for the National Native Association of Treatment Directors as a national trainer for alcohol and drug treatment programs in Canada. She is the principal research-writer for two counselor's training manuals.

In a newsletter published by the Wisconsin Winnebago Business Community, Vera Manuel tells us, "Because of my knowledge about multigenerational grief and healing I have determined that I should use all my gifts and understanding to attend to the healing of these wounds." Her play, *Strength of Indian Women,* does just that, illuminating the struggles of three generations of Indian women who gather to confront their pasts, heal, and celebrate the "coming of age" of the youngest member of their family. Set in a living room on a small British Columbia reserve, the elders prepare for thirteen-year-old Suzie's two-day fast by mending a dress made by her great-great-grandmother and worn by her grandmother, Sousette, when she, too, experienced her celebration of puberty. The mending goes beyond material items, however, as the elders confront their years in a Catholic residential school and the horrors they experienced at the hands of a priest and the nuns assigned as their instructors. In an attempt to heal their wounds, each of the elders reveals to Eva, Sousette's daughter and mother to Suzie, their terror of being sexually abused or whipped for trying to flee and the forced removal of their cultural identities at the hands of the Catholic Church.

Perhaps most intriguing, however, is the internal struggle between the women, each of whom has found her own way of coping with her history. For not only were these women abused but their individual treatment has caused them to either turn toward or against one another as a means of survival. While Sousette serves as the "peacemaker" of the foursome, we discover that her history with Eva involved abuse and a lack of physical love for her daughter. Obvious conflict also exists between the dark-skinned Lucy and the light-skinned Mariah due to the preferential treatment the latter receives at the residential school merely because of her pigmentation. Likewise, Agnes, the "ringleader" at the school, must overcome Lucy's ridicule for having turned toward alcohol and prostitution after escaping.

Ultimately, what we discover is that it truly is Manuel's strength as an Indian woman that forces all of us to acknowledge the atrocities of the past. As Eva reminds us, their chronicle of the past works not only to heal their own wounds but to ensure that their strengths will carry forward through each generation to follow. She says,

> When I hear your stories, I feel so lucky that you are one of the handful of girls who did survive. I can't imagine what my life would have been like without you. Even when you were not there, you taught me something. You taught me how to get through tough times, and how to survive. All of you went through so much. Someone should write about it. They should make a movie about how you survived. I feel proud sitting here among you. You're just like old warriors.

JudyLee Oliva (a descendent of the Chickasaw Tribe) came to playwriting through a traditional education in theatre: she earned an MFA in directing at the University of Oklahoma and a Ph.D. from Northwestern University in theatre and drama. She has won numerous awards for her plays, including an Agnes Nixon Playwriting Award for *See Jane Run*, Honorable Mention in *Writer's Digest* for *The Fire and the Rose*, Honorable Mention in the Alaska Native Play Competition for *Mark of the Feather*, and Honorable Mention in the Jane Chambers Play Competition for *On the Showroom Floor*. In addition, she has published two books on theatre and over thirty reviews and articles in *Theatre History Studies*, *Dramatic Theory and Criticism*, *Theatre and Religion*, and *Theatre Topics*.

Oliva admits, "[I]t took me a long time to figure out I could write about my background or lack of a background that I didn't know." As a result, she finds that, "What I'm having to do is break out of the strictures of what I was taught . . . but I realize there's just no way that the sounds and the words and the music that I hear can fit in that mold; it just doesn't fit, you know" (Roundtable). Despite, or perhaps because of, her struggle, Oliva creates vivid and moving works, as is evident in her play with music, *Te Ata*. Chosen as the first-place winner in the Five Civilized Tribes' Great American Indian Musical Play Contest in 2000, *Te Ata* shares the life, love, and struggles of Te Ata Fisher, a college graduate and performer of Chickasaw Indian legends intended to educate others about Native traditions and stories. Woven together like layers of memory, *Te Ata* chronicles the actress's life, capturing the poetry of her work, her love story with Dr. Clyde Fisher, and the challenges of transferring one's life from the red lands of Oklahoma to the world of New York City.

As the oldest feminist performance group in existence, Spiderwoman Theater (Kuna/Rappahannock) needs little introduction. Made up of sisters Muriel Miguel, Gloria Miguel, and Lisa Mayo, Spiderwoman Theater has existed since 1975 as a transgressive troupe dedicated to creating and staging political, social, and radical performance art. Its combination of dance, music, comedy, and drama provokes and educates, as is evident in the manuscript of *Winnetou's Snake Oil Show from Wigwam City.*

Throughout *Winnetou,* Spiderwoman Theater, along with cocreator Hortensia Colorado, confronts past and present through the Wild West show. The parody—the selling of Yataholey Snake Oil and audience participation in gunslinging tricks, as well as the transformation of a white man into an Indian through a series of rituals culminating in him holding a picture of an Indian man in front of his face—while poignant, provides comic relief while calling into question notions of authenticity, spirituality, and the ownership of cultural identity. The skillful juxtaposition of authentic video images of old powwows against the humorous yet artificial Snake Oil Show, as well as the weaving together of narrative, simultaneously awakens images of political correctness and Native stereotypes.

As is suggested in the description of the cast, each of the nineteen personas created on the stage emerge out of the four women, illustrating their personal struggles in coming to terms with the theft of their culture and questioning their own participation in "selling out" their heritage and identities. Yet the most powerful and telling message is captured in the closing lines of the text, where first Gloria and then the entire ensemble begin to take back and demand from their viewers some responsibility.

GLORIA: See me. I'm talking, loving, hating, drinking too much, creating, performing; my stories, my songs, my dances, my ideas. Now, I telling you, step back, move aside, sit down, hold your breath, save your own culture. Discover your own spirituality.
ALL: (*in chorus*) Now I telling you. Watch me. I'm alive. I'm not defeated. I begin. Now I telling you.

We wish to thank the members of the NAWPA Advisory Board for their support and assistance in the generation of this project; the Dean of Libraries at Miami University, Judith Session, for her continued support of the archive; and the Special Collections Staff of King Library, Miami University, for their hard work and dedication in ensuring that the NAWPA materials are accessible and well maintained.

Introduction

REBECCA HOWARD

The Native American Women Playwrights Archive (NAWPA) was conceived in 1996 as the result of a collaboration between a theatre graduate student and Dr. William Wortman, Humanities Librarian for Miami University in Oxford, Ohio. The student, whose ancestry was Cherokee and African American, was pursuing a research project concerning the work of Native women playwrights and was experiencing difficulty locating relevant resources. Dr. Wortman assisted the student in contacting a number of writers and performers, and the two began building a collection that would form the core of the NAWPA project.

The archive has seen considerable growth and change over the last 12 years, and continues to navigate the terrain of developing and promoting a collection that provides a "living archive" for writers who contribute work to the collection on an ongoing basis. The dynamic core of NAWPA continues to be the playwrights and their works, and the promotion, preservation, and attention that these works deserve in an atmosphere that is mindful of the complex issues surrounding such a collection. These issues become even more compelling considering the fact that the collection is housed and maintained in southwestern Ohio at an academic institution that is predominantly white yet takes its name from one of the indigenous groups that inhabited the area for centuries before the "United States" began to assert its sovereignty in the Northwest Territory following the American Revolution. It is also a region in which an organized, asserted Native presence has been reestablished in the last few decades after an absence of nearly 150 years. Being mindful of these issues while navigating this terrain involves identifying, constructing, and maintaining the critical connections that such an endeavor entails. These issues speak to the direction that the archive will take in the next several years, and requires the discussion, input, participation, and cooperation of many individuals within Native and non-Native communities.

The stated mission of the Archive is to

identify playwrights in North and South America, collect, preserve, and make their work more widely known, encourage performances and continued creativity, and help educate playwrights, theater companies, and audiences about Native American theater. Recognizing the difficulty all playwrights have publishing their work, we want NAWPA to play a positive role in the production of Native drama.

The archive was organized in three components to fulfill this mission. The first is the archive itself, which is located in the Special Collections department of Miami's King Library, which currently holds materials representing over sixty works by eighteen authors. These materials include manuscripts, as well as audio- and videocassettes of performances and lectures. The cornerstone of the archive is a significant collection of historical materials related to the ground-breaking work of the Spiderwoman Theater troupe, including numerous performance photos, posters and flyers going back more than two decades, and personal material from the Spiderwoman members, mostly reflecting the development and working process of the troupe, which was founded in 1975 by three sisters of Kuna and Rappahannock heritage: Lisa Mayo, Gloria Miguel and Muriel Miguel. Spiderwoman Theater is considered to be the longest-running women's performance group in existence. The sisters' work is grounded in feminist performance and emphasizes issues in the lives of Native women as they intersect with non-Native culture.

The second component is an online directory, located at http://staff.lib.muo hio.edu/nawpa, which provides an extremely accessible resource interface for individuals interested in learning more about works by Native women writers. The Web site includes listings of the works the archive holds for each author, a bibliography of additional publications by those authors and links to synopses of the works, a bibliography of works by writers who are not currently represented in the collection, an "Online Exhibit" of materials from the Spiderwoman collection, information concerning NAWPA conferences and other events of interest to Native writers, bibliographies of works by Native men playwrights, and links to related Internet sites. The site also allows users to request information and assistance by e-mail.

This "electronic archive" concept facilitates the management of and accessibility to information and resources, and provides an unprecedented opportunity to create a space where many voices that have traditionally existed "outside the canon" can gain access to public spheres of recognition and contact. Such technological venues also carry with them issues of representation and accessibility, issues that are changing constantly in their impact and shape. The participation of NAWPA in this rapidly shifting "global electronic village" (which is, of course, not truly global since not everyone around the world has, or wishes to have, access to the technology or information required to participate) is predicated on the desire to share information in the most responsible and effective ways possible while respecting the rights of the authors who have trusted their work to the archive. In conjunction with programming, this aspect is designed to ensure that these works are made visible beyond the library where they are housed.

The third component relates to programming. An inaugural conference, Women's Voices in Native American Theater, was held in February of 1997, accompanied by a performance of Spiderwoman's *Sun, Moon, and Feather.* A second conference in March of 1999 was titled Celebration of Native Women's Theater and included academic papers, performances, and a discussion of issues involving Native women's theater, including the production of the works by non-Native companies. Performances for this conference included another Spiderwoman piece, *Winnetou's Snake Oil Show from Wigwam City;* a performance by Shirley Cheechoo of her one-woman work, *Path with No Moccasins;* and a staged reading of Vera Manuel's *The Strength of Indian Women.* Since then, the archive has sponsored and/or facilitated staged readings of Diane Glancy's *Jump Kiss* and *The Woman Who Was a Red Deer Dressed for a Deer Dance,* Victoria Nalani Kneubuhl's *Ola Nā Iwi (The Bones Live),* and JudyLee Oliva's *Spirit Line.*

In examining the works in the archive, it is apparent that, within the diversity of the writers' experiences and styles, there are a number of similarities in the themes and structural choices the writers have made. The following discussion touches on the common thematic threads emerging from these works, examines some of the structural choices the writers have made, and considers the relationship of these threads and structures to dominant theatrical models. It is important to remember that the ideas discussed herein are ones that seem to recur in many of the scripts, but that these similarities are just that: similarities, not generalizations about the way Native women write. This collection does not presume to construct a paradigmatic model for Native women playwrights, for to do so would be inappropriate and insulting to the individuality of the writers involved. It is also important to note that the following discussion pertains to the entire NAWPA collection, not just the scripts included in this anthology (though space considerations make it impossible to mention all of the plays and authors currently represented in the archive). The quoted examples that follow are drawn from works that are not available (for reasons of length) within this published collection in order to give voice to a greater range of archive authors; works that are referenced but not directly quoted represent both archival works and some that are anthologized in this volume.

The first point of consideration is the common thematic threads that weave through the manuscripts included in the archive. Most of the scripts, not surprisingly, focus on women: their personal stories, their relationships with other women and their friends and families, and their cultural and personal identities as Native American women. Within this predominantly woman-centered focus, there appear to be four major common threads: (1) the tension between traditional ways and contemporary lifestyles, and the question of recognizing, defining, and claiming one's heritage; (2) an emphasis on intergenerational relationships; (3) the presentation and exploration of historical figures and traditional legends; and (4) the importance of anthropomorphized animals and embodied spirits.

The most common themes deal with the tension between traditional ways and contemporary lifestyles, and the question of recognizing, defining, and claiming one's heritage, as presented in plays such as *Mark of the Feather* by JudyLee Oliva. In this work, Mary and Elizabeth, cousins who are described as part white and part Chickasaw, have attended the Pottawatamie Pow Wow in Shawnee, Oklahoma. Elizabeth is gathering material for her thesis, entitled "20th Century Native American Spirituality—Cult or Culture," while Mary is searching for a deeper understanding of her heritage. Both women repeatedly use an "us-them" frame of reference. The tension inherent in their divergent views is conveyed in the following dialogue.

MARY: I'm claiming my heritage and you're denying yours.
ELIZABETH: Which is mostly white, isn't it?
MARY: I feel more red—at this moment.
ELIZABETH: You can't "feel" red or white. Not even you miss "I believe in miracles" woman.
MARY: You know, Elizabeth, you make fun of things you can't understand. I know how I felt when I heard those pow wow drums for the first time. I didn't breath [*sic*] . . . my heart stopped beating . . .
ELIZABETH: Get a stethoscope.

Elizabeth's cultural cynicism is directly at odds with Mary's desire to identify and explore what draws her to her Native blood. Her ensuing encounter with a man named Bird Runningdeer helps to guide and define her exploration, taking her farther away from her cousin's outlook.

Issues and questions involving the importance of heritage are often framed within the context of spirituality and religion specifically dealing with Native rituals and Christianity. For example, in the working draft of Marie Clements's *Urban Tattoo*, a collection of memory monologues, Rosemarie is sitting in a church, looking at the painted stars on the ceiling and saying:

Baby Jesus stars painted by an ancient French priest surrounded by Indians. This must have been his haven from us. His place to come when the brown faces engulfed him on the land. Here it was just him and his God and his painting hand and he controlled the stars here and the front door and the Good Indians could come and go as they liked as long as he was holding the door. I sneak in here when there aren't any good Indians around (or the good priest).

Much like Elizabeth in *Mark of the Feather*, Rosemarie seems to be commenting on the struggle between a culture's traditional spirituality and the appropriation, or overwhelming, of that spirituality by outsiders. The spiritual tension created by the development of blended belief systems becomes a central focus in these works.

The second common thread, the emphasis on intergenerational relationships, is exemplified by works such as Vera Manuel's *Strength of Indian Women*, in which four Kootenai elders prepare for the celebration feast and two-day fast that will mark the coming of age of Suzie, the granddaughter of Sousette, the elder who is considered the "peacemaker" of the group, and Diane Glancy's *Segwohi*, which foregrounds the conflict that can arise with the interaction between generational differences and cultural tension. Unlike Manuel's characters, Segwohi and his son, Peyto, are at odds over the passing on of ritual and belief. When Segwohi reminds his son that "We're here to obey the Spirit," Peyto replies that he is trying to make his own way while being pulled "one way and then another." He goes on to explain:

PEYTO: I don't hear the voices of the ancestors. I can't live what I don't see. I have to take part in the struggle I see before me. It's the real world, though it's only fragments of several worlds—and hopeless most of the time.
SEGWOHI: It's because you don't listen to the voices of the ancestors, Peyto. You can't hear them when you stay at the bar in town every night.
PEYTO: I have to have a guide who moves in *this* world—the one I see. You don't really hear me—

Other plays, such as *Bring the Children Home* by Marcie Rendon and *Emmalehua* by Victoria Nalani Kneubuhl, also focus on generational relationships and the passing on or reclaiming of rituals, practices, and languages that were lost or repressed for previous generations.

History and legend are present in nearly all of the authors' works in one way or another, with characters often making reference to the stories and beliefs with which they were surrounded as children. This continuous presence of the past is one of the most pervasive aspects of the writings in the archive, and it goes beyond a simple "thematic similarity," often creating an aesthetic atmosphere or tone rooted in a sense of timeless connection among past, present, and future. A number of plays present historical figures or events, including Martha Kreipe de Montaño's *Harvest Ceremony: Beyond the Thanksgiving Myth*, a depiction of the Thanksgiving story from the Wampanoag perspective; JudyLee Oliva's *Te Ata,* a biographical musical work that relates the story of Native performer Te Ata Fisher; and Victoria Nalani Kneubuhl's *Paniolo Spurs,* which offers a compelling portrait of Hawai'ian ranch life in the 1920s. Kneubuhl, in particular, has written numerous works presenting the history of Hawai'i's indigenous population in conflict with non-Native colonizers. Many are commissioned works, including *The Annexation Debate; Trial of a Queen: 1895 Military Tribunal; January 1893; Ka'iulani: A Cantata for Theatre;* and *The Conversion of Ka'ahumanu.* Retellings of Native legends appear in *Asivak's Creation Story,* by Jules Arita Koostachin, and *The Girl Who Swam Forever,* by Marie Clements.

The fourth thematic thread is the importance of anthropomorphized animals and animal and/or human spirits, who appear to assist or impede the lives of the human characters, as exemplified by Kneubuhl's *Ola Nā Iwi (The Bones Live).* Other works employ animal spirits that help move the story along or appear as major characters in their own right. For example, in *Your Dream Was Mine,* authors Shirley and Greta Cheechoo choose a somewhat mischievous woodpecker to accompany two sisters who have become lost after wandering from their wrecked car on the way to the wedding of their youngest sister. Appearing at first only peripherally, the woodpecker becomes a major player as the sisters continue their journey.

There are often multiple thematic threads woven into the same story, and operating at different textual levels, while other scripts do not employ any of these major themes as they address contemporary issues faced by women in all walks of life. Marie Clements's *Now Look What You Made Me Do,* for example, presents a graphic and compelling portrait of women struggling with domestic violence, while Denise Mosley's *Letters* tells the stories of several women and one adolescent girl through letters and diary entries.

In a structural sense, the similarity of these works is in their diverse challenges to (or negotiation with) traditional structural tenets such as linear narrative and binary conflict. Many of the works move back and forth through time, often employing a forward strategy that is episodic in nature and temporally fluid, a structure that is evocative of an oral tradition in which narrative events may progress in a manner that more closely resembles the ways in which memories actually occur in human experience. In addition, some of the plays tend to subvert the traditional dramatic framing of conflict as binary in nature and resolved through a predictably timed climax, and this subversion serves to highlight the intensity of internalized conflict and emotionally charged social interactions.

The consideration of the plays' structural elements depends on the lens through which a play is viewed. Monique Mojica observed that the dominant Aristotelian lens presumes that "there is a conflict between creating art and creating change. From an indigenous artist's perspective, this is a conflict fabricated from a foreign mind-set." A revised aesthetic in American theatre must spring from a perspective that views structural analysis through a different lens, one that encompasses a variety of experiences and traditions and sees them as complimentary, not conflictual and that respects the diversity of voices within our culture. We need to use a lens that redefines what is implied by "our culture," embracing the cultural richness of our society while still respecting the autonomy of the specific cultural influences that created the artist.

It is virtually impossible for any writer to develop her or his skills without being exposed to, and influenced by, the dominant literary canon. This does not mean that such exposure necessarily subverts that writer's perspective; on the contrary, that writer can, in turn, comment on and influence the fabric of the canon itself. Scholarly engagement with the canon over the last couple of decades has encompassed such terms as *margins, borderlands, fringes,* and *outsider,* language that is descriptively accurate but also could serve to perpetuate a psychology of exclusion. It is crucial to recognize and name the sources of oppressive and repressive sociocultural attitudes that serve to limit full participation in the dominant power structure for those individuals and groups who possess characteristics and attributes that mark them as "other." It may also be time to search for ways to subvert the psychology of exclusion by evolving beyond language that is, at its root, exclusionary and divisive. A more helpful vocabulary would recognize that the canon is informed, to varying degrees, by all participants who actively confront it and react to it with their contributions. The voices that are heard in the works of the NAWPA writers represent the potential for the construction of such a language.

Such a construction was begun at one of the events during the second NAWPA conference in March of 1999, an informal discussion with six of the playwrights whose works are represented in the archive: Diane Glancy, LeAnne Howe, Victoria Kneubuhl, Monique Mojica, JudyLee Oliva, and Marcie Rendon. The issues brought up in this discussion continued to resurface throughout the weekend and point to the complex intersections of, and bridges between, Native and non-Native perspectives, desires, goals, needs, emotions, and representations. The conversation that was begun at the conference also spoke to the differences and commonalities within and among Native communities and individuals and between writers who are creating from varying perspectives for varying reasons.

The primary thread that emerged from the discussion was the question of production and reception: who the authors feel they are writing for and whether or how a potential production is shaped by the author's desire to present her material to a specific audience for a specific purpose. Once again, the range of responses to this issue is quite varied and intensely personal.

Vera Manuel spoke passionately about her intense desire and need to write for a specific community. Her play, *Strength of Indian Women,* was, she explains, written to facilitate a healing process on both an individual and community level. She observed, "My whole life I've been really working closely with my people, with the struggles that I see my people going through, generational grief things that people are struggling with." She explained that after she wrote her first play, *Song of the Circle,* she "saw how powerful it was for healing, for people to be able to see their experiences, and what a powerful tool it was." Manuel expressed concern about how her plays are produced because, for her, the process of writing is "such a sacred experience that I am really concerned about where my words are going to end up, what's going to happen to them, because it was a sacred ceremony that brought them and they are connected to ancestors, to the ancestor's stories." She also noted that, even though she "always dreamed about writing a play . . . that's universal," she's aware that she is not willing to make accommodations that have been suggested to her as "necessary" if she is to get into "mainstream" theatre. She said, "I think of my audience, I think of my responsibility to my people . . . I think there's too many of our stories that need to be told as yet, that need to be written by us, from our experience. There's a lot to think about."

Other authors spoke of writing for a more universal audience. JudyLee Oliva remarked, "I have these big, huge visions of what I'd like to see onstage for all people, not just Native people, but I want my plays to speak to all people, so the reason why I'm writing right now is just to realize that vision onstage." Similarly, LeAnne Howe believes that, in the process of creating, "The question of audience is not important, it's about what I'm doing as an artist. What I'm doing with my community, who I call on to do it with; it's all got to be separate, you know?" Monique Mojica pointed out that, even though the question of audience "comes in somewhere down the road . . . in the process of creating, it doesn't come into it."

In seeing their work move from the initial creation of the text to a performance, most of the authors acknowledged that they had, at some point, encountered difficulties in the production or reception of their work. These difficulties seemed to center on the problem of people unable (or unwilling) to understand or "translate" a perspective that seemed clear to the individual doing the writing. Marcie Rendon described a children's play that she had written in which, at the end, the character of the grandmother "goes into the Spirit world." As it was directed, the grandmother simply died, causing many in the young audience to leave the theatre in tears. She realized that "it was one of those [experiences] where in my mind it was clear what I was thinking, and I thought it was clear on paper, but that's not how it got interpreted by the people who were reading it. And so one of the things I learned was, like when stuff is so internalized that you don't even think about it, that if I was going to put my stuff out there I had to think more clearly about how I was putting it out there or what needed to be explained. And then there's stuff that I refuse to explain." Even though authors of many genres struggle with interpretations of their work that are in conflict with their intent, some NAWPA authors felt that a common element in their work that has often been misunderstood by non-Native audiences, directors, and performers is the concept of a coexistent spiritual reality. Monique Mojica expressed her opinion that, "that characteristic, the awareness of more than one world, more than one reality, is something that is specific to Native women." Commenting on the broader issues of understanding and reception, Vera Manuel stated, "I feel like white people have to work harder to understand—why should we have to [keep] defining ourselves in the white context? Why don't they work harder to understand it . . . because it's not just our responsibility to de-colonize, it's also other people's responsibility."

The immediate impact of the weekend's discussions was the reaffirmation of the playwrights in structuring the direction of the archive. A subsequent meeting with the NAWPA Advisory Board in November of that same year (which included Marie Clements, LeAnne Howe, Monique Mojica, and JudyLee Oliva) confirmed the sentiment that the archive is important, unique, and necessary and work needs to continue in order to ensure that the collection gets the attention and respect that it deserves and will not become another example of Native works being relegated to a dusty box in an obscure corner of a museum (or library). Every aspect of the archive is continually scrutinized, reviewed, and revised as needed to reflect the vital nature of a collection that is such a cogent example of the vibrant (and sometimes contentious) intersection of the personal and the political. The Advisory Board has considered everything from the preservation and accessibility of the materials to the implications of the name.

The archive provides a compelling example of collaboration between Native and non-Native people who share a common interest in creating a space in which the voices of traditionally marginalized people can become an assumed, respected, and appreciated component of a larger cultural discourse. The archive will continue to be a dynamic and visible collection of works from a dynamic and diverse group of Native American, First Nation, and Pacific Islander women. Everyone involved in NAWPA has traveled a unique path in the world, and all of these paths have intersected within an organization that is a community where the voices of Native women playwrights are given visibility, respect, and the opportunity for dialogue as playwrights, women, and indigenous people. This anthology represents one step in that journey.

NAWPA Works Cited or Consulted

Brochure, Native American Women Playwrights Archive, 1996.
Cheechoo, Shirley, and Greta Cheechoo. *Your Dream Was Mine.* 1994.
Clements, Marie. *The Girl Who Swam Forever.* 1997.

Clements, Marie. *Now Look What You Made Me Do.* 1993.

Clements, Marie. *Urban Tattoo.* 1996.

de Montaño, Martha Kreipe. *Harvest Ceremony: Beyond the Thanksgiving Myth.* 1995.

Glancy, Diane. *Segwohi.*

Howe, LeAnne, with Roxy Gordon. *Big Pow Wow.*

Howe, LeAnne, with Roxy Gordon. *Indian Radio Days.*

Kneubuhl, Victoria Nalani. *Emmalehua.* 1995.

Kneubuhl, Victoria Nalani. *Ola Nā Iwi (The Bones Live).* 1994.

Kneubuhl, Victoria Nalani. *Paniolo Spurs.* 1994.

Koostachin, Jules Arita. *Asivak's Creation Story.* N.d.

Manuel, Vera. *Strength of Indian Women.* 1996.

Mojica, Monique. *ETHNOSTRESS.* 1997.

Mosley, Denise. *Letters.* 1996.

NAWPA Author's Roundtable. www.lib.muohio.edu/nawpa/roundtable.html.

Oliva, JudyLee. *The Fire and the Rose.* 1997.

Oliva, JudyLee. *Mark of the Feather.* 1997.

Oliva, JudyLee. *Te Ata.* 1996.

Rendon, Marcie. *Bring the Children Home.* 1996.

ETHNOSTRESS: Women's Voices in Native American Theatre

BY MONIQUE MOJICA

Originally presented at Miami University, Oxford, Ohio, 1997.

Good afternoon. I am here to talk to you about Post-Colonial Traumatic Stress
Disorder, also known as—

ETHNOSTRESS!!!!!!!

The first known incidence of this dis-order

this dis-ease, disease

was found on the shores of this continent, yes, this continent 500 and 5 years
ago,

and has now reached epidemic proportions.

Unbeknownst to you, you could be suffering from Post-Colonial Traumatic
Stress

Disorder.

Yes, *you* could be a victim of
ETHNOSTRESS!!!!!!!!!

1. Are the goals of Social Change and for artistic performance totally fused in
your work or are they in conflict in any way?

2. To what extent is the style of your work drawn from traditional modes and to
what extent is the creation of new styles generated for persuasive or political purposes?

3. If there is a fusion between an Indigenous perspective and a Western perspective does this create a conflict in your work?

I will begin by saying that I am tired of these questions that impose a dichotomy
rooted in Western European thought to Native artists' work and our existence.
Either/or. It is a way of thinking that presumes that there is a conflict between
creating art and creating change. From an Indigenous artist's perspective this is
a conflict fabricated from a foreign mind-set. It feels like splitting hairs to answer
questions that assume that we are compartmentalized into modules that never
intersect. Or that because as contemporary Native theatre artists who have
influences from many different sources that these sources must necessarily be in

conflict. Well, sometimes they are, sometimes they're not, but the "conflict" within the artistic work is in direct relation to the conflicts within the experiences of contemporary Native life. By this I don't mean to uphold the "caught between two worlds" popular romanticized victimization of the contemporary Native world, nor do I wish to present that experience as only one thing.

It is a different thing to grow up a Hopi in a desert culture than it is to grow up a Powhatan in the American South or on a Cree trapline in the North, or planting corn in the mountainous soil that nobody else wants if you are a Mayan in the Highlands of Chiapas, or if you come from several generations of urban Native peoples in the large cosmopolitan centres who have intermarried among nations. The experiences are many, the voices must be many. We are different and we are profoundly related, from our origin stories and the oral histories of the migrations of the people—we are relations. To what we share in our experiences of invasion, colonization and ongoing genocide, we are family. We are different and we are alike. More different than alike? Or more alike than different? Is the glass half full or half empty? Are you an Indian first or a woman first? What do you do with the non-Native part of your heredity when you identify yourself as a Native person? These questions are an exercise in reducing us into bite-size pieces that make us more palatable to Western tastes, more acceptable to the foreigner's mind-set. How many white artists are called upon to justify their influences? How many of them acknowledge or are even aware how they have been influenced by us? The truth is that after 500 years of forced "influence," of being denied the right to declare who we are, and learning how to deny it ourselves, we are greater than the sum of all our parts.

> If you are profoundly disoriented by flesh-colored band-aids,
>> you may be suffering from Post-Colonial Traumatic Stress Disorder.
> If you are allergic to milk, WHITE flour, WHITE sugar and alcohol,
>> you may be suffering from Post-Colonial Traumatic Stress Disorder.
> If you find yourself talking back to Walt Disney movies,
>> you may be suffering from Post-Colonial Traumatic Stress Disorder—or—
> ETHNOSTRESS!!!!!!!!!

There was a time when I was studying that I bought into the fabricated conflict between politics and art. In the early seventies, there were Native occupations and resistance movements all over the U.S. and Canada and I had a hard time justifying spending 6–8 hours a day training in a studio when there was a war going on outside. I left my studies and joined the Movement. I eventually returned to dance and theatre, recognizing that those are my strengths. Not an acceptable choice of a major among Native American studies students at the time. Twenty-five years ago there was no Native voice in theatre much less a

Native women's voice. (The Native American Theater Ensemble was formed in 1972 and Spiderwoman Theatre in 1975. To my knowledge, these were the first in North America.) Then, being a Native actor meant taking on another culture's perspective, all of the time. When I was in university that is exactly what I did whether I was studying Shakespeare, Chekhov, Tennessee Williams or performing with the Black Theater Workshop. While I will agree that it is part of the actor's craft to do the research that immerses the actor totally in the character's world, I longed for the opportunity to bring with me into my character studies the truth of my experience, the rhythms of my stories, the belief systems of my cultures. This is not to say that I devalue the study of any of the aforementioned playwrights. It is when the "dead white men" are held up as the "only" and the "best," "the fathers of all theatre," and the exclusivity of the canons of "great literature" is used to uphold a status quo that includes the continued annihilation of the world's Indigenous people that I begin to have a bit of a problem.

> If you only bring the television in from the garage so that you may watch the
>   riots in L.A.—or Toronto,
> you may be suffering from Post-Colonial Traumatic Stress Disorder, P.C.T.S.D.
> If you lose your identity and your nationality every time you put your foot
>   across a border,
>   "You must produce a tribal band card stating your blood quantum."
>   Mmmongrel-g-r—ped-i-gree-gree-g-r-r-r
>   "In addition, you must produce a letter, on tribal letterhead, declaring
>   your
>   family lineage at least as far back as your grandparents proving that you
>   are
>   51% or better Native American."
>   Mmongr . . . blood . . . gree quant . . . lineage . . .
>   "Oh, but are you an Indian in Canada?"
> If you are *still* in "Recovery from Discovery,"
>   you may be suffering from Post-Colonial Traumatic Stress Disorder—or—
>   ETHNOSTRESS!!!!!!!!!

As I have grown as a theatre artist so has my conviction that my art is my resistance; there is no boundary between the two. As a result, my work is propelled by what I most need to heal in my life. Whether my work explores questions of identity or discloses the sexual wounds imposed on Native women as a consequence of being used as the sexual commodities for the conquest; whether I am reclaiming Native women's history and exploding stereotypes; or examining the internalized racism within those of us who come from the nations in the American South whose lineages have mixed with African peoples; what compels me to create is the need to heal within myself, within my family, within my community, among our nations. To shine light into the hidden corners where there is only fear, shame and shadow and transform our dis-ease into something that can help make the people whole. It is the role of the artist to perceive things differently. It is the role of the actor to show how that perception feels.

In isolation, these symptoms do not appear to be fatal

> *BUT*
> it has been known to kill on contact.
> KILLS ON CONTACT through:
>> Measles
>> Influenza
>> Syphilis (and other Sexually Transmitted Diseases)
>> an-an-an-AAH-Choo!! the
>> Common Cold
>> *OR*
> It has been known to lead to a long, lingering death from:
>> Drug Addiction, Diabetes, Tuberculosis, Suicide, Family Violence,
>> In-grown Toenails, , and—
>> ". . . *for Thine is the Kingdom and the Power and the Glory,*
>> *forev* . . . , *forev* . . . , *forev.*"
>> Post-Col-mat . . . traum stress olonial alone colon-eth-eth no . . . no.
>> Disor-Disor-Post??

I would like to read a quote by Floyd Kiva New, one of the founders of the Institute of American Indian Arts in Santa Fé, New Mexico. He wrote these words in 1969, and I consider them a visionary statement. I'm taking this quote from an article by Hanay Geiogamah from the Fall 1991 *Canadian Theatre Review* issue on Native Theatre, which I edited.

> We believe that an exciting American Indian theatre can be evolved out of the framework of Indian traditions. We think this evolution must come from the most sensitive approaches imaginable in order not to misuse or cheapen the original nature of Indian forms, most of which are closely tied to religion.
>
> We believe that young Indian people must be trained in the fullest degree regarding all aspects of theatre: the history of universal forms, the technical aspects, acting, speech and movement. Against this understanding they must then be led to examine Indian culture for that which is theatrical, and then find ways to interpret those unique aspects for contemporary audiences in true theatre settings. Indian theatre ultimately will be born from this group. . . .

Indian theatre cannot be developed overnight, but will come only as a result of an educational process in which Indian artists are created who can then make their own statements. To understand this point fully, one must acknowledge the fact that no pure traditional form of Indian theatre presently exists—one must be created.

Twenty-eight years later, we are still in the process of creating this theatre. It is a process that has involved many of us standing in different places in the circle. At the age that I am now both chronologically and as a mature artist, the lines between my many different influences have become blurred, they have become a whole. They are another body of experience, another "way." I am currently searching along with other Native theatre artists for a methodology for this "way" so that I may do intentionally what I have done unintentionally in structuring my work. Many times there are things I can identify in my work only in retrospect that I would like to consciously build into a piece from its inception.

For example: nearly a year after my stage play *Princess Pocahontas and the Blue Spots* was produced and I was preparing the manuscript for publication, I realized that the play had a very definite structure. There are 13 transformations, one for each moon in the lunar year. Of those 13 transformations there are 4, one for each of the 4 directions, where there is a transfiguration of three women who are one. Thirteen moons, four directions. Sacred numbers in Native cultures. This was not a structure imposed on the work but rather informed by it. This organic emergence of theatrical structure is something I inherited directly from Spiderwoman Theatre. My Auntie, Muriel Miguel, the director of Spiderwoman Theater, directed this piece and it is through her influence that I gained trust in this process. I believe it is one of the cornerstones of developing Native Performance Culture. I had a similar realization about the elements inherent in my work while talking to a North Carolina Saponi/Tuscarora friend who is doing his masters degree at the University of Pennsylvania. He was doing linguistic research on the premise that there is a way that Native peoples speak English that is specific, much in the way that this has proven to be so for African American English. I began to bemoan the fact that since English is my first language and I don't have the privilege of speaking either of my original languages, I didn't think that those elements were present in my speech. His response was to pick up a piece from *Princess Pocahontas and the Blue Spots,* "Nubile Child," which you heard earlier. He identified for me where my English sentence structure and syntax came directly from an Indigenous language I've never spoken; and where my frequent use of repetition and rhythm has a ceremonial purpose: it's used to create a heightened reality. Wow, was I surprised! So we know that this Native "way" is a persistent and natural occurrence in our work. What we don't know is what would happen if we approached the work with the intention of creating from within the framework of these structures, forms and rhythms.

In Toronto in the early '80s, when Native Earth Performing Arts was founded and Native theatre artists first started creating our own work, one of the most essential concerns was just to get the stories out there, to establish our voice, in our own words. What followed were works that told what it's been like to be us. These shows were created largely to explain "us" to "them." The audiences were predominately white and the plays were pretty conventional in performance style. Some of that began to change with some Spiderwoman imports as Muriel and Gloria Miguel became involved in Native Earth's productions. Other artists, such as Vancouver's Margo Kane, began to push the boundaries of performance style by using Native storytelling as a base. Another big concern was to bring our communities into the theatre, a place where they were not used to going because up until this point they did not see themselves reflected. We needed to create an audience of Native theatregoers in order to dislodge the work from the stuck place of "white people don't get it." For example: during the second month on the road with a national tour of Cree playwright Tomson Highway's *The Rez Sisters,* we hit Winnipeg, Manitoba. Now the city of Winnipeg is known as the largest Indian reserve in Canada; nevertheless, when the cast showed up at the theatre on the first day of rehearsal, security was called because there were "Indians in the building." But something else happened on opening night in Winnipeg. My opening monologue in this play was entirely in Cree, and when these words left my mouth in front of a predominately Cree audience, I realized that I was playing to people who understood the words I was saying. Their response upon hearing their own language from the stage for the first time was so overwhelming that I almost wasn't ready for it. For the rest of that run the women in the cast were grabbing Indians off the streets and sneaking them through the stage door just so we would have a Native audience.

For the past 6 years I have been collaborating with a friend and fellow theatre artist who has remarkable creative vision in regards to conceiving a contemporary Native theatre. Now, I could introduce his credentials to you by saying he is one of the few Native theatre artists in Canada to be sent to study in Europe. He trained at Denmark's Tuqak Theatre and in Italy with Grotowski. I prefer to identify Floyd Favel Starr as a Plains Cree from the Poundmaker Reserve in Saskatchewan who during his stay in Europe regularly took himself to the ocean to speak Cree over the waves so that he wouldn't forget his language. I would like to read some excerpts from an article Floyd wrote for the same *Canadian Theatre Review* issue on Native theatre.

Behind me I have left pieces of myself, voluntarily and involuntarily, as offerings and sacrifices, broken and scattered like glass. It is the shattered memories and dreams that I cling to and try to piece together in some semblance of sanity. This is my bundle that I carry with me—my grandmother's words, a friend's advice—and each new experience adds to this bundle. All that is essential to me I carry on my back and in my heart. As a Plains Cree this is important to me. This is my culture, as an Indian, as an artist and as a nomad.

. . . Grotowski was one of my teachers and he used to say that my main task at his centre was to pick up the skills needed to go back and learn among my people. Skills such as picking up and remembering songs, developing a body flexible and free enough to learn intricate movements of dances, and nurturing memory to learn and absorb information and stories. These forms are the key to understanding ourselves and our relationship to the forces of nature. This is important for when I am old I want to be able to pass on our culture to my children and grandchildren. As an oral culture, we are always one generation from extinction; therefore I will do my small part toward our continuing survival as a distinct people.

. . . Grotowski told me a story once; he told me a story of a mustang who was separated from his herd. A herd of jackasses discovered him and adopted him. He grew up like a jackass until one day the mustangs reappeared. They began to remind him that he was a mustang. This was Grotowski's way of calling me a jackass, which says something about his teaching tactics: blunt and hard.

. . . All my experience is part of my culture, my bundle. I add a bit here and there, a story, a song, an experience, and will continue to do so until it's time to leave this earth. In this way one's understanding of culture is formed and continuously rejuvenated. We are in motion, never the same.

. . . Maybe that is why we create, to have a dialogue among ourselves and others with images, sounds and words; to put some order into the chaos.

In 1991 Floyd asked me to join him at a training centre for Native performers in Ontario called the Centre for Indigenous Theatre. He had just been appointed director of the Native Theatre School and was very excited about what he named "Native Performance Culture." One definition of "Native Performance Culture" as Floyd envisions it is "to identify performance principles inherent in the ceremonial and social cultures of the Natives of this continent, for the purpose of constructing a contemporary theatre methodology."

In other words, to create a theatre that has at its centre the way we use movement, the way we use oratory and song, using the structure of our stories, and the symbols that connect us to the Sacred. I was hooked! I had never before had anything to name the journey we were on, nothing to encompass the process.

In initiating this research, Floyd brought together a training team because this idea has also always contained a strong training component, otherwise there wouldn't be any actors with the skills to perform this work. The team over the years has included Pura Fé, a North Carolina Tuscarora singer/songwriter grounded in blues and jazz and the lead vocalist of the a cappella group Ulali; Muriel Miguel, a Kuna/Rappahannock actor with a background in modern dance and traditional Native dance, as well as the Open Theater and the director of our theatrical elders, Spiderwoman Theater; Sadie Buck, Seneca clan mother and lead singer of the Six Nations Women's Singing Society; Jani Lauzon, an actor, puppeteer and blues vocalist; Maariu Olsen, a Greenlandic Inuit actor and mask dancer; Louis Mofsie, a Hopi/Winnebago traditional dancer and singer and leader of New York City's Thunderbird American Indian Dancers; various Native guest artists such as traditional singers, dancers and drum and rattle makers; and non-Native guest artists such as voice master David Smuckler. The core of the Native Performance Culture research project team remains Floyd and myself with Muriel Miguel, Pura Fé and Sadie Buck.

On the 50th anniversary of the liberation of Auschwitz, I got a call from Floyd. He was very excited. "Monique," he said, "I've been thinking. We don't have a memorial to our dead! We have no collective day of remembrance." We make personal and family offerings to honor our dead, and there are community dead feasts, but as a people we have no memorial to the 60 million of our relatives who were wiped out during the first one hundred years of the invasion, nor for those who followed over the next 400 years. That is when Floyd and I decided that our work would be this memorial. Memory is a prerequisite to building memorial. Creating art out of the memory of ruins and fragments became one of the themes of the work. Floyd had long been drawn to Butoh dance and other post-Hiroshima art from Japan. I am the child of a Holocaust survivor, and my father provided access to a large body of literature, songs and art that came out of the Nazi concentration camps. During the winter of 1995, we had the opportunity to take some of these ideas into the studio with an ensemble of professionals and apprentices. Utilizing all the skills and strengths that we had among us from our diverse training and backgrounds, we did a 6 week research project in Native Performance Culture at the Banff Centre for the Arts in Banff, Alberta. What we were able to develop at this time far exceeded what we had imagined and culminated in 2-hour-long improvisations where we layered images from Hiroshima, concentration camps, My Lai, wove our personal stories of "ruin" into them, told it through the form of a traditional Inuit Raven dance (raven is the trickster in Inuit culture) and set it at Wounded Knee after the massacre. Sounds really heavy, huh? Well, our safety valve was Pura Fé, acting as disk jockey. We set it up so that if she saw things getting beyond painful she would put on Leonard Cohen's "Dance Me to the End of Love" and we had to drop whatever we were doing, grab the closest partner and dance. This to me was a turning point, and we had the beginnings of our first piece. It also left us with a crucial question: What happens when you create art out of atrocity?

Native Performance Culture was born out of the experience of the continuing Holocaust against Aboriginal peoples. It is our response that we transform the ongoing genocide into something healing for the people. From this position, I will say that one of the main thrusts of Native Performance Culture is the "decolonization" of our theatre.

Other symptoms of this syndrome include:

Loss of belief or Anomie
Loss of joyful belief.
The belief that the earth is round,
The belief that the sun rises in the East and sets in the West and
        that the moon is alive.
The belief that every being has the right to breathe air, drink water and take up
        space.
The belief that we are connected to all things and that there is
        enough for all.
The belief that I am standing here at this moment on the Earth which is round.
        Loss of joyful belief.
Loss. Loss. Loss of . . .
I am.
I am, I see . . .
I am, I see I spe (ak) I spe (ak)
I come from . . . I am . . .
I come from . . . I am . . . death
I come from . . . I am . . . killed . . . again and again.
I come from . . . I am . . . not . . .
        I am not here standing at this moment on the earth not round
Post-Colonial Traumatic Stress Disorder.
De-Colonize your mind
De-Colonize your mind
De-Colonize your mind
        your mind, your mind.
Body
Mind
Spirit
Ethnostress . . .
De-Colonize your mind.

I recently had the opportunity to examine some of the impulses for my work when I was asked to be on a panel on criticism at Toronto's Theatre Passe Muraille. For me it begins with the word, the gesture, the story, the character, the journey or healing. But I am also deeply connected to the clown character. Why clown? What else can one do with the rage? I'd like to read something from my response to the criticism panel of the Passe Muraille Papers:

> When I ask myself "What is my source or sources?" I always go back to the same place. Sound, movement, storytelling, transformation and the energies of the beings, that for lack of better terms, are called the Sacred Clowns, Tricksters and Contraries. In my culture, and in many of the Indigenous cultures of the world, these are the critics. The Clown is a hard critic, even merciless. But whether we are talking about the Clowns who enter sacred ceremony to scandalize, scare, ridicule and make the people laugh, or of the many epic Trickster stories passed on through oral tradition to teach us our history and how we are to behave in relation to other beings on the earth, these Contrary beings, our critics, are never exempt from getting caught in their own traps. Although it is not the people who criticize them, it is they who criticize the people.

Why clown? If I didn't have theatre I think my alternative would have been to blow something up or to blow myself up. The Trickster is an outlaw, a harsh and brutal critic, a teacher, a disrupter, a mutable creative force neither good nor evil neither male nor female. A cultural hero and buffoon. This energy has given me a persona through whom I can put my tongue on the rage, through whom I can push the pain to its most absurd point. The Coyote. The first and most irreverent absurdist. Other influences on my sense of the absurd come from loving the absurdist playwrights as a teenager. Beckett, Ionesco, Albee, Stoppard. And among them, Spiderwoman Theater, who have taught me to push the boundaries of the absurd. What else do you do with the rage? What else do you do when you are confronted every morning with the realities of genocide? Turn it on its ear, turn it inside out, pull it apart like silly putty. I turn my rage inside out and what do I get? A silly hat covered with tacky tourist beadwork, some of which was beaded by my grandfather, a portrait of poor ol' Princess Pocahontas in her Elizabethan ruff, the state flower of Virginia. Coyote. TRANSFORMATION! Coyote in drag becomes the quintessential Indian Princess, "Princess Buttered-on-Both-Sides." I use Coyote as a foundation layer for building many characters from Shakespeare's "Ariel" in *The Tempest* to a composite Hindu goddess, "Atmani," in Dilara Ali's *Mango Chutney* to "Mad Etta" on the CBC Television series *The Rez*.

Coyote is always with me now. My husband tells me that I see something absurd in the most unlikely places. I don't look for it, but I know that Coyote has been shopping for my clothes for quite some time now. Coyote sits on top of my computer, dangles his paws off the edge of my desk, licks my face and then urges me to go downstairs and raid the refrigerator. I try to strike a bargain, I explain that I really need to get this work done, that I have a deadline but what does he care? He has a taste for frijoles refritos and is pushing me off my stool.

There is a conflict between criticism that comes from within the context of a culture and criticism that comes from an outside worldview. Again I'll read from the Passe Muraille Papers:

> All the criticism referred to in the paper is rooted in a euro-centric source. So, what does that mean to my work, the work of the Native theatre community or to any artist who does not work from a euro-centric aesthetic and experience? What it means most often is that critics who see our work are not only viewing it from outside the theatre community, but don't even share with us common cultural sign posts or emotional responses to symbols. Never mind that the form, structures and rhythms of our stories are different. As long as a theatre artist remains true to a non-euro-centric aesthetic she or he is not likely to garner a "good " review. What is not understood must be "bad" or (even worse) "inaccessible" to the mainstream. The flip side of this is when a certain playwright or theatre company receives a seal of approval from a reviewer and achieves flavor-of-the-month status. At this point we pass into a phenomenon that I will never understand, where no matter how dreadful the work, the show receives a shining review. In the Native theatre community this only happens when the show is packaged as a formula that is recognizable to the reviewer. But then, afraid they don't understand the experience, the art is not critiqued. So once again, the community suffers, and the art is not nurtured.

Floyd Favel Starr writes, "We describe a methodology of the theatre as a series of laws encoded in structures." I will add that it matters very much what those structures are. For example, one of the ideas we are researching is to take Native architecture as a model for theatrical structure. If we build a play following the structure of how a tee pee is raised we will have a very definite structure that is different from anything European. What would happen if we use the Pueblo homes as a model? Or the Mayan pyramids? Or a longhouse? What would result from writing dialogue based on the call and response songs of the Southeast? Or a soliloquy written in the rhythms of the heightened ceremonial language of Iroquois oratory or Cree prayer? What would it sound like to create dialogue the way my mother-in-law, a Tzotzil Maya, has dialogue? Well there would be two simultaneous speeches; one telling the story and the other in constant affirmation: "Yes, this is the truth. It is as you say. We are here together in the same sacred universe. I bear witness to what you say." I don't know if they will work but I am hungry for the chance to try these things.

In closing, I'd like to offer another quote from Floyd Favel Starr:

> The teaching, theory and performance practiced in this country are based on European principles of performance expression and aesthetic and this needs to be remedied.
>
> Theatre in my case is a vehicle in which to explore the cultures of this land. At the same time my tradition and other traditions of this land become the reference point from which to explore theatre, and someplace in our bodies they are in active reconciliation.
>
> . . . Somewhere there is a forgotten campsite that is close to my family's heart. It is in this camp on the banks of the North Saskatchewan River where my great-grandparents died during the flu epidemic of 1918. Nobody visits the graves as their placement in history has faded away. In this camp are the cornerstones upon which to build the possibility of a theatre that takes its inspiration from the bones of the dead, and the ashes of long dead fires.
>
> . . . some time ago I dreamt that Grotowski died and we buried him in the graveyard on top of the hill on my reserve where my ancestors are buried.
>
> . . . one interpretation of this dream I feel is that I should bury deep into Mother Earth, into the soil that has my ancestors remains, my work and theatrical experience. From here the earth and the ancestors, spirits of this land will inform the style, methodology of what the work shall be, how it shall define itself.

Nya weh, nuedi, kolabal, hi-hi. All my relations.

Asivak's Creation Story (English and Swampy Cree Versions)

JULES ARITA KOOSTACHIN
WITH JENNIFER FELL HAYES

Produced by Koostachin Productions, 1995.

Characters

Narrator—A Trickster Spirit of both genders who watches over all people.

Nipisha—A Cree and an Inutituk word. In Cree it means flower. In Inutituk it means a magnetic fish (fish that sticks to you).

Ottanafaycaso—A Cree word meaning spider, which is a unisex spirit and guardian.

Setting

A long time ago when the world was at peace and the trees were tall and plentiful.

Glossary of Terms

Inuit—Nation from the Northwest Territories.

Inninu—Otherwise known as the Cree Nation.

Asivak—A Inutituk word meaning spider; it is also a unisex name.

NARRATOR: A long time ago when the world was at peace and the trees were tall and plentiful, there lived two legendary children. Even before the invasion of the white men, these children were destined to meet. They were to meet one another to pass on the souls of their ancestors. The Inninu boy was named Ottanafaycaso, and the Inuk girl was named Nipisha. One day Nipisha was traveling in search of a place to sleep after hunting for her village. Ottanafaycaso was also hunting and found that he traveled out of his Inninu territory. He was too tired to travel home and decided to settle in the first clearing he could find. He set up camp next to a creek and a short tree. Later that night, he fell into a deep sleep, and was awakened by a loud banging on his tent. In fear, he ran outside in his underpants, ready to fight with his spear. To his surprise he saw a very angry girl about the same age as himself. She was standing there with her hands on her hips ready to scream at any given moment. Ottanafaycaso started to laugh in her face, and he noticed that she was serious. She started to chase him around the camp with her spear.

NIPISHA: Get off my campsite Inninu!

NARRATOR: Nipisha stopped running and watched Ottanafaycaso in amusement. He caught his breath and started to laugh even louder.

OTTANAFAYCASO: Funny, funny girl. You make me laugh. Now if you please, get off my campsite.

NIPISHA: This is my place of rest.

OTTANAFAYCASO: You know it's very strange that you are out here in the wilderness by yourself. Should you not be with a brother or even your father?

NARRATOR: Ottanafaycaso saw anger in Nipisha's eyes and started to back away from her. This time he was not laughing.

NIPISHA: What did you say to me? No wonder the Inuit hate the Inninu. I will have you know that I am known for my incredible hunting abilities. And I do not need a boy or even a man to take care of me. Let me repeat that I don't need a boy's help, especially yours. You stupid Inninu!

OTTANAFAYCASO: All right then Inuk, we will have a competition at sunrise then?

NARRATOR: They both went to sleep in the tent and woke up with the sun.

NIPISHA: Okay, stupid Inninu, wake up! Let's go! Let's go!

OTTANAFAYCASO: My name is not Inninu, and I am not stupid! Let's go then.

NARRATOR: They both went outside and started the competition. They spent the day hunting and trapping. They tied. They went back disappointed. They ate their game for supper and went to sleep angry. The next morning Ottanafaycaso found Nipisha standing over him holding her spear in her hand.

NIPISHA: You! Inninu! You must leave now, I am tired of seeing your proud face. You snore too loud, too. I have proven that I am good as any hunter, so now you must leave.

OTTANAFAYCASO: Why are you being so mean? No! I do not snore. (Pause) You know you are right; you are a very good hunter and trapper.

NIPISHA: I know that already. It doesn't matter what you think. The point is that you are disrespectful of girls. You doubted me before you knew anything about me. Yes! You do snore. I thought I was sharing the tent with an angry bear last night.

NARRATOR: They stand staring at each other in silence for a few moments. Nipisha tries not to laugh.

OTTANAFAYCASO: I am so sorry. I do not want you to leave. You have shown me a new way of thinking. I should have known better than to doubt you. (Pause) Hmm . . . an angry bear?

NIPISHA: Anyway, your new name will be Angry Bear.

NARRATOR: The two children start to laugh.

OTTANAFAYCASO: I have to tell you of my awful dream last night.

NIPISHA: I had a dream, too. I was scared by it.

OTTANAFAYCASO: Mine was about us. Dreams guide us and we need to listen to them. I dreamt that men, with long black coats, have taken our villages from our families and friends. I woke up crying because a voice kept telling me to stay where I am, here with you.

NIPISHA: I had the same dream. But I want to go home and see for myself.

OTTANAFAYCASO: You can't! Please stay, we will be safe here together.

NIPISHA: I don't even like you.

NARRATOR: They both sat in silence staring at each other. They cried together for weeks, for their families and friends back home. They came together as friends and prayed to the Creator and their ancestors for courage. They burned traditional medicines and felt peace as the smoke (their prayers) were lifted to the sky.

NIPISHA: Now that our ceremonies are completed, we can create a new home for ourselves.

OTTANAFAYCASO: I will be honored to be your friend forever.

NARRATOR: A special friendship was formed that day. They stayed together for the rest of their lives. As adults they created new souls, ones with mixed blood. Their oldest son was named Asivak, a legendary hunter and trapper. Asivak was known as the strongest soul, because he was created by the love of enemies. His soul traveled and survived centuries of invasions, until he found his spirit guides Ottanafaycaso and Nipisha, his parents. At one time the Inuit and the Inninu were enemies, and through the devastation of losing everything and everyone they loved, they found hope in each other.

Asivak's Creation Story
(Swampy Cree Version, James Bay, Ontario)

NARRATOR: Wayscatch palmmashe tacoshe weemestigoshu. Napew Guyta-cochin oma aski. Guyetaw Inninu laskimesqaiw. Tabescotch guy gaskiowak adamenaogig. Otaskiwak. Guynoesh guytashekneewak endamenaogig. Payagway egishegak. Ottanafaycaso eshekneecaso Inninu napew. Guyosame guytotaw waysawonew guywaytinuk. Guymisscum oski aski. Guygitchi-ayeahschosue. Guygapayshow guyyahtea mitchisue. Nesta Guyatea nipaw.

Maygwatch itipayskanick guypaytum gaygwano amatwayegit awaynican.
Guysayguyso aweenasuit aweemasheget wanaweeteamay. Guygosqwaytum
awamat esqwaywa apeesheshit Nipisha eschinacasuit. Etacona emeshanik
mistikono. Ottanafaycaso guypafu guyswahao Nipisha. Guypamitchisahue
megwamay.

NIPISHA: Macha Nette! Inninu!

OTTANAFAYCASO: Asto kneeweepapin. Macha nette guytiton.

NIPISHA: Kneenataski ota wayscatch ota dochiittan.

OTTANAFAYCASO: Gaygwan aganapayo waychi gunawmut chinana gachiesk
itwe.

NIPISHA: Guyswayhue anima aytwit. Gaygwan anima waychi itwayan gaskihun
itaminahowan daski. Mona, tawinimow. Napew she-nanagachihit gaguy-
nanagageeeteasea-ne nina.

OTTANAFAYCASO: Gagoochitananu awaynican gaygaskihuit endaninahut.
Agoessqeeuil.

NARRATOR: Tabeschut guygaskiowhat endaminagik. Guygitchee ayeahschuse-
awak guyateanipawak.

NIPISHA: Inninu, waniska ago machagitoeta.

OTTANAFAYCASO: Mona gagatotan ota ochee aski. Gaygwannaspitch way-
cheegis-waysea-anne.

NIPISHA: Waysa mona gayguystaynimow esquill.

OTTANAFAYCASO: Kneemitchinawaysun. Gayguytotan esha. Mona, wayscatch
gawaknee guyskisun agee guyskinohamaweeun. Gaygwan aminagik, Nipisha.

NIPISHA: Guypayshe esshegeeshahook ota tawashetat gaygwanno Gitchi Man-
ito. Bayshegayshehook shewapamitan geegaynita wahegahut oskiacha. Gee-
whoshetieanne gamemashiek achah nesta minwhen metomenshegun.
Ottanafaycaso nesta Nipisha ochachagoak guyganoamegowak gehetacik
aski.

NARRATOR: Ottanafaycaso mona ochi guytoetao guyhitao guywechewaol Nipisha. Guysaguy ittowak naspitch. Guynatawego geegesh. Nipisha guywinew
Asivak. Ota cha gwa guypapa ni wa. Misoway Inninu Otaski.

Bring the Children Home

MARCIE RENDON

Premiered at Children's Play Theatre, Minneapolis, Minnesota, 1994.

Characters

Grandmother (Min-di-way): is quite old, and at this point very crabby. She has lived a long, full life and is tired and wants peace of mind and serenity. She has gone into the woods to die. She feels that she has fulfilled her life's purpose and is ready to meet the Creator. She has gray hair, is short, and walks with a cane. She was a mother, an elder and a wise woman. She provided guidance, healing, compassion, and direction to the rest of her village. She has raised many children in her day. She feels she has the right to be crabby after being so good her whole entire life. A little eccentric now, she can see the spirits and occasionally talks to them.

Youth (O-day-mi-nung): an undefinable youth in terms of race, ethnic heritage, and sex. Has no past. Is born in the now. Knows that he belongs somewhere, with someone, but with who? Knows that he is connected to other humans, but where and how? Is searching for himself. Does not see the spirits.

"Bad" Spirit (Matilda): hates her name, hates her body (tries to make her legs longer, her nose better, her arms stronger), encourages Oday to get into trouble, and when she doesn't get her way she throws a tantrum. Is always changing her hairstyle—ponytail on the right, on the left, two on either side, one hanging in the middle of her forehead.

"Good" Spirit (Gi-way-di-nung): gets the giggles, is filled with awe and wonder. Quick, light on her feet, feels feelings. When she has to she will kick Oday in the butt, tweak his ears, or smite him on the forehead to get his attention—all in a very playful but sincere way. He has to listen to her. She is feisty.

(For the most part, the fairies stick close to Oday's side, except when they are fighting with each other, or when Matilda is throwing a tantrum or off stretching her legs and arms out or fixing her hair a new way. The fairies are fascinated with Oday, and both try to win his attention.)

Maigun: Undeterminable age. First appears as a drunk then as a man. Is actually a wolf spirit.

Crow and Eagle: Spirits present throughout play.

Windigo: Spirit symbolizing decay/cannibalism of Western society.

Chorus of youth: hip hop/rap.

(As a writer, it is my hope that, with the exception of the GRANDMOTHER, MATILDA and MAIGUN, the characters could be played by either male or female performers.)

Setting

Present time.

Act I: Daytime. Woods in the winter. Snow. Circle of Jack Pines.

Act II, Scene 1: Early evening fading to darkness. Further into the woods.

Scenes 2–3: Daytime fading to dusk. The edge of a small town.

Act III: Part of the stage is set as a clearing on the edge of the woods. The other part will later reveal a house with a front door leading into a kitchen/living room where a young woman is sitting at a table, and a back door leading into a bedroom.

ACT I

SCENE I

circle of jack pines
snow
winter setting
Characters onstage:

Windigo spirit, wearing decayed-looking outfit, snowshoes—he is an extremely feared spirit—name is whispered if spoken out loud. Eagle spirit flying east to west and back around—screeching as if in protecting mode. Crow sitting calmly on stump.

Windigo begins dancing song of death with mournful wind sound in the background. Eagle continues to fly east to west then begins circling in the clearing in the center of the jack pines. Crow flies south to north cawing.

EAGLE: I fly east to west and back around
    guardian of the spirit world
    I guard the doors of east to west
    I fly between the space of dawn to dusk
    I've named each child before it's born

(Bodies under snow in circle of jack pines begin to move slightly. Oday rises out, falls back asleep on top of snow.)

CROW: I fly south to north and back around
    guardian of the healing winds
    I guard the doors of south to north
    warm spring winds lift my wings
    I know each child's name before it's born

(ODAY awakes again, begins shivering from cold and fear. Lays back down in curled up ball, burrows back under snow. EAGLE and CROW perch as if on guard over ODAY.)

SCENE 2

(Windigo winds his death march across stage. EAGLE and CROW brush more snow over ODAY. GIWAYDINUNG rises out of snow. MATILDA peeks out but is too afraid to come out fully.)

MATILDA *(whispering to CROW and EAGLE)*: Windigo—crazy maker
GIWAYDINUNG *(whispering)*: Windigo—cannibal
CROW AND EAGLE *(echo)*: Windigo
he steals the souls of young and old
feeding on decay
GIWAYDINUNG *(uses rattle to chant at WINDIGO, pushes him out of circle of*
    pines—offstage):
    every child needs a mama
    every child wants a dad
    loving arms to hold them
    when all the world seems
    bleak and cold
    the only job of old ones
    is to protect the young
    or else the night will get so dark
    no one will see the day

(Fairies settle back under snow. EAGLE dances more intensely, eagle whistle blows. CROW flies from north to east to south cawing. Then settles silently into trees, snow, etc. Stage becomes silent and dimly lit. ODAY once again rises out of snow, looks at himself in bewilderment, looks around at the world as if in a dream.)

ODAY: Wow! This is wild! Oh, man, this is toooo much. This is toooo much.

(Sees bodies still moving visibly under snow. Hears sound of owl—Eagle screeches. Oday scared, curls back up in ball. Once again Eagle and Crow brush snow over him.)

SCENE 3

Mindiway enters stage, mumbling to herself, no possessions except what she is wearing and her cane. Is not really dressed for winter but doesn't seem to notice. Has thrown a scarf over her head.

MINDIWAY: Let me tell you—I've had it! Mindiway do this. Mindiway do that. Grandma can you help me. Never a moments rest. Here I am—an old woman—can barely walk and people STILL want me to help them. Ever since I was a little kid it was Mindiway do this. Mindiway do that.

My mom, she'd holler, "Mindiway take this soup over to old man Still-day—and you be nice—he's an old man—don't be getting' smart with him either." Mindiway this. Mindiway that. Never a moments rest. And then my OWN kids . . . Mama this . . . Mama that . . . always wanting something.

(Turns tender as if remembering. Matilda and Giwaydinung are peeking out listening.)

Not that I didn't love them . . . but puh-leaze—shouldn't there be a law that mothers get some rest sometime? Constant noise, constant chatter . . . aah, finally some silence. I can finally hear the quiet.

(Sits listening to the silence . . . can frown or grimace if there is any noise in the theater)

After my kids grew up, thought I'd get some of my own time, but oh no, they had to have kids—then it was: Grandma can you help me, Grandma what was it like when you were growing up . . . no END to the questions . . . cute little rug-rats, but no end to the questions—why, why, why . . . aah, quiet, peace and quiet—gentle on an old woman's ears—I'm just gonna sit here in the quiet until that old man Windigo comes to get me.

(Laughs, almost a cackle)

That's how I'd finally get the little brats to leave me alone, tell them if they didn't be quiet Windigo would come and get them.

(Laughs again)

Well, old man, come and get me. . . . I'm ready.

(Begins hollowing out space under one of the trees)

Been threatening for years. One day I'm just gonna get up and walk outta here . . . One more question and I'm gonna leave.

Finally did it too.

Let me tell you, once you get old everyone thinks you know everything. The questions never stop. Yesterday, old man Stillday's great-granddaughter comes to my house—right in the middle of Jesse Raphael—asks me, "Komis?" called me Komis! Wasn't even her grandmother, but she says, "Komis, can you tell me how to make that soup your mama used to make?"

I tell you I tried . . . tried to sit there just calm, telling myself, now Mindiway you just stay calm . . . but I tell you all I wanted to do was listen to my show or the wind blowing outside . . . soon as she started askin' me about soup all I heard was the wind blowin' in the jack pines and I knew I had to go.

Soup—she wanted to know about soup—and if I told her carrots and rabbit legs she would have used carrots and beef—or knowin' kids these days she would have used carrots and tofu—veggies, everyone running around thinkin' they're a rabbit, nibbling on leaves, I tell you.

But the wind was callin'—I said, hold on granddaughter, I got the recipe in the back room—soon as I was in back I grabbed my scarf and headed out the backdoor—enough is enough.

(Laughing) She's probably still sitting there waiting for her soup recipe. Me? I'm done, no more questions, just quiet, comes a time we all deserve a rest. . . . I'm gonna sit under this tree and never move again. . . . Been hearing that old Windigo for years; instead of him chasing me, I'll just sit here and wait for him.

(Crawls under tree)

Guess I won't be needing this.

(Throws cane, and folds arms over chest, closes eyes and listens to the quiet. Cane hits snow that begins to move. ODAY rises out of snow, brushing self off. Looks around like lost.)

GIWAYDINUNG: Oooh, a wonder child!

(ODAY looks at self and body in wonderment, examines movement of arms and legs. MATILDA and GIWAYDINUNG are watching intently.)

ODAY: Wow.

MATILDA (*whispering loudly, fusses with hair*): Whadda ya mean a Wonder Child? It's just another human!

ODAY: This is too much. What in the world is going on?

GIWAYDINUNG (*shakes her head no, whispering excitedly back*): Uh-uh, it's a Wonder Child! I wonder where the child has been. I wonder where he'll go. I wonder what the future holds and how the child will grow. Wonder of wonders, another perfect gift.

(*Mindiway peeks out, looks around, doesn't see ODAY just the fairies, irritated, scoots back under tree. ODAY is too preoccupied with himself to see MINDI-WAY. MATILDA starts a snowball fight with GIWAYDINUNG. ODAY thinks the snow is falling on him off the trees. Picks up cane and looks around.*)

ODAY: Someone's here.

MATILDA: You are such a dunce. A child is just a child. Their noses run in winter, they tend to scream and cry at night, the only thing they're good for is to help me make my mischief every day and every night. You think each child is perfect and I've proved you wrong a hundred times. You got the last one, now this wayward child is mine.

GIWAYDINUNG: Sweetie, I don't think so. This Wonder Child is mine.

MATILDA: Sweetie?! (*putting finger in mouth, gagging, mutters to audience*) She thinks every child is precious, a wonder to the world. A child without a past doesn't know which way is home. A child without no parents, no family of its own, will surely get so lonely it'll be a snap to shape and mold.

(*GIWAYDINUNG spins ODAY around so he is facing the tree MINDIWAY is under.*)

ODAY: Who's there?

(*MINDIWAY scoots farther back to tree trunk, ODAY sees movement, crouches down.*)

ODAY: Come on, I see you, who are you?

(*MINDIWAY feigns sleep, deafness.*)

ODAY (*right in MINDIWAY's ear*): HELLLLOOO.

(*MINDIWAY jumps, grabs cane from ODAY, crawls out from under tree.*)

MINDIWAY: What's your problem kid? Didn't your people teach you any manners? Can't you see I'm trying to rest?

ODAY: Rest? It's freezing cold out here!

MINDIWAY: So? I like the cold. You don't like the cold . . . leave.

(Mumbles to self and crawls under different tree)

ODAY: I don't think this is my day. Lady!?

MINDIWAY: Hmmh.

ODAY: Excuse me?!?

MINDIWAY: I said, you don't like the cold . . . leave!

ODAY *(after long silence, close to tears)*: I can't.

MINDIWAY: What do you mean you CAN'T?

ODAY: I don't know where I am. If I don't even know who I am how in the heck am I supposed to know where to go?

(By now crying, GIWAYDINUNG crying with him, MATILDA busying herself with her hair, GRANDMOTHER trying to ignore him but crawling farther out from under tree)

MINDIWAY: Hey kid, knock it off. Where'd you come from?

MATILDA: Yeah, blubber-mouth, stuff it.

(ODAY points to snow, CROW caws, EAGLE whistles.)

EAGLE: The child is lost and no one cares
 without his name he can't be claimed
 his spirit name he must recall

CROW: The children wander all alone
 there is no place to call a home

GIWAYDINUNG: The only job of old ones
 is to protect the young

MINDIWAY: Criminy, are you ever going to give me a break? Who made me the patron saint of wayward souls? I told you, I'm too old for this. I can't be traipsing all over the country trying to find this one's home. I thought I got to rest once and for all!

(CROW caws, EAGLE whistles.)

MINDIWAY: *(mutters to self, then)*: All right kid, what do you need?

ODAY: I want to go home.

MINDIWAY: Well go.

ODAY: But I don't know where to go.

MINDIWAY: Pick a direction kid, any direction.

MATILDA: Yeah, kid, pick a direction, any direction. Follow me.

GIWAYDINUNG: Don't listen to her. *(Shoves him towards Mindiway)*

ODAY: I can't just go wandering off by myself. What if I get lost?

MINDIWAY: As far as I can tell you already are.

ODAY *(close to tears again)*: Why are you being so mean? Who are you?

MINDIWAY: A witch!! Relax! I'm a tired old lady. And I'm sick to death of answering everybody else's questions, including yours. Who are you?
ODAY (crying): I don't know.
MINDIWAY: You don't know?
ODAY: No.
MINDIWAY: No clue?
ODAY: No.
MINDIWAY: You're in tough shape kid.

(ODAY cries harder.)

MINDIWAY: Get a grip kid, it's easy enough to fix. I'll call you Kid.
ODAY: Kid?
GIWAYDINUNG: Kid?
MATILDA (laughing): Kid!!!!
MINDIWAY: You got a problem with being called Kid?
ODAY: Well it doesn't exactly tell me who I am.
MINDIWAY: Well, if you don't know who you are, you wouldn't know even if I told you. My name is Mindiway
ODAY: Min-di-way.
MINDIWAY: Means Crabby Old Lady!
ODAY: Crabby Old Lady. Mindiway. Fits. Why do. . . (GIWAYDINUNG slaps her hand over his mouth to stop his question.)
MINDIWAY: That's right kid. No questions. I'm sick to death of questions. These guys here (gesturing to EAGLE and CROW, ODAY looking confused) say I got to help you, but I don't need to answer any questions while I'm doing it. Build a fire. Soon as it's morning I'll take you to try and find your people. But NO questions, you hear?

(ODAY jumps up and starts gathering firewood and building a fire. Mindiway retreats under tree. MATILDA wrecks his logs and sticks as soon as his back is turned. GIWAYDINUNG finally gets a long branch, and using it like a sword keeps Matilda back from the fire so ODAY can finish making the fire. Bored, MATILDA falls asleep on tree roots. ODAY crawls under tree with MINDIWAY, and she grudgingly covers him with part of her scarf. She falls asleep first.)

ODAY: Who am I? Grandma, can't you tell me just who I am and where I've been? There is no future without a past. Grandma can't you tell me, just who I am and where I'm going?

(As he falls asleep, GIWAYDINUNG sings to him.)

GIWAYDINUNG: You, my child, are the answer to questions not yet asked. You are the sunshine after tomorrow's rain. You had a name from whence you came. They know you where you're going. From the future they gently call your name.

(*Fades to darkness*)

ACT II

SCENE 1

MINDIWAY and ODAY are on their journey. It is evident they have been traveling a ways. It is early evening.

MATILDA is whispering in ODAY's ear trying to get him to ask MINDIWAY anything at all: How? What? Where? Who?

GIWAYDINUNG blows dandelion seeds into MATILDA's face. MATILDA sneezes. GIWAYDINUNG scoots closer to ODAY.

GIWAYDINUNG: Stop being a nuisance. I tell you this child is a gift.

MATILDA: What do you mean? A gift? He doesn't even know who he is. Any lost child is mine! They can't think for themselves . . . pooooooor babies . . . always looking to belong . . . suckers!!!!

GIWAYDINUNG: We'll see.

(*GIWAYDINUNG stands back and looks at MATILDA's hair. MATILDA self-consciously notices and begins rearranging her hairstyle. GIWAYDINUNG runs up alongside ODAY. ODAY is walking alongside MINDIWAY. He looks like he is about to talk but hesitates because he knows he can't ask any questions.*)

GIWAYDINUNG (*whispering to ODAY*): You came from there . . . journeyed here . . . where you go is up to you.

MINDIWAY: What'd you mumble kid?

ODAY (*surprised*): Nothin'.

MINDIWAY: I heard you mumbling to yourself. You got somethin' to say, say it out loud.

ODAY: I didn't say anything.

MINDIWAY: Well, then quit thinkin' so loud, you're disturbing my quiet.

ODAY: I don't dare say anything.

MINDIWAY: What do you mean, you don't dare say anything?

ODAY: Well, just about anything I can think of to say might be a question. Like I kinda wonder why you have a name that means something and mine is just Kid.

MINDIWAY: NO questions, any questions, I'm outta here. Had enough questions to last me TWO lifetimes. Grandma this . . .

ODAY: "Grandma that . . ." It just doesn't seem fair that just because you are
    worn out with questions I can't ask any. This whole world is brand new to
    me, and I'm expected to figure it out myself!
MINDIWAY: Well, Kid, who said life is fair?
GIWAYDINUNG: We all need someone . . .
MATILDA: Maybe you. I take care of me and so can you Kid . . . dump this old
    lady now . . .we can travel faster, faster . . .without any old baggage along
    . . . you want to know life, listen to me.

(MATILDA trips over a root.)

GIWAYDINUNG *(to MATILDA)*: If you don't watch, you can't see.
(To ODAY): It may be true that life's not fair
    but Eagle dances on the wind
    travels east to west and back again
    whatever you put out
    comes back again
    the circle never ends

*(MATILDA catching up, keeps kicking her toes into the ground as if trying to
make them shorter.)*

MINDIWAY: Wish that wind would die down. I can't hear myself think. We
    better get someplace soon, I'm about to drop.

(She lowers herself onto a tree stump.)

ODAY: I'm so hungry I see spots in front of my eyes.

*(As GIWAYDINUNG and Matilda vie for his attention in front of him, Oday
faints from hunger.)*

*(Lights dim and come up on MINDIWAY and ODAY seated on the ground in a
small encampment. It is almost dark out. A couple of small children are running
around playing tag. A weary mother is sitting nursing a baby. The father is giving water to MINDIWAY and ODAY. The family is clearly very poor. MINDI-
WAY awakes first, looks around suspiciously. ODAY sputters on his water,
comes awake.)*

ODAY *(catching herself)*: Where . . . *(looks at MINDIWAY)*
MOTHER: Would you tell them kids to be quiet. I'm trying to get the baby to
    sleep.
FATHER: Hey, you two settle down. Get over here, sit down, you're waking up
    the baby.

(MATILDA distracts them and they run farther back and keep playing, getting

louder instead of quieter. GIWAYDINUNG is hovering over the mother and baby, as the baby starts to fuss. She strokes the mother's hair, the mother swats at her like she is a fly bothering her. GIWAYDINUNG turns her attention to the baby.)

FATHER: I'm Jack, my wife Antonia, and our children—Chad, Kim and Baby—can't say as if we've come up with a name that suits the little one yet. And you?

MINDIWAY: Mindiway.

(FATHER looks at ODAY, who looks away confusedly to MINDIWAY.)

MINDIWAY: Call him Kid. Can't say as how the little one knows who he is yet.

FATHER: Not every child does. The world is filled with young ones not knowing who they are or where they belong.

MINDIWAY: Hmmph.

FATHER: So where did you come from?

(MINDIWAY points with her lips in the direction they came from.)

FATHER: Where you going?

(MINDIWAY points with her lips in the opposite direction, eyeing the pot of cooking food as her head turns.)

FATHER: Ain't much that way but trouble.

ODAY: I think she's probably used to trouble. She doesn't like questions. Answering them gets her crabby.

(Oday eyes food. FATHER is uncomfortably stacking and restacking four bowls, eyeing his family as he counts the bowls again.)

ODAY: We haven't had much to eat lately.

MOTHER: Us either. . . . *(voice rising)* Would you tell them to please be quiet!

(Only Matilda comes running back.)

FATHER *(uncomfortably)*: There isn't much here to share . . .

MATILDA: Keep it, keep it . . . the old lady wanted to die anyway.

GIWAYDINUNG *(hands on hips, to MATILDA)*: You, I do not believe . . .

MOTHER: Shut up you two!!

(The two children come running back subdued. MATILDA trips the youngest, who falls on the mother and baby. The mother jumps up, reaches to slap the child and GIWAYDINUNG steps between and receives the slap.)

MINDIWAY (*standing rapidly with her cane, angry*): Never hit a child! Sit down woman, are you starving mad? I said, sit down!

(*Even MATILDA jumps back at the sound of her voice. MINDIWAY grabs one of the bowls from the man and ladles stew into it.*)

MINDIWAY (*in a little kinder voice*): Here woman, eat.

(*She continues dishing up for the rest of the family, who eat hungrily. GIWAY-DINUNG, recovered from the slap, zaps spirit lights at the pot of stew. MATILDA is back by a tree stretching her legs and arms and hitting her nose and rearranging her hair.*)

MINDIWAY (*to ODAY*): Every child you hit, a star in heaven dies.
GIWAYDINUNG: The night will get so dark no one will see the day.
MINDIWAY (*to the father*): Our only job as old ones is to protect the young.
GIWAYDINUNG: Or else the night will get so dark, no one will see the day.
MOTHER (*who is crying softly*): I just get so tired, and they make so much noise.

(*Rocking baby in her arms*)

MINDIWAY: Oh daughter, don't I know it. But that's no excuse to forget who you are (*starting to sound crabby again, takes baby from her and puts her in hammock in trees*). You go rest, we can put the little ones to bed. They'll probably fall asleep themselves now that they've eaten.

(*GIWAYDINUNG blows a gentle breeze that swings the hammock gently back and forth.*)

FATHER (*embarrassed, looking in his empty bowl he's just finished*): You two must be starved, and now you fed us, instead of us treating you like guests.

(*GIWAYDINUNG zaps more spirit lights at the stew. FATHER gets up to look in the pot and is surprised to see more in there. He hurriedly dishes up two more bowls and hands them to ODAY and MINDIWAY, looking bewildered. MINDIWAY shrugs and eats hungrily. Lights dim to campfire light.*)

GIWAYDINUNG (*singing softly to mother and father, as lights dim even further*):
Every child needs parents
rested, strong and sure
in this forest there are people
looking for a place to call
their own
when they arrive tomorrow

welcome them into your home
if you reach out and ask for help
someone will surely
lend a helping hand
every child needs a father
rested, strong and sure
sometimes the hardest part
of being a dad
is admitting
it's a job
we can't do all alone
sleep well my mother
dream a new world
into being
where every mother
has a helping hand
dream a new world
into being
where every child
gets a guiding hand
sleep well and
dream a new world
into being

SCENE 2

Scene is at the edge of a small town.

GIWAYDINUNG *(entering and going to edge of stage, to audience)*: He thought he'd found his family, but the journey continues on.

MATILDA *(still clumping around, doing her version of body building)*: Yeah, well, I thought that family would suit him fine, but nooooo, old crab butt leads him on.

(An old man, drunk, smells, is dirty, is staggering down the street. Rests against a light pole by a convenience store, gas station. Symbol for the gas station is an eagle. A small child dressed all in black sits quietly on a curb, playing with the dirt, stones, throughout the following scene. OLD MAN has trouble walking, one eye is swollen shut. GIWAYDINUNG is skipping, dancing. MATILDA is clumping, stretching legs, arms, fussing with hair. MATILDA rushes up to man and takes deep whiff, seems thrilled with his smell, checks his hair for lice. Flicks them at GIWAYDINUNG. GIWAYDINUNG looks at MATILDA's

shoulder as if she sees one there. MATILDA starts to freak, shaking out her hair and shirt/dress.)

MAIGUN *(begins talking to light pole)*: I am Maigun! Used to be people respected Maigun. Don't nobody show no respect any more. Young people these days. Ain't like it used to be. Used to be could go lay down in Cockroach Park and wake up in the morning your pint still on you. Now, man can't even walk down the street without some rag tag, million-dollar-sneakered dude, thinkin' he got the world tied around his neck on some fifty dollar, gold chain! Think they're some big men, takin' an old man's dollar fifty. Chump change, pocket change, no change . . .

(Spots ODAY and MINDIWAY walking on the street)

MAIGUN *(TO ODAY)*: Hey, bro, you got fifty cents for the bus? Nah, don't spose you got the time of day for me, huh?! Well let me introduce myself cous (cousin), I am Maigun. You know what that means? Loyal, that's one thing. . . . Bet your grandma's name is Mindiway. Heh, heh, heh.

(Notices neither one is laughing)

The wolf, that's me, we protect our own—people nowadays turn their back on their own, attack the guy lives right next door—pow, bullet in the head cause the neighbor's barbecue smoke blowed inta their yard—world gone crazy. Now me, I knows how to take care of my own—yeah, cous, Maigun, that's me. You got a name cous?

(ODAY shakes his head no.)

MAIGUN: Life's hard enough without knowin' who you are. *(Peers at Mindiway)* Don't I know you, ain't you one of them Fiiiine-day girls? Weren't you at Crow Fair back in '86? Damn, girl, you ain't aged a bit.

(Stumbles while trying to look cool. MINDIWAY smiles, is a little bit pleased. MATILDA's laughing, walking like an old lady trying to be sexy. ODAY looks embarrassed, wanting to get away. GIWAYDINUNG is curious, pensive, eyeing a group of young people standing on farther corner. MATILDA rushes over to join them as they enter the store.)

MINDIWAY: Never been to Crow Fair.
MAIGUN *(holding on to light pole, peering at ODAY)*: Nah? This your grandkid?
MINDIWAY: I don't think so.
MAIGUN: Looks just like you.

MINDIWAY: Hmmph.

MAIGUN (tired): Don't matter, a kid's a kid. We end up takin' care of 'em all just the same.

MINDIWAY: Ain't that the truth

MATILDA (sticking head out store door): Pssst, kid, over here. Leave the two old lovebirds a chance to reacquaint themselves.

(ODAY, who has been eyeing the store, unaware of MATILDA, checks his pockets as if looking for change.)

MAIGUN: Kid, got some change? I could get me and your grandma here somethin' to drink.

(Winks at MINDIWAY with his one good eye, starts to retch, leans on pole, slides down till sitting on ground. ODAY, full of discomfort, starts to walk towards store, the eagle on the gas symbol catches his eye, he turns to look back at the old man. ODAY keeps going to store.)

MINDIWAY: When was your last drink?

MAIGUN: 'Bout three thish morning.

MINDIWAY: Looks like you need more juice.

ODAY: Looks like he's had enough to me.

MINDIWAY: Whatta you know, Kid? (She reaches into pocket and pulls out a miniature, gives old man a sip, but hurriedly pulls it back after one swallow.) Sometimes the only cure for poison is more poison.

MAIGUN: Thass right, kid (on the verge of passing out).

MINDIWAY: Gets so that a fresh drink of water could kill a body.

MAIGUN: But my soul ain't dead, I am Maigun (is out).

GIWAYDINUNG: The shadow of the night.

MATILDA (back from store with popsicle and chips, talking to Oday): Shadow of a used-to-be. Ain't nothin' but a drunk. Check it out Kid, those kids in there are havin' fun, candy, pop and gum. A sugar fix is what you need.

MINDIWAY: Kid! Kid! Where'd your ears go?

ODAY: Wha . . .? Let's go, this guy stinks!

(MATILDA starts jumping with glee.)

MINDIWAY: Hush.

ODAY: Well he does. Come on, I want to go. You got anymore magic in that pocket? Like some money for some pop?

MINDIWAY: Questions!!!

ODAY: Tough

MINDIWAY: Tough, huh?

(*MINDIWAY sits on grass running hands over grass as if looking for something. OLD MAN is passed out. ODAY goes into store.*)

MAIGUN (*barely coming to*): Better give that kid his name before he's really lost.

MINDIWAY: I don't even know it myself yet. Think you're so smart, you name him.

MAIGUN: Your job, not mine.

MINDIWAY: Well he don't have to act so darn pathetic all the time.

MAIGUN: You're not exactly Mother Teresa yourself.

(*ODAY comes out with other kids who have bags of candy and pop. MATILDA runs over and whispers in ODAY's ear, who takes a pop from one of the kids and doesn't give it back. MINDIWAY is searching the ground. Kids point and taunt them.*):

> Is that your ma and dad?
> Ooooh—ug-ly.
> Hey, old lady, whatchu lookin' for?
> Looks like a witch.
> Hey, kid, where'd you come from?
> Yer ma a witch?
> Ahh, leave him alone, Kid!? You my homie, huh?
> You just move here?
> Look at your old man's eye.
> Must have AIDS.
> Catcha later, kid.

(*They drop wrappers on ground, run off laughing. Oday is left standing with pop he's stolen, looks dejected. Walks slowly back to Mindiway.*)

MINDIWAY (*under breath*): Brats! Where'd you get that pop kid?

ODAY: I dunno.

MINDIWAY: What da ya mean you don't know? Didn't pop outta the sky.

ODAY: They gave it to me.

MINDIWAY: And they gave me a ham dinner. Ain't right to steal. Throw it away.

ODAY: Huh?

MINDIWAY: Throw it away.

ODAY: I just got it.

MINDIWAY: Throw it.

ODAY (*taking big gulp*): Uh-uh.

MINDIWAY (*menacing, old man stirs*): Now.

(ODAY, intimidated, walks to trash by pumps, taking big gulps and throws it away. Matilda is sorry for him, peers into trash after pop. Makes face at GIWAYDINUNG.)

MINDIWAY: Kid?

ODAY: Huh?

MINDIWAY: Get me a stick

ODAY: A stick?

MINDIWAY: A stick, I didn't stutter.

(ODAY searches and finds stick. MINDIWAY, with GIWAYDINUNG peering over her shoulder, digs out plant and root. ODAY sits at a distance watching. MATILDA is doing her workouts. MINDIWAY mashes up plant and root and mixes the rest of the miniature in it. GIWAYDINUNG moves closer to ODAY.)

ODAY: Wha. . . *(GIWAYDINUNG puts her finger to his lips.)* You are a witch.

MINDIWAY: Huh?

ODAY: You're mean.

MINDIWAY: Hmmph.

ODAY: Let's go, he stinks.

MINDIWAY: He's sick—gonna put some medicine on his eye here.

ODAY: He's drunk.

MINDIWAY *(as she starts putting mixture on old man's eye)*: So?

ODAY: Gross.

GIWAYDINUNG: Not everything is what you see.

MATILDA: He's just a drunk.

ODAY: Yech, you could catch whatever he's got, slime running out your fingers by tonight.

MATILDA: Snot and pus, blood and guts. *(Makes gagging noises)*

MINDIWAY: You got a lot to learn.

ODAY: Them kids asked me to go to the park, shoot some hoops.

MINDIWAY: Better stay here.

ODAY: You ain't my mother.

MINDIWAY: But I'm all you got.

ODAY: I'm gonna go.

MINDIWAY: You could get lost.

ODAY: I already am.

(Getting up and walking off in direction kids went, MATILDA gleefully runs after him.)

MINDIWAY: I'll be here.

GIWAYDINUNG *(to grandmother)*: The journey isn't over, it's only just begun.

MINDIWAY: Yeah, well you don't have to be so chipper, this guy really does stink.

GIWAYDINUNG: Yeah, I guess.

MINDIWAY: The kid's gonna get hurt.

GIWAYDINUNG: I guess.

MINDIWAY: Are we almost through?

GIWAYDINUNG: He has a lot to learn.

MINDIWAY: I don't have much time.

GIWAYDINUNG: You have enough and so does he. This guy here will help you both, I promise, wait and see.

MINDIWAY: You know I'm old and tired, I thought my time was done.

GIWAYDINUNG: Not yet, grandma, not yet—you two rest, there's more work to be done.

MINDIWAY: You think I'm just gonna lay out here on the street with some old drunk?!

GIWAYDINUNG: No one will see—rest.

(She envelopes them with fog.)

SCENE 3

Lights out.

Lights come up, it is dusk. There are people on the street, hot summer night. Group of people standing on a porch, in darkness. Fog dissipates around MINDIWAY. She is alone, starts slowly waking up through first part of following scene. ODAY walks onto stage with other youths; they are teaching him hip hop moves. Mindiway watches. MATILDA and GIWAYDINUNG are finishing hot-dogs, watching ODAY. Both get up, MATILDA dancing towards ODAY, on the way transformed into a young person dressed in street gear. GIWAYDINUNG walks through trees (bushes) comes out dressed more fancy, in red, still a spirit that ODAY can't see. She copies dancers moves. MATILDA is the center of attention. ODAY is watching.

GIRL: You have fun today?

ODAY: Yeah.

GIRL: Whatcha gonna do now?

ODAY: I dunno.

GIRL: What about your grandma?

ODAY *(looking confused over to where MINDIWAY is just waking up)*: Oh.

MATILDA *(making complicated dance move)*: Hey kid, can you do this?

ODAY *(laughs)*: I can try.
BOY: You learn fast.
GIRL: Hang around.
GIRL: You'll learn a lot.
MINDIWAY *(yells)*: Kid!
GIRL: Your grandma's callin'.
MATILDA: She always hangin' on you? Ain't you got a life?
ODAY: Well, I want to go home.
BOY: Shoot, my folks don't even know where I am.
CHORUS FROM PORCH:
  Daddy's on a bender
  mama walks the streets
  pushing baby's stroller
  weary to the bone
GIRL: Mine would kill me if they knew I was out here.
CHORUS FROM THE PORCH:
  Daddy's working late again
  board meetings to attend
  mama's at the health club
  getting fit and trim
BOY: Ain't seen mine in a year.
CHORUS FROM THE PORCH:
  Daddy's at the crack house
  children all alone
  mama walks the streets
  rarely left alone
BOY: Left me at that stupid group home, didn't bother to come back.
ODAY: Don't you get lonely?
BOY: Lonely?
MATILDA: Lonely, we got each other bro.
GIWAYDINUNG:
  everyone needs a daddy
  everyone wants a mom
  the children of the world
  can't be left to fend alone
  there are so many dangers
  the nights are cold and long
  although we have these muscles
  sometimes the mind
  loses all control

CHORUS FROM PORCH:
  wanna buy a tree
  bud for you and me
MATILDA: Hell, Kid, you don't even know your name.
BOY: How you think you're gonna find your folks without even a name to go
  by?
CHORUS FROM THE PORCH:
  the night is dark
  no one can see
  have a rock
  this one's on me
MINDIWAY: Kid!
GIWAYDINUNG:
  we all need a daddy
  we all need a mom
  the children of the world
  can't be left to fend alone
  there are so many dangers
MINDIWAY:
  the nights are cold and long
  every child that's hurt
  a star in heaven dies

*(A shot rings out on the porch, all the children hit the ground, MINDIWAY
jumps up and runs across the street, hollering, "Kid, Kid." The other kids and
people on the porch run in all directions. MATILDA runs with them. GIWAY-
DINUNG hides in bushes. On the edge of the sidewalk, MINDIWAY falters,
reaches for her heart, falls to ground as ODAY slowly gets up, watching her.
When he realizes she is hurt he runs over.)*

ODAY: Mindiway, Mindiway, get up, what's wrong, get up!

*(Tries to get her to sit up, starts crying, sirens are heard way off in distance.
OLD MAN from the morning, clean, strong, walks out from trees.)*

OLD MAN *(picks up MINDIWAY and carries her)*: Come on kid, we got to get
  her home.

(Lights out)

ACT III

SCENE 1

Lights up just on a clearing on edge of forest. GRANDMOTHER is lying on ground, ODAY and OLD MAN are sitting by her. On the other part of the stage in darkness is a house, with a front and back door. The back door is into a bedroom. The front is into a kitchen /living room where a younger woman is sitting at the table. But right now the lights are on just ODAY and the OLD MAN with MINDIWAY lying on the ground.

ODAY *(to OLD MAN)*: Who are you?

MAIGUN: Maigun.

ODAY: I thought you were a drunk.

MAIGUN: Not everything is what it seems.

ODAY: How come you have a name and I don't?

MAIGUN: You do.

ODAY: Then what is it?

MAIGUN: She didn't tell you?

ODAY: Uh-uh.

CROW *(in tree)*:

    you had a name

    from whence you came

    they know you where you're going

    from the future

    they gently call your name

ODAY: What if she dies and I never get home?

MAIGUN: Guess it's time to apply what you've learned.

ODAY: But I don't know anything!

MAIGUN: Doesn't look like this is the time to whine, kid.

(He gets up and walks off, leaving a canteen of water behind.)

ODAY:

    grandma

    can't you tell me

    just who I am

    and where I've been

    there is no future

    without a past

    grandma

    can't you tell me

    just who I am

and where I'm going
seems I've been alone
for so long
with no one to help me
pick me up when I fall
that I can't reach out now
to grasp the hands I see extended toward me
grandma
can't you tell me
just who I am
where I've been
and where
I'm going

ODAY (*hollering after MAIGUN*):
I'm so lonely
on this journey
so small and all alone
somehow I need some guidance
to teach me right from wrong

MAIGUN (*hollering back*): Faith, kid, faith—time to practice what you've learned.

ODAY: Come on Mindiway, wake up, you can't die on me now. (*When she doesn't answer*) Who am I? Wake UP!! (*Then bursts into tears*)

GIWAYDINUNG'S VOICE (*softly, from offstage*):
who are you
a little boy
a grown man
who are you
or will you always be
running to and from
hiding from
the you
you could become

CROW: You my child are the answer to questions not yet asked
the answers are all around you
whatever you need will be given

(*CROW drops a branch on ground. ODAY picks it up and pokes at the ground. An eagle whistle is heard. ODAY notices the plant he is digging at; it is a straw-berry plant. He sits as if remembering. The OLD MAN is watching from a dis-*

tance, the CROW caws. ODAY is mashing up the plant leaves in his hand when he notices the canteen. He puts the leaves in the canteen and shakes it up. The CROW caws again, the EAGLE whistle is heard. ODAY holds up MINDIWAY's head and gives her a sip, then another one.)

MATILDA: The little brat thinks he's a doctor. He was better at shooting hoops.

GIWAYDINUNG: Shut up once and for all would you! You got the right idea Kid.

MATILDA: Gives her any more of that, her old ticker's going to go into overload.

(ODAY looks at MINDIWAY, confused. Picks more plants and mashes them in his hands and rubs over her breastbone. MINDIWAY starts to stir.)

MATILDA *(sarcastic)*: Oh, wow, a miracle!

MINDIWAY: Uhh, uhh.

GIWAYDINUNG: Come on Grandma, not yet.

ODAY: Mindiway.

MINDIWAY: Uhhhhh, uh.

ODAY: You okay?

MINDIWAY: Egh, Kid, you tryin' to kill me? What is that?

ODAY: Don't know.

MINDIWAY: Lemme see.

(Oday shows her plant.)

MINDIWAY *(looking at plant)*: Odayminung, heart berry.

MINDIWAY *(to ODAY)*: Help me up, we got to finish this journey today.

(They struggle up and into a walking position. Mindiway leaning on Oday, they walk off towards house as lights come up on that part of the stage.)

MINDIWAY *(pointing at back door)*: There.

ODAY: Here?

MINDIWAY: Sure thing Kid. Get me in there. Just gotta lay down for a bit.

(They enter back door. ODAY helps MINDIWAY into bed.)

MINDIWAY: Go out front, there's a girl sitting there. Old man Stillday's daughter. Tell her I had to lay down. If she gets nosy, tell her you're my grandson's son, visiting from town.

(ODAY starts to leave room.)

MINDIWAY: Kid, if she wants to know your name tell her you're Odayminung.

(ODAY turns and looks at MINDIWAY.)

CROW: Odayminung.
MATILDA: Odayminung?
EAGLE: Odayminung.
GIWAYDINUNG: Odayminung.
ODAY: I have a name?
MINDIWAY: You always did. But now you know. Heart berry, heart medicine. Kid, you're good for the heart.

(*As he leaves room, room turns blue.*)

MINDIWAY: Heart medicine.

Conclusion

Stage on MINDIWAY's side goes dark, lights on that side come up blue. MINDIWAY is in blue light in tree, ODAY is seen sitting and talking at table with OLD MAN STILLDAY's daughter. MATILDA is under tree GRAND-MOTHER is in. MATILDA's doing her version of workouts, looks angry and disgusted. Lights go down. CROW caws. EAGLE whistles.

The Girl Who Swam Forever

MARIE CLEMENTS

Produced by Savage Media, 1995.

Characters

Grandmother/The Old One: The girl's dead grandmother/An ancient Sturgeon/Old, gentle, and deep.

Forever/The Girl: A young Katzie girl of sixteen that is running from a Catholic mission school/ The Girl-Sturgeon in myth. She has a dreamlike quality and moves with the ease of a fish.

Ray/Brother Big Eyes: The Girl's Brother. Older and cooler. A great dancer/The Owl in the myth. Birdlike in movement and attitude.

Jim/The Fisherman: The Girl's lover/A young non-native fisherman.

The Church Frogs: Voices of the church. Nightmarish. The church conscience of the Girls. They take bodies as nuns and priests, dressed in black with large frog heads.

Setting

The play is both underwater and on land. Real and myth. Movement based. Using slides/video and soundscape to create both worlds.

Time: early sixties

Time: The beginning

"The Katzie descended from the first people God created on Pitt Lake. The ruler was known as Clothed with Power. This first chief had a son and a daughter. The daughter spent her days swimming and transformed into a sturgeon. The first fish to inhabit the Pitt Lake. It was from this girl that all sturgeon descended. After she left her brother wept uncontrollably and Clothed with Power took the silklike hair of the goat and transformed him into an owl-like bird that could only be seen by the Katzie descendants. It is only by human hand that a sturgeon can die and those that wish to take a sturgeon must first seek spirit power from her brother the white bird. Sometimes the sturgeon will make itself available to the fisherman. Sometimes a song must be chanted to which a steam will emerge and the sturgeon will make themselves caught floating to the surface belly up."—Old Pierre

"It is said that the white sturgeon are somehow involved in the whereabouts of souls of those who drown and whose bodies are never recovered from the river."—Robert Joe, A Ghost in the Water

From the darkness a voice speaks—large, dark, and old. A light splashes down into the darkness creating a filter that shows layers of blue from the highest/lightest to the darkest bottom. The light rests on the race of the OLD ONE. She rocks in a rocking chair on the bottom of the river, the light catching her face to and fro.

THE OLD ONE: Sometimes you don't know your own story from the bottom up, or from the top down, until it meets you. Meets in you. Words and silence, swimming and falling to the middle, circling each other in a dance of remembering. A remembering transforming. A dream from the here and now to the beginning, and again from the here and now to the beginning again.

(The light dims on the OLD ONE. The stage is left in darkness. Pairs of sturgeon eyes appear from the darkness.)

(The OLD ONE remains in the dark as the GRANDMOTHER. A dim light is brought up on a bed surface. It looks like mud but is the figure of a girl covered by a blanket. A brief projected image of a sturgeon on the blanket. It moves as the girl stirs.)

THE OLD ONE: A story begins from the darkest part of us to the deepest. From our unknown the lightest thing can surface. From the youngest the oldest thing can be born. To know this thing is to name an instinct you had before you knew how it sounded. An instinct you had before you knew how you looked. You swam, you flew, you sang, you loved things that did not know you existed and some that did. This thing will come to you and ask to be heard, to be seen, to be loved and that will make you bigger.

(As she sits up the sturgeon image vanishes. Small bulges appear under the blankets.)

FOREVER: It is hard to hide anything here. The smallest bulge can lead to a full day of prayers. The smallest apple stolen from the kitchen, the smallest piece of bread tucked inside, or under, can give you away. I can't sleep for trying to think about what I am going to do. I lie awake at night, night after night, and stare up into the ceiling and ask the darkness for an answer, but all I get is God's eyes looking at me, and it is not an answer he is giving me but a dirty look.

(As she mouths words to a song, her GRANDMOTHER sings the song softly finally reaching her hand over and gently stroking her GRANDCHILD's hair.)

FOREVER: So I close my eyes hoping he won't be able to see me and I try to sing or mouth words that my Grandmother used to say to me when everything went dark. Dark when my father disappeared, dark when my mother disappeared, dark until all that was left was the sound of my grandmother's soft words and her hands coming, appearing out of that darkness, stroking my head and hair and tears, until those old hands took my pain in their creases and smoked them.

(The GRANDMOTHER's hands disappear.)

FOREVER: I know my father and mother didn't really disappear but it feels that way when people die. One minute they are here, right here, and the next they are gone, just gone, and no matter how far or hard you look for them they are just gone. My father was swept away by the river and my Grandmother says my mother . . .

GRANDMOTHER: . . . couldn't take it anymore.

FOREVER: I wonder if she died of "I couldn't take it anymore."

(Light up on the hands of her GRANDMOTHER intertwined lying on her lap rocking in and out of the light as she goes back and forth.)

FOREVER: My grandmother's soft words would end then and she would take those smoking hands and weave them together and leave them in the middle of her lap for the longest time, her eyes bent on them, rocking a pain back and forth.

(FOREVER reaches over and touches those hands.)

FOREVER: "It's alright Grandma, it's alright." I try to remember everyone sometimes. I remember my Grandmother best because she disappeared not long ago, and sometimes I don't think she's disappeared at all. I remember her hands and the sound of her words. I remember pieces of everyone—my father's strong arms pulling up fishnets, my mother's long black hair and my brother. I need to see my brother just to make sure he hasn't disappeared and either have I. This place can make you feel like everything has disappeared. Tomorrow I'll take my leave of absence and steal as many apples and pieces of bread I want from the kitchen. I'll bulge out everywhere and run. I know they'll come after me but I'll go to the places I remember and they don't know and maybe they won't find me this time. Sister Alphonse says that God sees everything. And I won't argue that, but if he sees what I know, and I know he knows because I can feel him giving me a dirty look. He knows, but he hasn't told anybody here and that's a good sign.

(Darkness)

(The sound of a train approaching. We hear it before we see it. A train light blares on her like a confession light getting brighter and brighter. The sound of the train increases with growing intensity, wheels turning and a train passing throughout. The voice of the OLD ONE whispers as the train.)

FOREVER: Every time I see a train I feel like trying to catch it. I feel like running with it as fast as I can. Trying to keep up with it until the very moment it rushes past whispering that you could be part of it . . . if you could just run fast enough. "Run Faster." It whispers right in your ear and then swims past like it wanted to tell you something else but changed its mind. It leaves you like a giant sigh. "We could have gone somewhere."Anywhere. I think of my brother, words unspoken. I think of Old Al's leg that was cut off by a train. I think I like my body parts.

(The sound and image of the train passing)

FOREVER: I watch it pass. I think about an elder who wanted his spirit guardian to be a locomotive because it was so strong and made of steel. It had an iron history but saw the future. I should have been made of steel.

(A train blast)

(The image of trees taking over. Forever walks through the trees and sits on a swing. Forever's eyes are closed, listening to the woods, and approaching steps.) *Voice-over—replies of "I don't know, I haven't seen her, etc., from the reservation filter under the action.)*

(The outline of boy hiding behind a tree and looking at her)

FOREVER: I was swinging on the swing, swinging good sounding lies back and forth trying to think—what to tell my brother, when I felt these eyes on me. I kept my eyes closed so I could hear the sound of leaves crying out crunch by crunch . . . getting closer . . . smashing the upturned leaves like hands curling and caught under a weight foot, by noisy foot. *(To herself)* I hear you . . . do you think I have no ears ? *(She yells at him)* "Hey, do you think I have no ears?" Quiet. Just the sound of his eyes on my body. You know, blue eyes . . . eyes lookin' at you like you were some kind of strange sight . . . like white boy eyes lookin' straight at your private parts as you walk by. Quiet. It made me madder and madder that he could look at me that way and I was the one who was supposed to be embarrassed.

(She jumps from the swing and yells in his direction again.)

FOREVER: "I'm gonna tell my brother you know. I'm gonna tell my brother about you and if he doesn't get you I will." . . . Quiet.

(Sound of leaf steps going and the increasing sound of frogs ribbitting)

FOREVER: Then the sound of fast crunching leaves and frogs. Someone saw me and they will talk . . . talk up a damn ribbit storm gossiping . . . getting me caught. Damn him and these damn noisy frogs. "I could eat you little frogs. I could stick you with a big pointy stick clear through and barbeque you, so watch what you say."

(The frogs become silent.)

FOREVER: Quiet. So quiet. Quiet. I felt guilty. I shouldn't have yelled. So quiet I could hear my conscience getting closer and I knew God had finally told them and they were looking for me and they were getting closer.

(The sound of the croaking frogs becomes more humanlike; voices of her church conscience.)

(The outline of priests and nuns appear between the trees. Their faces reveal them to have frog faces. The sound and actions of the church frogs become nightmarish and menacing. A drum has been placed at the middle of her and the circle is being stretched painfully. The green of the forest fades into the dark red of roe taking center on her stomach. They pull at her.)

FOREVER: Finally placing their hands on me. Tugging and pulling and stretching a confession any way they could. Tugging at my words and pulling them till I don't know what I just said. Stretching any truth to lies. Pulling my body till this bulbous middle shifts itself from fear. This fear moves in me and dislodges this foaming guilt that makes me sick every morning scared everyone will see this bulge. I don't tell them the skin on my stomach is starting to stretch like I was making a drum. I don't tell them. I don't confess anything. I don't tell anybody. Anything. They would sneak peeks at my drum. I cover my belly.

(A CHURCH FROG hits her stomach with a drumstick. A loud drumbeat sounds.)

(She crouches doubled up and sick. The sound of leaves crunching and approaching steps. She hears them but doesn't look up. BROTHER BIG EYES walks to her. Throughout the scene they are moving from the forest to an abandoned boat.)

FOREVER: Ray?

BRO. B EYES: Yeah. It's me. Are you okay?

FOREVER: Yeah.

BRO. B EYES: You don't look okay.

FOREVER: I'm alright now. I just felt kinda of sick, that's all.

BRO. B EYES: You sure? How did you know it was me?

FOREVER: I didn't. How did you know it was me?

BRO. B EYES: I didn't. I was just going to see if you were at the boat and I heard all this frog racket and thought somebody must be here. So I thought it might be you.

FOREVER: Oh.

BRO. B EYES: So?

FOREVER: So what?

BRO. B EYES: You know, so what? I wasn't expecting you till the holidays.

FOREVER: Why, you would have dressed for it?

BRO B EYES: At least shaved.

FOREVER: You're shaving now?

BRO. B EYES: I was always shaving.

FOREVER: Now you were always shaving.

BRO. B EYES: Okay, okay I finally got this amazing, growth.

FOREVER: Scary.

BRO. B EYES: Besides being there. What's wrong?

FOREVER: Nothing. I just needed to see you. You know. I just needed to . . . I miss her. I thought maybe by being here . . .

BRO. B EYES: Yeah, I miss her too.

FOREVER: You should miss the way she dressed you.

BRO. B EYES: She never dressed me . . . Okay, she helped . . . I like the way I'm dressed.

FOREVER: Real Tough.

BRO. B EYES: What?

FOREVER: I said you look real good. Really.

BRO. B EYES: Well, you're not going to look too good with a bald head.

FOREVER: Only if they catch me. They said they were going to shave my head if I ran away again and they caught me. They are not going to catch me this time.

BRO. B EYES: You better hope not because you'd look really ugly with no hair.

FOREVER: I think I'd still look pretty good.

BRO. B EYES: Oh yeah, they'll be lining up to marry you. Your only hope would be to marry Old Al.

FOREVER: Perfect. He has no teeth and he has a wooden leg.

BRO. B EYES: Well, you are getting older and if they catch you you'll have no hair. I think you'd make a real pretty bald, legless couple and have real ugly babies.

FOREVER: Thanks. (*She turns away.*)

BRO. B EYES: What's wrong?

FOREVER: Nothing.

BRO. B EYES: I was just kidding.

FOREVER: I know.

BRO. B EYES: Hey . . . don't worry . . . we'll think of something. Maybe they're tired of running after you.

FOREVER: Ray?

BRO. B EYES: Yeah.

FOREVER: Do you ever see Grandma?

BRO. B EYES: Forever?

FOREVER: Don't look at me that way. I know she's dead but do you ever see her?

BRO. B EYES: No, but sometimes I can feel her and sometimes I think I dream of her when I'm sleeping but when I wake up I can't remember the dream but I feel like she was there. Just for a second. You're not gonna go all weird on me are you?

FOREVER: Too late.

BRO. B EYES: Way too late.

BRO. B EYES: Well, I should go see how the search party is doing. They'll be looking for me to say my good words . . . "No, I don't know where she is." Do you think they think I'm lying?

FOREVER: When are you coming back?

BRO. B EYES: As soon as I can. You'll be alright here.

FOREVER: Yeah, I know.

BRO. B EYES: I'll bring you some stuff. You okay? You sure?

FOREVER: Yeah, sure.

(*She sits under the abandoned hull of a boat that is made of the ribs of a fish skeleton.*)

(*BROTHER BIG EYES goes to leave and then stops and watches her settle into the hull of the boat without her knowing he is watching her.*)

BRO. B EYES: I could feel she wasn't telling me everything. I could feel a change. I thought maybe they had done some things with her at the mission school that she didn't think she could tell me. Some things that nobody here wanted to hear but it came out anyway. Came out in strange ways. In mother's crying through the night and father's loading and reloading their guns and then simply having to put them down, placing them down, the

weight of having to put them down, the weight of that moment of helpless-
ness leaving a hunch in their backs forever. The weight of that rage never
leaving their bodies. It wasn't their way. It wasn't our way. Would it be my
way? I don't know. Rage comes easy to me. It bunches up in my fists heavy
until I let them fly. In this flying I come to understand a power. I know it is
a power misused but I feel this power and it feels old, and I know it knows
me, and knows what I am up against, and comes to me to make the fight an
honest one, or at least even. At least even.

(He exits)

*(FOREVER gets comfortable in the boat. A blue light fades up on the hull of the
boat. She dips her foot in and then her body and finally is submerged in the
color of water.)*

FOREVER: Now that I'm here, I can't stop thinking about him. Thinking about
the first time I saw him. I'd seen him before, everybody here has seen
everybody before. But it was the first time I really saw him. And I think it
was the first time anybody had really seen me.

*(A light dims up on the water tower and reveals the shadowy figure of a man
looking down.)*

FOREVER: I was just getting out of the water after a swim. And I felt something looking at me.

(She looks up at him. He climbs down and crosses track to the other side.)

FOREVER: Somebody looking at me. Somebody was way up on the water tower
looking down. We looked at each other. I couldn't see his face but a body
that positioned itself so comfortable, so arrogantly there like he thought he
was an eagle or something and at any moment he could leave. . . . He came
down from the tower and walked over to me and just said Hi.
JIM: Hi.
FOREVER: Just like that. He said he'd been watching me swim. He said he'd
been watching me swim, every day for a few days and that I looked like I
could really swim.
JIM: You look like you were born to swim.
FOREVER: I said, "What were you born to do? He said, he was . . .
JIM: . . . "Born to be wild."
FOREVER: We laughed. But it was more than that. It's that feeling you get when
you meet someone and know that you are different from each other because
it is obvious, but what makes you stand and stare is that you know you are
same in ways that you can't explain yet—you just recognize each other.

(Scene fades with them just standing and looking at each other.)

(BROTHER BIG EYES stands on the railroad tracks between either side of town. He carries a bag full of food to give to FOREVER.)

BRO. B EYES: I can feel them talking. I can't always make out what they are saying but I can tell they are talking and talking, and that talking has something to do with something they don't know anything about. Sometimes that talking comes with a laughter. A laughter that comes out and then turns its head on you, and turns into a whisper. That whisper turns into a hush. Some kind of civilized hush . . . that I wish I could break. I feel they are talking not about me but about mine but I can't hear it all, and it makes me nervous. Edgy. It makes me think this has something to do with Forever and that . . . that is . . . not acceptable. My sister is not for them to even talk about. Somebody's been where they shouldn't be. Because I can feel them talking about it. They know something I don't know and that is dangerous.

(FOREVER sits in the hull of the boat looking out over the water. BROTHER BIG EYES watches her and walks in.)

BRO. B EYES: Hey, how come you look so sad? What's wrong?
FOREVER: Nothing.
BRO. B EYES: Oh come on—it's me.
FOREVER: It's not important.
BRO. B EYES: Forever?
FOREVER: What?
BRO. B EYES: Why did you run away this time?
FOREVER: *(No response)*
BRO. B EYES: Forever! *(He goes to push her playfully and winds up a punch.)*
FOREVER: Like hell, try it. *(She winds up.)*
BRO. B EYES: Don't swear.
FOREVER: Don't tell me how to talk.
BRO. B EYES: Didn't those priests and nuns teach you nothin'?
FOREVER: Nothing. Didn't they teach you nothing?
BRO. B EYES: Nothing for years and look at me now.
FOREVER: Yeah . . . look at you now.
BRO. B EYES: They're still out there looking for you, you know.
FOREVER: I know.
BRO. B EYES: And sooner or later they'll find you.
FOREVER: I don't think so.
BRO. B EYES: And take you back to . . .
FOREVER: Straight back to . . .
BRO. B EYES: To . . .

FOREVER: Divinity.

BRO. B EYES: Scary word!

FOREVER: It's a scary place . . .

(Long pause)

BRO. B EYES: Did something happen there?

FOREVER: Just the usual.

BRO. B EYES: I don't know then. . . . Is this about a guy, Forever? If it is I'll tell them where you are myself.

FOREVER: No you wouldn't.

BRO. B EYES: Don't push me.

FOREVER: OOOOooo now that's scary. What makes you think it's a guy?

BRO. B EYES: What makes you think I'm so stupid?

FOREVER: I won't answer that.

BRO. B EYES: If it wasn't a guy you'd have already told me what was wrong.

FOREVER: Maybe it's none of your business.

BRO. B EYES: You're my business.

FOREVER: Why?

BRO. B EYES: Because I'm your brother.

FOREVER: So?

BRO. B EYES: So tell me about it.

FOREVER: I can't . . . yet . . . things are just changing that's all. I'm changing.

BRO. B EYES: Changing . . . what does changing mean?

FOREVER: I never used to have to explain things to you.

BRO. B EYES: I never used to have to ask. Do I know him? It's a him isn't it? This whole thing is about a him isn't it?

FOREVER: No, it isn't.

BRO. B EYES: Don't lie.

FOREVER: I'm not lying.

BRO. B EYES: Well I hope he knows who your brother is. Because if you ran away to be with some asshole you're both going to be sorry. Do you hear me, Forever?

FOREVER: No. . . . Of course I hear you, you're yelling right at me.

BRO. B EYES: I'm not yelling.

FOREVER: Yes, you are.

BRO. B EYES: No I'm not.

FOREVER: Yes, you are. . . . Ray, I missed you too.

BRO. B EYES: I didn't say I missed you.

FOREVER: You didn't have to.

BRO. B EYES: Yeah, well I'll see you later. I got some things I have to take care of.

FOREVER: Like what?

BRO. B EYES: It's none of your business.

(BROTHER BIG EYES exits. FOREVER lays down in the boat and falls asleep.

(DREAM MUSIC filters up.)

(The boat begins to rock with the music. Just the hands of her GRANDMOTHER steering the motion. Water light dims and fills the stage to a deepwater darkness filtering light. FOREVER floats down into the dream—the river. THE OLD ONE takes her place at the bottom of the riverbed in her rocking chair. A sturgeon image grows from her, making her bigger and bigger as she talks.)

THE OLD ONE: A hundred years I have been talking but no one has listened. I
    weigh 800 pounds with words spoken but not heard. 800 pounds I have
    grown 100 years to reach you but still nothing. Nothing until I heard my
    voice swimming inside you. I took those 800 pounds of silence and spun
    them in years of circles to create you. You are made of words in my silence.
    You are made of a silence that is me before everything.

FOREVER: I do not see well here.

(BROTHER BIG EYES floats by on a bicycle.)

FOREVER: It is dark like a great dream.

(CHURCH FROGS counting apples)

FOREVER: I cast my shadow and the bottom of my world moves fishlike.

(She moves. Her shadow is larger than her girl body and sturgeonlike. Similar sturgeon shadows gather around her.)

FOREVER: That is all I have to understand.

(Garbage descends down to the river bottom. Beer bottles, an old boot, a bicycle wheel, bones, flecks of sawdust.)

THE OLD ONE: It is crowded here with all that has been discarded. There are
    my people, some bone white from the journey. Some calling to join us from
    under the sawdust. Some—still some—large with words unspoken. It is
    crowded here with all that has been discarded . . . sunken boats and bones
    and me . . . sunken boats and bones and me.

FOREVER: It is cold here. And hot here. And cold when it should be hot, and
    hot when it should be cold.

THE OLD ONE: No one knows where to dream anymore. No one knows where a
    million year old dream can go. So we rise up to lay on your banks, not
    because we have given up but because we are dreaming of a new beginning.

(FOREVER rises up with the light and returns to her sleeping form.)

FOREVER: Grandma? *(in sleep)*

(Blackout)

(BROTHER BIG EYES enters from a high perch and looks down on FOR-EVER as she sleeps. He takes the drum and stirs a thinking circle. He slowly lays the drum down and falls asleep on his perch.)

(JIM approaches her and wakes her gently. The following scene is more about what isn't said than what is.)

FOREVER: Hey . . .
JIM: Hi . . . What are you doing here?
FOREVER: What are you doing here? You first.
JIM: I heard you might be, or somebody might be down here somewhere.
FOREVER: Who did you hear it from? My brother?
JIM: If I heard it from your brother I don't think I'd be here.
FOREVER: Right. I wanted to . . . talk . . . talk to you . . .
JIM: I was thinking about you.
FOREVER: I need to tell you something and it's real . . .
JIM: About . . .
FOREVER: Us . . . Oh God/ . . . (Shit did I say)
JIM: /Oh shit
FOREVER: /God.
JIM: You wanted to talk to me about God.
FOREVER: You wanted to talk to me about Shit.
FOREVER: No./ . . .
JIM: /No . . . I just wanted to know you were okay.
FOREVER: Are you okay?
JIM: I think so.

(Long pause)

(He slowly silently digs in his pocket and puts his rosary beads in her hands.)

FOREVER: He knew but he didn't want to know. He didn't want to hear the words. I started crying. I couldn't help myself. He put his rosary beads into my hands . . .

(A drumbeat comes in softly and then louder as a heartbeat, mixed with water sounds, a low song.)

FOREVER: Do you think these will help? . . . Small round cool beads in my sweating hands. . . . Do *you* think these will help? . . . That's when *his* hands starting sweating. He just stared at me. Quiet for a long time. So quiet he was almost begging me not to tell him so I just sat there and he just sat down. Me wishing he would say something and him wishing I wouldn't say anything. So quiet I started listening to my insides. I could hear Grandmother's voice inside me. Right inside my stomach with it. Listening, guggling, bubbling through my veins. Not so much words but a song she used to sing to me when I was a kid and scared. Vibrating through my body like the heartbeat of a drum. He got quieter. I asked him if he could hear anything.

FOREVER: Can you hear anything?

JIM: No.

FOREVER: No? No . . . I wasn't about to tell him about my Grandmother was there inside me too . . . he looked scared enough. I wanted to tell him, to ask him . . . to say . . .

JIM: I can't hear a thing.

FOREVER: You can't hear a thing. I know. I know . . .

(*They stare at each other.*)

He looked at me like he felt sorry for me. I looked at him the same.

(*He finally exits. She lies back down and holds herself. She falls asleep.*)

DREAM MUSIC: Old to new.

(*THE OLD ONE enters speaking in Katzie and English. She takes her place as the storyteller in her rocking chair. BROTHER BIG EYES wakes up in his dream. He places the drum in the sky and raises it to become a moon. He dives into the water as FOREVER falls into it.*)

(*THE GIRL and BROTHER BIG EYES echo some of the Katzie words, remembering fragments of their language.*)

FOREVER: I am dreaming.

BRO. B EYES: I am dreaming.

THE OLD ONE: The Lord Above gave my forefather a wife by whom he had two offsprings, a son and daughter. These children never ate food, but spent all their days in the water—

(*FOREVER and BROTHER BIG EYES begin to move in slow motion, as if through water.*)

F/BBE: I remember the river.

THE OLD ONE: "My friends," he said, "you know that my daughter spends all her days in the water. For the benefit of generations to come, I have decided she shall remain there forever."

BRO. B EYES: Forever?

THE OLD ONE: He led her to the water's edge and said, "My daughter, you are enamored of the water. For the benefit for generations to come, I shall now change you into a sturgeon."

(FOREVER begins to transform and move like a sturgeon, the image of a sturgeon appears on her as she moves.)

THE GIRL: I am floating under the water softly.

THE OLD ONE: "Thus the sturgeon was created in Pitt Lake, the first fish that ever ruffled its waters."

THE GIRL: I do not see well here. It is dark.

THE OLD ONE: "Oetectaan's son mourned so inconsolably for his sister that at last his father summoned the people again."

(BROTHER BIG EYES transforms into an owl. He takes his place on his perch as an owl. He grabs the moon and begins drumming with the music.)

THE OLD ONE: "He plucked the finest and silkiest hair from the mountain goat, laid it on the boy's head and limbs and transformed him into a bird. 'Fly away,' he said. 'Hereafter the man who wishes to capture your sister, the sturgeon, shall seek power from you.'"

BROTHER/GIRL: It is far down, this dream.

BRO. B EYES: I see everything.

THE GIRL: I cast my shadow and the bottom of my world moves fishlike.

BRO. B EYES: I cast my shadow and the bottom of my world moves under my wings.

THE OLD ONE: Sometimes the sturgeon will make itself available to a fisherman.

MUSIC: "Last Kiss" fades up and over original dream music.

(BROTHER BIG EYES, seeing the fisherman and hearing the strange music, tries to drum as loud as the song. Lights fade him out musically and visually.)

(Lights up on JIM as a fisherman on the water tower. The fisherman lowers his fishing line—a long huge string of rosary beads—and lifts her up. Sturgeon images dance on the screen around them.)

FOREVER: I like to dance and you like to pray and sometimes when you fall you fall for me and we dance. Oh we dance.

(The two embrace and discover each other.)

(He lifts her up and a cloud of steam covers them. . . . THE OLD ONE continues . . .)

THE OLD ONE: Sometimes a song must be chanted to which steam will emerge and the sturgeon will make herself caught floating to the surface belly up.

(Underwater sex scene)

FOREVER: I am so close to hearing your words
   I am too close.
   I am so close to believing your words
   I am suffocating.
   I am so close to your words I can't hear that
   your words have become a hook.
   I swallow those words.
   Some bubbling from your mouth.
   Some coming from your eyes.
   I swallow them all.
   Blue sky eyes and all.
   Swallow till they reach the bottom of me where
   everything is silent and still. Unspeakable
   and dark. I have fallen for your words and you
   have fallen into me.

(Steam finally takes over the stage and covers everything but the image of THE OLD ONE rocking.)

THE OLD ONE: It is said that the white sturgeon are somehow involved in the souls of those who drown and whose bodies are never recovered from the river.

(THE OLD ONE disappears. Whiteness fades and leaves FOREVER waking up trying to surface from the dream, confused by her form.)

FOREVER: I came up between the log booms, sticks squishing each side of me till I became smaller and browner, and they became as wide as a forest, few breaths in between. I had been dreaming to the top and got caught between the worlds.

(BROTHER BIG EYES drops from his perch and confronts her.)

BRO. B EYES: Forever?
FOREVER: What?
BRO. B EYES: It's him isn't it?
FOREVER: Him who?
BRO. B EYES: Jim Harding.
FOREVER: Jim who?

BRO. B EYES: You slept with him didn't you?

FOREVER: You don't understand.

BRO. B EYES: What's to understand?

FOREVER: If you just let me explain/

BRO. B EYES: /Explain what, that my sister is sleeping with every guy in town?
. . .

FOREVER: It isn't like that.

BRO. B EYES: No, let me guess . . . you're in love . . . you are both in love and
you're gonna get married. You're 16. He's white for Christ's sake.

FOREVER: It's not about that.

BRO. B EYES: What's it about? Do you want to tell me what it is about? What!
Let me guess this white guy is going to take you away from all of this, is that
right is that right is that what he said "Huh"?

FOREVER: He didn't say anything.

BRO. B EYES: I could feel them talking you know . . . talking all over my back
as if I couldn't see who left their looks on me. Talking all the time and all
the time it's you this is about you and some guy you let touch you. Everybody knows Forever. EVERYBODY and the whole town will know by now.
Look at you. Look at what he's done to you. Gave you a little more than you
expected didn't he?

FOREVER: Stop it. *(She tries to cover herself.)*

BRO. B EYES: Didn't he?

FOREVER: What . . . don't look at me that way?

BROTHER: You're pregnant aren't you?

FOREVER: *(Nothing)*

BRO. B EYES: Aren't you? Tell me the truth!

FOREVER: I always tell you the truth. Yes . . . yes!! Alright.

BRO. B EYES: Did you tell him?/ What did he say?

FOREVER: /I think he knows but . . .

BRO. B EYES: What did the great man say?

FOREVER: He didn't say anything.

BRO. B EYES: I'll change that. He'll have a lot to say . . .

FOREVER: Ray don't . . .

BRO. B EYES: Ray don't what???

FOREVER: Don't . . . don't do this . . . calm down . . . *(She tries to settle him
down.)*

BRO. B EYES: It's already done . . . don't touch me. Don't come near me.

FOREVER: You promised you'd always be there . . . you promised you'd never
disappear. Please Ray, you're the only one left I . . . can . . .

*(BROTHER BIG EYES stops and is about to give in but leaves. FOREVER
wanders through space lost and trying to put herself together.)*

FOREVER (*whispering*): I can . . . I can . . . I can I can . . .

(*The area turns green. Sound of rain coming down and the CHURCH FROGS. She is wet and standing in the forest. CHURCH FROGS—croaking soft prayers of baptism, then, louder and harsher prayers. They should be under the following but rise to it and her desperation. An image of herself as the mission school-girl appears on her or the chorus.*)

CHURCH FROGS: You kneel down on the floor in front of everybody. Tell them you're sorry you ran away. You're no different than the rest of them! How we gonna beat the devil out of you. . . . The devil is strong in you. So strong. Are you feeling dirty because of what happened? These wild little Indians, pagans.

FOREVER: I was baptizing myself in the rain, asking forgiveness for the fact. I thought the rain would stream down my body in rivers and make me clean again. Stream down my hair, my eyes, my neck, downstream over my breasts to the middle of me. The very middle. My own ceremony. Drops of holy water washing. No priest for me this time. No confession. Just me and the Virgin Mary talking straight cause I thought she might understand because she had a baby even though she was a virgin. Anyways, it doesn't hurt to ask.

(*The image of herself as a woman appears. The woman is sexual and nude. She lays the beads over herself.*)

I took my lover's beads so I could wear them day in and day out. I wore them so I could feel them lay on top of me. The cross at the end stretching and pointing below my belly reminding me. My first time with a man. I wore them so I could count each bead according to what I was praying for. Him or me. Or him with me. Or me with memory of him between my legs . . .

(*Image of herself large with pregnancy*)

I wonder if I could unhook this child from me, this dream from me. If I could pull the pieces from me that did not fit. Red fleshy bits of blood and me left at the end of a hook and weighing down on this webbed net . . .

I could've gutted myself right there just to see if like a fish I would die swift and spineless, mercifully headless. No dream, just the red stain of blood left on the pier joining the other stains of death ingrained into the wood.

(*She takes the beads and is about to stab herself with a cross.*)

If I could take this knife and cut the ancient and new from me. Cut the circle from my gut and take that circle, wash it in the river and see what it is made of. Is it flesh, my flesh? Or dreams that do not fit between these worlds.

(The image of a sturgeon appears on her.)

When it is all said and done throw my bones in the river brother . . . this place is too hungry and greedy and needy for me. Throw my bones in the river. I have given all I know . . . and leave knowing nothing. Throw my bones in the river throw my bones in the river brother . . . hurry I want to go home!

(The shadow of THE OLD ONE–Sturgeon comes from behind her fishlike. The CHURCH FROGS back away and fade. Her GRANDMOTHER's hand reaches in the light and gently rests her hand on her Grandchild's head and strokes her hair. She sings softly.)

GRANDMOTHER: It will be alright . . . shssh . . . it will be alright. I am here Forever. I am here . . .

(She places her hand on FOREVER's stomach.)

Here. Here. These pieces, these stories have found a place in you. Found a place to grow from the beginning and circle to include everything that is you and circle to include everything that is us. Here. Here. It circles and in this motion a million year old dream surfaces. A dream that is being made smaller by the loudness of a dream silenced. Here. Here. Let this dream breathe. Let its breath flow in you, taking you, shaping you with its memory and your future. Here. Here you will grow stronger. Here. Here you will grow larger in the knowledge it will never disappear from you. Here. Here. Let us swim. Here. Here. Let us dream. Let us dream. Let us swim away on land.

(The sound of a train approaching in the distance getting closer. The train's mechanical sound is mixed with the low sound of the sturgeon. FOREVER turns and runs for it. BROTHER BIG EYES is searching frantically for her.)

FOREVER: All I know was that I was running.
THE OLD ONE: All I know was that she was swimming.
BRO. B EYES: Forever!
FOREVER: Running and then swimming forward.
BRO. B EYES: Come back. . . . Come back. I didn't mean it.
FOREVER: Running and running . . .
THE OLD ONE: Swimming and swimming . . .
BRO. B EYES: Seeing everything but her.
FOREVER: Falling into place.
BRO. B EYES: Forever!
THE OLD ONE: She fell from the sky and landed here large.

FOREVER: Swimming.

THE OLD ONE: Bigger than your mind can imagine.

FOREVER: Reaching out and away.

THE OLD ONE: Longer than her black braids.

BRO. B EYES: Where are you?

THE OLD ONE: Quieter than your conscience.

BRO. B EYES: I'm here for you.

THE OLD ONE: More patient than a human century.

BRO. B EYES: I'll be right here waiting for you.

FOREVER: Running and swimming.

BRO. B EYES: Seeing you.

THE OLD ONE: Swimming and swimming.

FOREVER: Like steel.

(We see FOREVER catching train. Image of her looking out of a train. The train becomes a white sturgeon and a train, a white sturgeon and train, white sturgeon, train. Like it is dancing between the two.)

BRO. B EYES: Pieces flying together.

THE OLD ONE: Stories meeting.

FOREVER: And swimming away on land.

BRO. B EYES: Getting smaller and smaller.

THE OLD ONE: Meeting in you.

FOREVER: Seeing everything.

THE OLD ONE: Circling in you.

FOREVER: Taking everything.

THE OLD ONE: Into a beginning.

BRO. BIG EYES: Disappearing.

FOREVER: Into the city.

(The sturgeon train gets smaller and disappears from sight. BROTHER BIG EYES takes the moon from the sky and drums and sings, water sounds fade up. Owl-like he perches. His song becomes a wailing and begins to mix with tears of the rain.)

BRO. B EYES: I'll wait for you. I'll be right here waiting for you.

THE OLD ONE: She was a watery thought one murky night. She formed out of our insistence. Taking shape and shore. Taking pleasure, conceiving a dream for the Old Ones. A dream that has washed up alive on our banks. Changing form but not intention. We dream a new beginning to this end.

(Image of train entering the city)

FOREVER: *(Voice-over)* I am swimming Grandma. I am going to have this baby, this dream. Maybe it will have blue eyes and brown skin. Blue eyes so it won't have to stare at us anymore because it would know us, because it would know itself.

(The carcass of a sturgeon is strung up and cut open.)

(The image and the cry of a new child)

(A leaping sturgeon)

THE OLD ONE *laughs.*

THE BEGINNING

Acknowledgments and Sources

The playwright is indebted to Wayne Suttles and Diamond Jenness, editors of *Katzie Ethnographical Notes: The Faith of a Coast Salish Indian.* The Genesis story, the second dream in *The Girl Who Swam Forever,* is taken from Old Pierre's retelling of the original story. Thanks also to Terry Glavin for *A Ghost in the Water,* published by New Star Books; to Agnes Pierre and the Pierre family; to Nelson Gray, author of the play *Talker's Town,* produced by Savage Media. *The Sturgeon Song* was written and composed by Wayne Lavallee. Finally, thanks to the Westminister Fish Company.

Harvest Ceremony:
Beyond the Thanksgiving Myth

MARTHA KREIPE DE MONTAÑO
WITH JENNIFER FELL HAYES

Characters

Theresa White Cloud/Elder Sister (a Wampanoag in the past)/Catherine (a Pilgrim in the past)

Bill White Cloud/Tisquantum (a Wampanoag in the past)/William (a Pilgrim in the past) and Moshup (Wampanoag culture hero in storytelling scene)

Mattie White Cloud (a teenager)

Younger Brother (a Wampanoag from the past)/Bartholomew, Catherine and William's son (a Pilgrim in the past)

Spirit from the Past

Musician (background music and sound effects)

The audience members will be placed in-role as Pilgrims and helpers and be told that they will be asked to take part in the play as actors. They will receive name tags complete with actual Pilgrim names. During the interactive segment, they'll be called by their "Pilgrim" names.

Setting/Costumes

The time is the present, a few days before Thanksgiving. The play takes place in two time periods—the present and Dream Time. Dream Time is what it was like nearly 400 years ago (1620). In scenes that take place in the present, they wear jeans and T-shirts or any contemporary clothing. In the very first part, they use their real names when they introduce themselves.

Most actors play multiple roles. In the dream scenes, Mattie's parents appear as historic characters. Dad is Tisquantum, Mom is Elder Sister, and Aunt Molly is The Spirit from the Past. They also take the part of Pilgrims and change costume by putting on "Pilgrim" capes and hats over their buckskin, all in full view onstage. The Wampanoag wear Eastern Woodlands style buckskin clothing in dream scenes. The Spirit from the Past wears a white buckskin dress.

Interactive Teaching Section

In the teaching section, the actors step out of role and teach the following skills using pantomime and reproductions of tools the 17th-century Wampanoag would have used:

1. Using a fishnet and a spear, TISQUANTUM teaches through pantomime how to catch fish with the dip net and how to spear fish with a spear whose tip is made from the spine of a horseshoe crab. He explains that some of the fish is eaten and some is used for fertilizer.
2. Using pantomime, ELDER SISTER makes a mound of earth over a fish, and plants four seeds of corn in the top of the mound and plants beans and squash at the bottom of the mound so the beans will climb up the corn stalk and the squash will spread out underneath. She explains that these three crops were planted together and are often called the Three Sisters.
3. Using a deer blade hoe (made from a deer scapula bone), YOUNGER BROTHER shows how to weed the garden. Then, using real dried corn on the cob, he shows how to pick the corn and how to husk and shuck the cob to get corn kernels.
4. SPIRIT shows how corn is put into a corn pounder made of a hollowed wooden log and is made into cornmeal by pounding it with a wooden pestle. Then some is used for food and some is stored to be used later.

Note: the play starts with everyone dressed in everyday clothes.

SCENE I

MATTIE: Hi everyone, welcome to our Museum. I'm glad you've come and that you've all arrived safely. We'd like to share a bit of history with you, but before we begin, we'd like to acknowledge and thank all of the things that are truly important to all of us . . . all the things that we could not live without.

DAD: We'd like to acknowledge our Mother, the Earth, who provides us with everything we need for life. We recognize and offer our thanks to our Elder Brother the Sun, who gives us warmth and who causes everything to grow; to our Grandfathers, the Winds of the Four Directions who give us air to breathe. We honor our Grandfather Water, who nourishes the plants and who gives us something we all need to survive. We thank and recognize all the animals of the earth and all of the plants. We consider them to be our Brothers and our Sisters and they give up their lives to provide us with our food, with medicine, shelter and clothing. We need all of the forces of nature—

EVERYONE: all of us. Without them there is no life on this planet. We are all related—

AUNT MOLLY: Mother Earth,

MOM: the Grandfathers of the Four Directions,

YOUNGER BROTHER: Water,

MATTIE: our Brothers and Sisters,

DAD: the Plants and Animals.

MATTIE: That was a Native American Thanksgiving prayer. Native Americans have always given thanks. We were taught these things in the very beginning of time and just because we may live in apartments in big cities, none of us could survive without them. According to Native American tradition, all people everywhere and the plants and animals—all are related.

MATTIE: My name is _____ and I play the part of a teenager called Mattie in our play. (to the rest of the cast) Why don't you introduce yourselves.

DAD: And I'm _____. I play Bill White Cloud, Mattie's Dad. He's a Kiowa from Oklahoma. I also play the part of Tisquantum in the past. Tisquantum was called Squanto by the English. He's a Wampanoag. There will also be a time when I play William, a Pilgrim.

MOM: My name is _____ and I play Theresa White Cloud, Mattie's Mom in the present. She's a Potawatomi from Kansas. I also play Elder Sister, a Wampanoag from the past, and a Pilgrim named Catherine.

YOUNGER BROTHER: And I'm _____. I play Younger Brother, a Wampanoag from the past, and a Pilgrim named Bartholomew, son of William and Catherine.

AUNT MOLLY: Hi I'm _____ and I'll be playing the part of Aunt Molly in the present. She's a Wampanoag from Massachusetts. I also play the part of the Spirit from the Past.

(*Actors ad-lib . . . Okay let's get going, have a good show, etc.*)

MATTIE: Hey, we forgot our musician.

MUSICIAN: I am _____ and I play the music and sound effects you'll be hearing throughout the play. (*To actors*) Do you want to help me out? (*Gives MOM, DAD and YOUNGER BROTHER a rattle*)

MATTIE: You were great guys. Now it's time for our play. During the play, some of you will be asked to be "Pilgrims" to actually help us with some acting. I think we're all ready to begin. Here we go!!! Imagine yourselves in my family's kitchen. The time is the present, 1999. I'm having dinner with my Mom and Dad. (*She places MOM and DAD in tableau positions . . . then claps her hands and they come to life.*)

SCENE II

The White Cloud family kitchen in New York City.

MOM: More pie, Mattie? Mattie more pie?

(She can't hear because she has earphones on and is listening to rap music.)

MATTIE: YEAH!!

DAD: *(holding the ear phones away from MATTIE's ears so she can hear)* "Yeah"! "Yeah" what?

MATTIE: *(fresh)* Yeah more pie!

DAD: Mattie, whatever happened to "yes, please . . ."?

MATTIE: Just kidding, Dad! I just like to see you get all riled up. Yes, please Mom. Good cornbread.

MOM: Have you much homework tonight?

MATTIE: I've got some math and that big history project.

DAD: Mattie, your manners are terrible. Don't wipe your hands on your shirt. When I was a teenag . . .

MATTIE: Sorry, Dad. *(uses her napkin exaggeratedly)*

MOM: Have you started your history project? And your Dad's right, your manners . . .

DAD: When I was your age . . .

MATTIE: I got a couple of books out of the library, and my textbook has some stuff in it . . .

DAD: Hey—I'd like to get a word in edgewise!

MOM AND MATTIE: *(in unison)* Sorry.

MOM: What were you saying?

DAD: When I was a teenager I had some respect for my parents—I didn't have to be reminded—

MATTIE: OK, OK, Dad. Chill!

MOM: Chill!?

MATTIE: Sorry! But things are different now—it's not the same as when you were growing up. And that reminds me—all the guys in my class were talking about turkey and dressing today, with Thanksgiving coming up—Chris's Mom makes a pumpkin pie from her grandma's recipe, and she says it's really cool—and all her family get together, it sounds great. I can't believe we're not going to eat turkey on Thanksgiving. Why can't we celebrate like everyone else?

DAD: Mattie, surely you know why we aren't. I can't believe that you don't know . . .

MATTIE: I think we should join in and celebrate like everyone else. We're Americans aren't we?

MOM: Didn't you hear Aunt Molly talking when she was here last week? I know when she was here she . . .

MATTIE: Yeah, yeah, she told me how her Wampanoag family fast in remembrance, and how some of them march in protest every year in Plymouth. It just seems . . .

DAD: It's a day of sadness and mourning for them, Mattie.

MATTIE: But that's all in the past right? Why can't we get on with now? It doesn't sound so terrible in my history book . . .

MOM: That's just it! The history books leave so much out! The truth about American Indians is seldom taught in schools. Have you finished, Mattie? Give me your plate, please.

MATTIE: Here Mom. I know the Europeans needed Indian help to survive—

DAD: I bet your books don't say they repaid this help by taking the Wampanoag land and nearly wiping them out—

MATTIE: Well, no. Here Mom, let me help you. *(helps with dessert)* But didn't historians write these books? Surely they—

DAD: And who were the historians?

MATTIE: Oh! The Europeans, of course. I didn't think about that. *(running off with the pie, sticking her finger in and around it)*

MOM: *(chasing her)* Mattie! For heaven's sake wait until you are served!

MATTIE: Sorry Mom, it just smells so good.

MOM: Want some pie, Bill?

DAD: You bet Theresa—my favorite. But why don't you serve Mattie first, before she passes out?

MATTIE: *(grins)* Thanks, Dad. *(taking big scoops onto her plate)* I can't believe the Europeans wrote their own version of history. I thought history books were supposed to give you the facts—

DAD: Now you know you can't always believe what's in books. It's true—they left a lot out. And very few people know what really happened—all we have to go on is some writings the English left, and of course they were very biased.

MOM: *(clears plate)* Thanks, hon.

MATTIE: If nobody really knows what happened and even if the English were biased, I think we should just forget all about it and get on with today.

MOM: We're really concerned that you learn the truth about this, Mattie—we have a responsibility to pass the truth on to you kids. Now that we are in the East, we need to learn what happened to the Native people here. I've asked Aunt Molly to come over while Dad and I go grocery shopping.

MATTIE: AW, MOM!!! Aunt Molly's really nice and all, but she talks too much and I've got a bunch of homework and I need to call Chris and Savannah about basketball practice—

MOM: Chris and Savannah can wait and this is to help you with your history project—Aunt Molly's a Wampanoag from Massachusetts, and she can tell you traditional stories—

MATTIE: *(scraping up the last of the pie from her bowl)* Well Mrs. Hunter did say we need to record some oral history.

MOM: More pie, Bill?

MATTIE: YEAH!

DAD: Mattie.

MATTIE: Just kidding. I can't resist, Dad! Thanks, Mom.

MOM: Can you clear the rest of this away when you're done? *(knock knock)* Oh, there's Molly now.

DAD: I'll go.

MOM: I'll get the coats.

DAD: *(to MATTIE)* Mattie, I want you to be polite and respectful to Aunt Molly. She's been very kind to this family ever since we came to New York. Do you understand?

MATTIE: Yes, Dad.

(DAD reentering with AUNT MOLLY who is carrying a basket)

AUNT MOLLY: Hi Bill. *(hugging)* It's sure gettin' cold out there.

DAD: Here let me take your coat. *(hangs it on coat rack)*

AUNT MOLLY: Hi Theresa. *(kiss)*

MOM: Hi Molly.

(DAD nudges Mattie on back of head.)

MATTIE: Hey Aunt Molly.

AUNT MOLLY: Hi Mattie.

MATTIE: You want some pie?

AUNT MOLLY: Sure. It smells good. I don't think I need my arm twisted to eat some of that.

MOM: Well we're going now. Enjoy yourselves.

DAD: Have as much pie as you like, Molly.

AUNT MOLLY: *(hugs and kisses, bye)* Thanks Bill. I'll call you tomorrow Theresa. Bundle up and stay warm out there.

DAD: Mattie, remember what I said.

MATTIE: Yes, Dad. Later.

AUNT MOLLY: *(eating pie)* How's everything, Mattie?

MATTIE: Oh pretty good.

AUNT MOLLY: And school?

MATTIE: Fine, thanks.

AUNT MOLLY: Mmmm this is delicious! Your Mom makes a mean cherry pie. Oh, I brought you something Mattie.

MATTIE: *(trying to be enthusiastic)* A little basket . . . neat. And—what's this at the bottom?

AUNT MOLLY: It's a piece of cornbread.

MATTIE: What's a piece of cornbread doing in there?

AUNT MOLLY: Traditionally, at harvest, we take little baskets like this and leave them in the woods. They're offerings—

MATTIE: Offerings?

AUNT MOLLY: Yes—a way of giving something back to the earth in thanks for what we have received.

MATTIE: OK. *(putting basket down)*

AUNT MOLLY: Well your Mom said that you had this history project coming up and she wanted me to come over and tell you one of our traditional Wampanoag stories that my grandmother used to tell us in the wintertime, when I was little. Do you remember what Wampanoag means?

MATTIE: *(thinking)* People of the First Light.

AUNT MOLLY: Right. This story that I'm going to tell you is about a long time ago when no other people lived here but the Native people.

MATTIE: Let me clear your plate away, and set up my tape recorder.

AUNT MOLLY: OK, here, I'll help you. *(While clearing ad-lib a couple of lines about basketball or dinner on Thursday, or pie.)* Are you ready?

MATTIE: OK, all set.

AUNT MOLLY: *(acting out story with other actors, MOSHUP wears mask)* A long, long, long time ago there was a giant, whose name was Moshup. He lived here upon the mainland, until it became too crowded. So he waded over to Martha's Vineyard and settled in Aquinnah. The Wampanoag tried to follow Moshup to the island and to prevent them from coming he created great storms to push them away. Then Moshup thought about it for a while and decided that he should allow the Wampanoag to come to his island so he could teach them the right way to live.

He taught the Wampanoag how to build their lodges, how to till the soil and catch the abundant game and whales and smaller fish that lived in the ocean. Moshup began dreaming of strangers coming from a faraway place to inhabit his island. He did not want to go through the strife of teaching another people how to live, all over again. So he decided to pass this responsibility on to the Wampanoag whom he had taught so well. Then Moshup disappeared just before the coming of the Europeans he had seen in his visions. But some people believe that he returns, now and then, to check up on the Wampanoag in the form of a great white whale.

MATTIE: That's the end?

AUNT MOLLY: Mm huh.

MATTIE: Good story. Mrs. Hunter's going to like that.

AUNT MOLLY: I'm glad you liked it. Now you think about this a little. Because these old stories have inner truths and meanings for those who take the time to look for them. Well that's it. I guess I better get going.

MATTIE: Don't forget your little basket Aunt Molly—

AUNT MOLLY: Oh no, that's for you. It's just a little reminder that Native people from all over the Americas have always given thanks to the Creator and all the Grandfathers for providing us with all we need.

MATTIE: Thanks.

AUNT MOLLY: I can see by that funny look on your face that you think that's a little bit weird and old-fashioned.

MATTIE: No really, I—

AUNT MOLLY: (gently) These aren't my rules Mattie. They were given to us a long time ago. And just because us city folk don't grow our own food, it still comes from the Earth and we were told that the Earth is our Mother and we must take care of her and share all that we have. So this is for you. Good night, dear. (exits)

SCENE III

MATTIE: How come grown-ups always talk like that? About a long time ago. Why is Aunt Molly stressin' on me? Her and her stupid basket! (tosses basket) Why is everyone getting on my case? If Mom and Dad and Aunt Molly want to live in the past, it's fine by me, but why can't they just leave me alone?

(MATTIE begins studying at the table and falls asleep. . . . SPIRIT enters picking up the basket. It begins to glow.)

SPIRIT FROM THE PAST: Mattie—Mattie, wake up—

MATTIE: (wakes up, confused) Who—what is it—

SPIRIT FROM THE PAST: Don't be frightened, I mean no harm.

MATTIE: Who—who are you? How'd you get in here?

SPIRIT FROM THE PAST: I'm the Spirit from the Past. You summoned me into your dream through the basket.

MATTIE: No, I didn't. Go away!

SPIRIT FROM THE PAST: I can't go away once summoned. I've come to take you on a journey to the past and you are bound to go. (beckons Mattie)

EVERYONE: (except MATTIE) Bound to go—bound to go—bound to go . . .

MATTIE: (breaking out of spell) Wait a minute, I didn't summon you, I want to UN-DREAM you.

SPIRIT FROM THE PAST: You are BOUND to follow me. Come, we are going back to the year 1620. *(SPIRIT leads MATTIE)*
EVERYONE: Back in time—back in time—back in time . . .

(Choreic speaking "back in time" as undercurrent throughout)

TISQUANTUM: Travel swift and light
ELDER SISTER: Over three hundred years
TISQUANTUM: Back to Massachusetts, to Rhode Island
ELDER SISTER: Back before the Europeans came,
YOUNGER BROTHER: Before they gave their foreign name . . . to—our—land,
SPIRIT FROM THE PAST: When the land was ours
SPIRIT FROM THE PAST: The land of our ancestors,

("Back in time" stops and everyone says "Back to Sowams")

EVERYONE: Back to Sowams.
ELDER SISTER AND SPIRIT FROM THE PAST: *(sing)* Travel through the years, travel on the wind,
SPIRIT FROM THE PAST: Back through the centuries
Through the seasons to winter—
To winter 1620.
EVERYONE: The winter wind has icy breath

(icy breath, icy breath, icy breath . . .) ("icy breath" in the undercurrent throughout by everyone)

TISQUANTUM: And *(icy breath, icy breath undercurrent)* Native people . . .
ELDER SISTER: Exposed to new diseases,
SPIRIT FROM THE PAST: Are sickening and dying.
SPIRIT FROM THE PAST AND ELDER SISTER: *(sing)* Back in time—Back in time
SPIRIT FROM THE PAST: To when the land was ours
The land of our ancestors,

(These are said at the same time, with the "back to Sowams" ending it.)

ELDER SISTER AND SPIRIT FROM THE PAST: *(sing)* Back in time, back in time, back in time . . .
TISQUANTUM AND YOUNGER BROTHER: Back to Sowams, Back to Sowams, Back to Sowams.
EVERYONE: BACK TO SOWAMS.

SCENE IV

The village of Sowams

SPIRIT FROM THE PAST: Here we are, Mattie. We're in the village of
Sowams, 40 miles to the southwest of the place where a ship called the
Mayflower is anchored.
MATTIE: The *Mayflower*? The ship with the Pilgrims?
SPIRIT FROM THE PAST: The history books call them "Pilgrims," but they
were refugees and adventurous businessmen who came here to make
money from the land. This is the principal home of Massasoit, the great
leader of the western Wampanoag. *(The Spirit turns to go)*
MATTIE: Spirit—where are you going? Don't leave me here—

*(MATTIE begins to shiver with cold. ELDER SISTER enters, carrying a basket
of corn.)*

SCENE V

ELDER SISTER: What are you doing here child? You're not from here are you?
MATTIE: Who . . . I—I'm lost—
ELDER SISTER: Are you from Patuxet?
MATTIE: I—I—I
ELDER SISTER: I hear all our people there are sick and dying. Poor girl, I see
you are shocked and chilled. Come with me, you shall have the warmth of a
fire and some food. *(She leads her to where YOUNGER BROTHER is
pounding corn in a wooden corn pounder and packing it in woven baskets.)*
(In a whisper to her brother). I think she's a survivor from Patuxet.
YOUNGER BROTHER: *(without turning)* I'm glad you've come, Sister, there is
so much to do packing the tribute food. It takes longer to do, now that so
many of our people have died. And since our enemies the Narragansett
were hardly affected, they will soon attack us. *(turns and sees MATTIE)* Oh,
have you come to help too?
ELDER SISTER: Brother, I told you this poor child comes from Patuxet—I
found her cold and wandering outside—she seems confused and in shock—
YOUNGER BROTHER: No wonder, if she has had to suffer the loss of her family and friends. Those boat people have brought evil to us—
MATTIE: Boat people?
YOUNGER BROTHER: The hairy white people who arrived in boats, child—
surely you remember—the people who brought sickness and disease to
your village?
ELDER SISTER: Brother, her wits wander, from the shock of losing her family,

or else she would remember. Come child, sit and eat some of this corn-bread while we pack the tribute food. It must be ready for the Sachem's Great Giveaway at the midwinter ceremonies. *(packing food in baskets)* When you feel stronger you can help us take it to the Sachem.

MATTIE: Sachem?

YOUNGER BROTHER: You surely have not forgotten Massasoit, our Sachem—our leader? He will give all this corn and more to those who do not have enough for themselves.

ELDER SISTER: Gently, Brother, she will remember soon enough, perhaps.

YOUNGER BROTHER: The village herald has announced that the hairy white people have built crude shelters where the Patuxets used to live. What do you think it means?

ELDER SISTER: It looks like they have not just come to fish and to capture our people for slaves, but they are thinking of staying.

MATTIE: They captured people for slaves?

YOUNGER BROTHER: You don't remember? Perhaps you remember Tisquantum from your village?

ELDER SISTER: The boat people took him as a slave to their country over the ocean—

YOUNGER BROTHER: That is how he learned their language.

ELDER SISTER: When he got home, he found the bones of his people—your people too—scattered on the ground. All dead from the plagues.

MATTIE: Plagues? Like in the Middle Ages?

YOUNGER BROTHER: Why doesn't Massasoit drive them away?

ELDER SISTER: They are really no threat to us. They are pitiful. They didn't bring enough food to last through the winter and it's too late to plant. They are so hungry they ate an eagle. *(reacts in disgust)* They shoot their muskets at our men. Massasoit wants us to stay away from there for now, and he has sent for Tisquantum because he speaks their language very well.

YOUNGER BROTHER: Poor girl, you are shivering *(puts a blanket on her)* Do not be fearful—we will take care of you. Hurry sister, there is much to do.

(As they begin to pick up the baskets, the SPIRIT reenters.)

SCENE VI

SPIRIT FROM THE PAST: *(freezes sister and brother)* Come, we are leaving Sowams. They will not remember you were here. Now we are going to Patuxet, Tisquantum's village, where the Europeans are camping amid the bones of the dead Wampanoag.

EVERYONE: *(rattles)*

The village of Tisquantum,

The village near the ocean,
YOUNGER BROTHER:
    Once alive and bustling
    Once a thriving home of Wampanoag;
ELDER SISTER AND TISQUANTUM: Now a death camp
EVERYONE:
    The bones of the dead lie white on the ground
    A place of the spirits of the dead.

(Cast becomes Europeans, starving and dying.)

SPIRIT FROM THE PAST: We are in Patuxet.
MATTIE: Who are those people? Why do they look so ill?
SPIRIT FROM THE PAST: They are the boat people, the Europeans. And
    they're in trouble. One or two are dying each day from malnutrition and
    exposure because they don't have adequate shelter, or enough food.

*(BARTHOLOMEW is tending to his sick father, WILLIAM. CATHERINE
enters.)*

SCENE VI–A

CATHERINE: How does he?
BARTHOLOMEW: Very weak. Oh, Mother, would that we had never come to
    this hideous and desolate wilderness, full of wild beasts and wild men.
CATHERINE: 'Tis a disaster. Will you take a little more water, William?
WILLIAM: *(weakly)* I would give my soul for a cup of my mother's soup . . .
    (coughing)
CATHERINE: He asks for soup morn and night—and I have naught to give
    him. *(Angrily)* We might as well all die now in this wild and savage land.
WILLIAM: *(moans)*
CATHERINE: *(suddenly remembering the corn buried in the graves)* The sav-
    ages waste corn by putting it in their graves. Such superstition. *(Rationaliz-
    ing)* What use is corn to the dead?
WILLIAM: *(moans)*
CATHERINE: *(She is thinking about the corn)* Bartholomew, what is of no use
    to the dead will keep the living alive.
WILLIAM: *(moans)*
BARTHOLOMEW: *(strokes his brow)* Try to sleep, father. *(Thinking out loud—
    to CATHERINE)* Yes, there is corn buried in the ground. . . . Mother, we
    need it more than they do. Why can't we dig it out of the ground, and bring
    it here for father?

WILLIAM: *(moans again)*

(CATHERINE sings a sad Pilgrim hymn; when finished she exits. . . .)

SCENE VII

MATTIE: They robbed the Indian graves?

SPIRIT FROM THE PAST: They robbed the spirits of their journey to the after-life. They took the corn and shell beads meant for the spirits of the dead. Desperation and starvation led them to do it.

MATTIE: Can't we stop them? Can't we help them get food another way?

SPIRIT FROM THE PAST: As you said, it was all in the past, so what does it matter?

MATTIE: Spirit, I'd like to go home, please.

SPIRIT FROM THE PAST: That is not possible, yet. Come—we must go to spring 1621.

EVERYONE: They didn't know how to survive. The white people, the boat people, the people with muskets.

SPIRIT FROM THE PAST: They did not know the Three Sisters, Corn, Beans and Squash or . . .

EVERYONE: The bounty of our Mother Earth.

YOUNGER BROTHER: They did not bring enough food,

TISQUANTUM: They did not bring enough food,

YOUNGER BROTHER: They did not understand the land,

TISQUANTUM: They did not understand the land,

(In position for the work sequence)

SPIRIT FROM THE PAST: Here we are Mattie. It's spring 1621. We are still in the village of Patuxet, now called Plimoth Plantation, where the Europeans are trying to survive with help from Tisquantum, whom the English call Squanto.

SCENE VII–A

MUSICIAN: Drum solo.

(Actors set up workstations. Drum when workstations are set.)

MUSICIAN: "Spring sound" on flute.

TISQUANTUM: Listen! The first, faint breath of spring.

MUSICIAN: "Spring sound"

EVERYONE: The sound of spring is carried on the wind:
Hear the sound Spring! Spring!

(In pairs, repeat the verse in a round)

MUSICIAN: "Spring sound"

YOUNGER BROTHER: Winter's icy grip is freed. Spring's approach is near.

ALL: Hear the sound!

SPIRIT FROM THE PAST: Spring, the time for planting, will soon be here.

SCENE VIII

TISQUANTUM: I have good news. Massasoit has signed a peace treaty with the boat people. We have agreed to do each other no harm. The boat people are very warlike people in their own country and they have developed weapons they call muskets. A military alliance with them will help us against our real enemies, the Narragansetts. And I have come to share with them a gift of our Sister Corn. I will show them how we plant her and how we take care of her. We will teach them.

TISQUANTUM:
> We paddle out in our canoe.
> Netting fish is what we do.
> Large fish we use a spear to catch,
> and the fish is tethered
> by a line we attach.
> We give thanks to the fish
> with a gift and a prayer.
> We take our catch home
> so then we can share.

ELDER SISTER:
> In Mother Earth we make a mound
> Put in a fish and pat it round.
> Make four holes for corn on top
> Squash and beans round out the crop.
> We say a prayer for it's plain to see
> We owe our lives to the Sisters Three.

YOUNGER BROTHER:
> Cut back the weeds
> With a deer blade hoe.
> Free the soil
> So the corn can grow.
> Pick the corn
> When the stalk is high,
> Shuck the cob
> Spread the kernels to dry.

SPIRIT FROM THE PAST:
    A prayer of thanks we always say
    For the corn we picked from the field today.
    We pound the corn with this tool of wood
    To make cornmeal. It is good.
    In woven bags all fresh and clean
    We store some more for times of lean.

TISQUANTUM: *(to members of the audience who have been put into roles as Pilgrims)* Europeans—Pilgrims, you have little time to lose. You have told us of your lack of food, your illnesses, your weakness.

YOUNGER BROTHER: Hear the sound of spring?

MUSICIAN: "Spring sound"

ELDER SISTER: Do you hear it? It is the time for planting; you must send us your representatives to learn our skills, or you will not survive the coming winter.

EVERYONE: We will help you.

TISQUANTUM: We will teach you our skills, but you must hurry!

EVERYONE: The seasons do not wait.

MUSICIAN: *(call and response four times with actors)* Way ah ho

EVERYONE: Hey

MUSICIAN: *(sends actors into audience)* Please bring the Pilgrims to us.

Procedure:

1. The Wampanoag characters each gather a group of Pilgrim audience members.

2. After they are given their name tag of actual Pilgrims who came over on the *Mayflower,* each group will concentrate on learning one or more skills with teaching objects. The "Pilgrims" and the Wampanoag use both pantomime and real objects to do the tasks.

3. The rest of the children are asked by Mattie and the Musician to call out "Hurry the seasons do not wait!"—every time they hear the "spring sound," to speed up the Pilgrims' learning process. During the course of the learning process, the sound of spring is heard from time to time as judged necessary by Mattie and the Musician.

4. Wampanoag Indians then teach their Pilgrim groups. The "Pilgrims" will eventually be able to demonstrate what they have learned; one person from each group will describe what their group learned so that the whole audience can learn as well.

5. The audience members are thanked and returned to their seats.

(After Pilgrims are seated:)

MUSICIAN: *(music to strike work stations)*

EVERYONE: The Wampanoag took care of one another
   They shared their harvest, shared their food,
   Shared, shared, shared, shared. . . . *(undercurrent)*

SPIRIT FROM THE PAST: Made sure no one went hungry.

ELDER SISTER: *(to Pilgrims)* I am happy to see life again in Patuxet. There has
   been too much death here.

TISQUANTUM: Now you have learned if you take care of the Earth, the Earth
   will take care of you.

YOUNGER BROTHER: And, in time, with our help, you might even learn to be
   Wampanoag

EVERYONE: Real People.

SPIRIT FROM THE PAST: But, after Tisquantum and his people helped the
   English, sickness visited the Wampanoag again.

ELDER SISTER: *(coughs and looks ill sinking to the floor)*

SPIRIT FROM THE PAST: The Boat People from across the water
   Brought diseases, brought sickness

EVERYONE: Shared, shared, shared, shared . . . *(undercurrent)*
   To these shores, all unfamiliar.

TISQUANTUM: Shared smallpox

YOUNGER BROTHER: Shared typhoid

ELDER SISTER: Shared bubonic plague

SPIRIT FROM THE PAST: Shared influenza

EVERYONE: Shared, shared, shared, shared . . . *(fade away)*

MATTIE: *(seeing misery and focusing on one of the sisters)* Does she die?

SPIRIT FROM THE PAST: Yes.

MATTIE: No, she can't die so soon! She was so kind to me.

SPIRIT FROM THE PAST: Like all Native Americans at this time, she has no
   immunity against the foreign sickness.

MATTIE: But it's so unfair.

SCENE IX

SPIRIT FROM THE PAST: Many diseases caused repeated epidemics amongst
   Indian people who had never encountered them before, and who had not
   built up any immunity to them. Millions of Indian people died.

MATTIE: I didn't know life was so hard back then. *(looking at Indians)*

(Turns to SPIRIT FROM THE PAST, takes a beat, and then says) Can we go
now?

SPIRIT FROM THE PAST: Not yet. We have to see what happened after the Pilgrims were given corn and taught how to plant and care for it. It is now the fall, after the harvest.

TISQUANTUM: The boat people are very thankful to us. Because they were starving. I showed them how to plant the seeds of corn we gave them and their crop did very well—they have a successful harvest of corn, much better than from the seeds they brought with them from their home. The corn will save them. And they have invited us to join them in their celebration, a "Harvest Home" festival. They promised to show us all of their weapons.

SPIRIT FROM THE PAST: The harvest home celebration was attended by Tisquantum, the leader, Massasoit, and 90 men. The celebration lasted three days and was accompanied by eating, drinking, and parading in the cornfields so the people could show off their weapons. They were anxious to impress Massasoit. And in the end, the boat people survived, all because of the generosity of the Wampanoag.

MATTIE: Did they ever learn to become Wampanoag?

SPIRIT FROM THE PAST: Well, they learned some things. They did learn how to survive and they took Native American food and made it their own. Many of the Indian place names are still used today and the roads that became interstate highways are built on our Indian trails. So to this extent, they did become Wampanoag. Then they wrote us out of their history books and their consciousness.

MATTIE: That's so awful! All those people died! *(Turning sadly)* Including Sister . . .

SPIRIT FROM THE PAST: But it's all in the past, so it doesn't matter anymore—Right?

MATTIE: *(doesn't reply)*

SPIRIT FROM THE PAST: You don't answer. But come, we have a little farther to go. We're going to a Thanksgiving in 1637.

MATTIE: Why another Thanksgiving?

SCENE X

SPIRIT FROM THE PAST: This one was different. The English often gave thanks to God for military victories over Indians. In 1637 they had a Thanksgiving to celebrate a massacre.

MATTIE: They thanked God for a massacre?

SPIRIT FROM THE PAST: A massacre of about 700 Pequot men, women and children at Mystic Fort in Groton, Connecticut. Their village was surrounded and set on fire . . . survivors were sold into slavery. We also know that more than three-fourths of the Wampanoag, including the whole village of Patuxet, died as a consequence of contact with the English just before the occupation of Plimoth Plantation. So these are a few reasons why some Native people have a day of sadness and mourning instead of Thanksgiving.

MATTIE: *(to audience)* So Pilgrims—your descendants will survive because of the Native Americans. Because of the help they gave and because of the land they shared. I wonder if those descendants of yours so far in the future will ever think about the great price that was paid for their survival? *(Turns to SPIRIT)* Spirit, how do we make sense of all this?

SPIRIT FROM THE PAST: If we don't learn from the past, we're destined to make the same mistakes again. We must move on, but ALWAYS REMEMBER.

MATTIE: But what about Thanksgiving?

SPIRIT FROM THE PAST: Each of us, in our own way, gives thanks to the Harvest that we all share. Native Americans have harvest and hunting ceremonies to give thanks.

TISQUANTUM: The African American people brought the Yam Festival.

YOUNGER BROTHER: The Jewish people have the Harvest Succot in the fall.

ELDER SISTER: The Chinese have a harvest festival in winter.

SPIRIT FROM THE PAST: *(to audience)* Everyone please stand. *(Join hands)* Join us as we hear an honor song. We will remember all those who gave their lives so that we may stand here today. Let us hope that by remembering it will help us in healing our country.

(An honor song is played. On the second verse, the lights slowly fade and the song becomes an undercurrent.)

MATTIE: *(steps up, holding the basket and speaks to audience while honor song is played softly)* Now I know that Native Americans have always given thanks, but they don't all celebrate Thanksgiving. I didn't understand this before, but I think I do now.

(Holds the basket up so it appears to float, song ends and lights fade while basket glows.)

THE END

Acknowledgments

I wrote Harvest Ceremony in 1985. It has gone through several incarnations, and along the way many people have helped shape the script. Dorothy Napp Schindel, the 1997 director, came up with the idea to make the play interactive by bringing audience members onto the stage. Her creative genius guided the 1997 cast in the development of the script, and her vision is responsible for the integration of music, lighting, and interpretive choreography. The script was improved immeasurably by a collaborative rewrite with Jennifer Fell Hayes, who further developed the character of Mattie, made the dialogue flow, and added the interactive learning sequence. Joe Cross and Donna Couteau, codirectors for the play in 1995, added an important scene at the end of the play that depicts a massacre of Native Americans in Connecticut and the honor song. Amy Tall Chief, who has contributed to the play for three years, added her insight and experience from several perspectives; that of an actor, assistant director, and stage manager, all of which helped to shape the presentation and the final version of the script. Melanie Anastasia Brown contributed the story of Moshup. Suzanne Paquette, Vickie Ramirez, Alexander Cuyaribo Santos, Erik Solorzano, Amy Tall Chief, and Jason Turner, who together make up the 1997 cast, deserve a special mention for helping to develop the script, which was continually evolving during rehearsals and performances. Nancy Eldridge, Jill Hall, Suzanne Paquette, Linda Coombs, and Tim Turner, of the Plimoth Plantation, and the Wampanoag Indian Program at Plimoth generously gave their time and advice. Although the script is mine, all of these people and more have helped shape it. I would like to acknowledge and thank them all for their contributions.

—Martha Kreipe de Montaño

Letters

DENISE MOSLEY

Created in 1996.

Characters

Tonya Blake, a black woman; age 14 and later age 26; a stewardess
JoAnne
Angel Henderson
Steward
Tomasina "Tom" Williams, androgynous voice
Darryl Worthington
Elizabeth Worthington
Lisa Worthington
Sonya
Mertyce
Cindy Bevins
Janice
Tommy
Stewardesses 1 and 2
Agent: female ticket agent for Blue Skies Airlines
Paging Desk Agent: intercom voice
Josh Jacobs

Setting

Act I
    Scene 1: 1973, Tonya's bedroom
    Scene 2: 1983, the middle of a busy airport terminal
    Scene 3: aboard the plane
Act II
    Scene 1: a campsite at night
    Scene 2: the airport terminal waiting area, Gate 8
    Scene 3: interior of the Worthingtons' elegant bedroom
Act III
    Scene 1: a busy airport terminal, ticket counter, Gate 10

ACT I

SCENE 1

It is 1973. Lights up with Marvin Gaye's "Let's Get It On" playing in the background. Records (45s) are scattered on the floor. A bed with frills is downstage. On the walls are pictures of recording stars: Marvin Gaye, the Marvelettes, the Supremes, and the Temptations. There is a stereo with the turntable playing Gaye's song.

On the floor in front of the bed sits TONYA at her vanity mirror. Wearing PJs and pink curlers in her hair, she is talking to JoAnne on the phone.

TONYA: Did you see Bernard today? He looks so good in turtlenecks with his varsity jacket. *(Pauses to listen, then squeals with laughter.)* JoAnne, stop! If your mama knew you talked like that—besides they say it's not the size but the way they use it. *(She smiles devilishly and laughs out loud again.)* If you don't quit embarrassing me, I'll hang up, JoAnne. You know I'm still waiting for Mr. Right. *(She flops down on her belly and opens the pages of a magazine, still holding the phone to her ear.)* Did you get this month's issue of *Teen Ingenues?* Uh, huh. I picked it up on my way home from Kramer's Drugs. JoAnne, *(expression)* did you ever notice how the pharmacist there looks stoned sometimes? I'm not kidding girl. I walked over to the counter once to check out the new miracle cure for corns . . . *(Listens)* No! I don't have corns. *(Sticks her bare feet up in the air to look.)* I just like looking at all the stuff near the drug pickup counter. You know, like that stuff they sell for feminine hygiene—douche! *(Pronounces it dou-che)* You know, douche! I asked the saleswoman if it was a dusting powder and she looked at me like I was trying to sell her dope; told me to go home and ask my mama. As if I would ever talk to Mama about my feminine hygiene—pleeease! *(Laughter)* I know, I hate those commercials. Anyway, as I was standing there at the cash register, I looked up at the druggist and he just stood there staring at his hands like they weren't his. *(TONYA picks up an emery board and begins polishing her fingernails.)* Oh, *Teen Ingenue* has a cute picture of Marvin Gaye in this issue. *(Listens and finishes fingernails. Begins to stick cotton between her toes and paint them.)* Well, you can have DeBarge and I'll stick with Marvin. I like older men. *(Sighs affectionately)* What? The pen pals section—wait, let me look. (*She puts down the nail polish to flip through the pages.*) Yeah, I got it. (*Reads to herself.*) Oh, he sounds really cute. I don't know, JoAnne. You never know what you'll run into with these letters. I mean, what if he's white! (*They giggle!*) Not like I care or anything. (*Sincerely*) Mama says love sees from the heart, not the eyes. (*TONYA's mama calls her name offstage.*)

MAMA: (*offstage*) Tonya, get ready for bed and get off the phone! I need to make a call.

TONYA: Oh, it's just Mama. I gotta go JoAnne. What colors are you wearing tomorrow? Brown and Yellow? Okay. Bye. (*TONYA hangs up and picks the cotton from between her toes. She also picks up the magazine and reads out loud.*) "Dear *Teen Ingenue*, I am 14 years old and very interested in sports, music, movies and science. My favorite hobbies are skating, experimenting with lab animals, like mice." (*TONYA looks at the audience and makes a face!*) Ooooh! "And some of my friends think I have a great singing voice and the ones that don't, don't count." (*TONYA looks at the audience again.*) Ummm! I wonder if he sings like Marvin Gaye? "I'm going out for basketball this year and expect to make freshman team." (*TONYA looks at audience.*) I like a boy with confidence. "I'm writing this letter hoping to meet someone who wants a long distance friend. Out here in South Dakota . . ." (*Tonya to audience, with a curious expression*) You know, he could be Indian. My great-granddaddy was full-blooded Cherokee. (*Smiles proudly*) That's where I got my beautiful high cheekbones! "There aren't that many blacks" (*TONYA looks at audience again with a wry smile.*) Never mind! "So I was hoping to get to know someone by putting my letter in this magazine. I hope it works. I could sure use another friend! Whoever reads this letter sees a friend. Write soon! Sincerely, Tom." (*TONYA walks over to her vanity and pulls out paper and pen from a drawer. She sits back on her bed and begins to write.*)

SCENE 2

It is 1983. In the middle of a busy airport terminal stands a disheveled, attractive woman. She is in her early twenties, black, and wearing a stewardess uniform, pulling the ubiquitous luggage-on-wheels behind her. She careens into a female passenger outfitted in a L. L. Bean wilderness outfit. The passenger nearly falls over TONYA's luggage.

TONYA: Oh, I'm so sorry. It was all my fault. I'm late for my flight—overslept and couldn't get the batteries in my WaterPik to work. (*All the while she is straightening out the woman's clothing and her own.*) Then I had to stop at the hotel commissary to buy a regular toothbrush. You know, a medium-soft never works for me. Leaves the chicken between my teeth. *(By now the woman is staring at her in fixed fascination—waiting for an exit—a breath in the dialogue.)* Now, I'm late and I'll bet you know what that's like. You look well traveled. *(She catches herself.)* I didn't mean worn out. Just aged. No! Not that you look old! Look, can I help you find your gate to make this up to you?

ANGEL: Uh, well, no. My gate's right here. Thanks anyway! *(She scurries into a nearby seat.)*

TONYA: *(looking up at the gate number and letter)* This is my gate too! *(Passenger looks concerned and rummages through her bag, pulls out a magazine and reads. TONYA rushes to sign in with the steward behind the check-in counter.)* I'm here. I'm here. I hope you didn't have to hold the plane. My alarm didn't go off and my toothbrush broke and I had to buy a manual one.

STEWARD: What are you talking about? *(Confused)* The next flight isn't due for 45 minutes and it's on time. Are you headed to Colorado?

TONYA: Yes. That's my flight. What are you talking about? 45 minutes? If that were true, I'd be early, I'm usually on time, but never early. *(She is exasperated and moving behind the counter to check the flight sheets. Papers slip from the desk to the floor in front of the desk. She scurries around the counter, with the steward behind her, and runs into her own luggage.)* Ow!! Oh no. My nylons. I can't go from Washington to Colorado in torn stockings. *(She bends over to inspect her knee. The steward holds up a hand and stops her from assisting.)*

STEWARD: Look, if you're going to Colorado, you've got time to change your hose. *(He gets up and goes back behind the counter.)* Tell me something. Did you set your clock back an hour last night?

TONYA: What?

STEWARD: Did you set your clock back an hour for daylight savings time?

TONYA: Daylight savings time? *(She looks relieved.)* Then my clock was *(At this exact moment, a clock alarm goes off in her luggage. She looks at the luggage and back at the steward.)* on time. *(She smiles a big vacuous smile.)*

(The steward goes back to his work, picks up the phone, and eyes TONYA like a teacher who has just gotten the wrong answer from a student. TONYA goes over to a seat nearby pulling her luggage. Out of a big bag she pulls a letter and begins to read.)

TOM: Dear Tonya, I'm writing you from the barracks because I got a case of the flu and couldn't drill today. The weather here in Germany is pretty cold but nothing like White Springs, South Dakota. I can't believe I'm here. Not in my wildest dreams did I ever believe that lettering for varsity basketball would have brought me to Germany. I love the people here and they really love sports. And it's incredible how clean they keep their towns and cities. My language is still a barrier, but I work on my German every day. How's this—Wo kann ich ein Paar der Unterwäsche der Männer kaufen? *(in German)* It means "where can I buy a pair of men's underpants?" Gotta cover the basics, you know? Uh, that was a joke.

TONYA: *(to the audience)* You can take a boy out of the states, but if you do, make sure he's got his Jockeys.

TOM: Anyway, our team looks really good this year. We hope to win the title so I've got to get healthy. They probably couldn't do it without me. I'm the best center God ever gave the U.S. Army.

TONYA: *(to the audience)* The confidence was much more charming when it came with acne and unexpected nocturnal erections.

TOM: I'm really glad you finally found a job you love. After putting all those years into a college education and a master's degree in marketing, it must have been really tough not being able to put it to use. The worst must have been knowing what you were worth and making pennies trying to convince some doctor's wife how cute she looked in her Diane von Furstenberg.

TONYA: *(to the audience)* He's so clothes conscious. *(A wry smile)* Must have been closest to his mama. *(Catches herself)* Not that he's any less a man. He presses 300 pounds and leg lifts nearly 400. I'll bet his mama can't compete with that.

TOM: I am really proud of you Tonya. The way you never lost heart and knew someday you would find the right job. I mean, how many stewardesses or stewards do you know with as much education as you—I'll bet not many.

TONYA: *(to the audience)* Honey, if you only knew! But just like my age, I'm not telling.

TOM: Can you believe it, Tonya? It's been ten years since I was introduced to you from a page in a teen magazine. The last ten years I've spent every day, except Sunday, excited, hoping the mailman (Excuse me, mailperson) . . .

TONYA: *(to the audience)* You can't just love 'em. You gotta train 'em too!

TOM: . . . had a letter or package from me to you. Thanks for loving me when I lived in the wastelands of South Dakota and for being the only one who understood why I joined the Army. Now I've got my pharmaceutical degree courtesy of Uncle Sam, and in exchange they'll get the greatest center in the next four years of history of any Army basketball team. I'm sorry I missed your flight into Virginia before I left for Germany. After ten years I would love to see and hold you in person instead of just a photograph. I guess you must really wonder by now if it's ever going to happen. Remember when you wanted to fly down to Quantico for my graduation and I had

to write to tell you to forget it? Sneaking out late the night before graduation and getting caught was really dumb. Being AWOL got me two extra
weeks in boot camp. I hated disappointing you and my family.

TONYA: *(to audience, her face is softened and sad)* It took me nearly a month to
find a dress that blue with these tinier than tiny crocheted white dots all
over. Another week to find just the right hat and shoes to set it all off. I
worked graveyard shifts at the Huddle House for the extra money because I
had classes during the day. I wanted him to see me and fall instantly in love.
I wanted to feel his strong arms around me in our first hug. I've kept the
entire outfit put away in my cedar chest. Still waiting for our first meeting.
(A brighter smile) I know it's just a matter of time. Don't get me wrong, I've
had plenty of dates and boyfriends. My social calendar is as full as it should
be for someone 24, attractive and fine. *(She sports herself in a model's
pose.)* But, there's something about Tom that separates the wheat from the
chaff—something unique, different. *(Heavy sigh)* Besides, what's the
hurry? This way I get to travel, see other countries and cities and I'm not as
compelled to rush off and get married. In a way I guess you could say Tom
is as good as birth control and in-laws combined, as long as he's out there in
the wings. *(She laughs)* I'm not as interested in marriage. *(Goes back to the
letter)*

TOM: I'll make it up to you someday, Tonya. Gotta run now. I gotta go over to
the medical center and get a prescription filled. Pretty soon I'll be the one
behind the counter counting pills and weighing doses.

TONYA: *(to audience)* And staring at his hands.

TOM: Did you know that pharmacists are very particular about their hands?
They inspect them often to make sure they're clean because of all the med-
ication they handle—you know to avoid contamination.

TONYA: *(to audience)* I knew that.

TOM: Take care lady and hope to see you soon—really. Love, Tom. P.S.—
Here's a picture of me with the team. I'm also the best-looking center in
this Army. *(TONYA takes the picture out of the envelope and lovingly outlines his face before kissing it. Light fades from her to the young woman
TONYA bumped into earlier. She is writing a letter to a friend.)*

ANGEL: *(voice-over of ANGEL writing letter)* Dear Callie, By the time this letter reaches you, I should be in Colorado. I guess you were right about my
needing to get away—to find a fresher perspective. But, I can't help feeling
that it won't really change anything. I haven't been camping since the trip I
took to Cumberland Island at age 13. At 31 the idea of sleeping in a bag
outdoors and mooning mother nature every time I need to go to the bathroom makes me feel foolish instead of excited. I guess what I really feel is
vulnerable. Every time I think about the last five men in my life I feel hurt

and very stupid. What is it about me that constantly draws in train wrecks? *(As ANGEL's voice-over continues, synchronously it blends with her voice as she puts the letter aside. All figures on the stage are in the dark, with a spotlight centered on ANGEL. The darkened figures' movements are slow and deliberate.)* First there was Jo with his "all I need is a chance" speech. I took him in, fed him, clothed and sheltered him until he finished his computer analyst courses. Once he'd found a good job he dumped me like last week's leftovers. He was followed by Paul who wanted me to lose 40 pounds so I could look more like Cindy Crawford. After losing ten pounds and eating rice cakes when I wanted Haagen-Daz, he dumped me for some blonde Baywatch look-alike that's old enough to be his daughter. Then there was the cowboy I met at the drugstore. He told me his daddy owned a steer ranch and was the wealthiest rancher in Abilene, Texas. Told me he had been disowned by his daddy when he decided to become a strict vegetarian, but knew one day the estate would be his and he'd turn the ranch into a conservation for abandoned wild animals. Well, he can be the first abandoned wild animal he saves as far as I'm concerned. It took me three months and three black eyes to realize that no one, not even me, deserves to be hit—ever. I don't care how rich their daddy is.

Then there was Charles, sweet Charles, pain-in-the-eyes Charles. He loved me so much that he called me at work six or seven times a day. After living with him three months I felt like an ant in the middle of a marshmallow. He wanted to be with me seven days, twenty-four hours a day. Even sitting on the toilet became a strategic effort. I got up earlier just to sit there to be alone before he put his head in through the door to see what I was doing. Maybe if I had just once lifted my butt and said, "What're ya think?" he would have gotten the message. *(Sigh)* But, he was so sweet. He cleaned, cooked, and made love gently. I just couldn't take his neediness. It was beginning to affect my work when the calls interrupted my board meetings. Being an assistant to the president of International Commerce Bank means my time is theirs from nine to five and sometimes after five. I'll never forget the day I told him it was over. He cried in my arms, like a child—just like a little boy. It wasn't until that moment that I realized that in some ways I was like a mother for him. I still remember the look on his face when the cab came. He picked up his bags and looked at me with this sweetest expression, "If you ever need anything, call me," he said. It took all the strength I had not to run after him, all the instincts of survival I had not to let that much love kill him and me—because I knew eventually I could one day hate him as easily as I'd loved him.

Then last, but not least, that was Richard. He came with a manual. He kept an index card near the bed so he could jot down all his daily activities. He created an itinerary for his Mercedes. A little calendar that marked the days he got it washed and waxed, the day his oil was checked, the day he got it detailed, the day the tires were to be rotated, etc. He had a list for every day of the week that included what time he got up, showered, ate breakfast, left work and so on. It detailed every activity for the entire day. At night I waited in bed, my foot tapping with sexual energy while he sat at the computer marking each activity off that was accomplished and not. Then he'd get busy with the one for the next day. By the time he came to bed, both my foot and I would be sound asleep. He would wake me up and say "Angel, wake up. This is the last item on my list today," while he fingered and probed for ten minutes before I relented and ten minutes later he was a paperweight and I was the last item on the paper underneath it. I really liked the fact that he had his own business importing and exporting electronics. I liked the fact he was financially independent, but I didn't like his obsession with his lists, and his business. He put in sixty hours a week to my fifty. The only time we spent together intimately was when it was penciled in. After three months of scheduled sex and romantic unromantic dinners I told him, over din- · ner, it wasn't working out. And the only reaction I got was, "Okay, let me check my calendar and I'll get back with you and let you know which day I'll move out." I felt like taking the fork in my hand and spearing his calendar-hand to the table. Instead I cut off a big piece of rare steak and chewed noisily. That was four weeks ago.

(*At this point, ANGEL returns to her seat, picking up the letter and pen. She begins to write as her voice merges with the voice-over. Her real voice fades as she finishes the letter with voice-over only.*) Callie, I believe with all my heart that there is a soul mate for everyone—somewhere. I still believe despite all the train wrecks I've had in my life that mine is still out there wondering where I am. (*Big sigh*) Maybe that's my problem. I keep hoping to find someone or something that exists only in movies and novels. Do you believe in soul mates, Callie? Write me care of Cindy in Colorado. Wish me luck in the woods. Love, Angel. (*Lights up and all activity resumes. ANGEL folds the letter and places it into an envelope. She pulls a stamp from her purse and places it on the envelope. She looks around for a nearby box. Finding none, she walks to the counter, to the STEWARD.*) Excuse me. Is there a mailbox nearby?

STEWARD: Yes, go back to the main terminal and just beyond the gift store, at the corner wall.
ANGEL: Thanks. How long before boarding?
STEWARD: Approximately 20 minutes if the plane lands on time and so far everything is on schedule. (*He returns to his papers.*)

(*As ANGEL turns to leave she passes what looks to be a family. She exits stage left as the family enters. The man is middle-aged with sandy hair and average build. He is wearing an expensive suit, holding a computer valise over one arm. He is followed by a woman holding the hand of a little girl. The woman is 20-something and much too fashionably dressed for an airplane flight and her hair looks like a newly minted dollar bill. She is thin and beautiful. The girl is clutching a red book with a lock and is dressed more casually, yet well. She sports pigtails, and a face similar to her mother's. She is 11 years old. They all look tense. They go to the check-in counter.*)

DARRYL: Excuse me. (*Rather loud and tense, expecting immediate attention*)

STEWARD: (*his back to DARRYL, he responds slowly*) Yes, tickets for three?
(*Eyeing them, he extends his hands for the tickets.*)

DARRYL: (*slaps tickets on the counter impatiently*) Yes. First class.

STEWARD: (*slowly removes each ticket slip and checks it against the computer. He never looks again at DARRYL.*) Your plane departs in 30 minutes, Boards in 10. (*He places the tickets back on the counter and walks away to other business.*)

DARRYL: (*picks up tickets and leads his family to seats nearby. The woman has an overnight case in the hand that isn't holding the girl's. They sit down and she opens it immediately. DARRYL eyes her with quiet exasperation while the girl looks on.*) Don't you have on enough makeup already? How much does it take for a short flight to Boulder?

ELIZABETH: (*answers flatly as though used to insults*) When I get there I'll let you know. Meanwhile, do you think you could make yourself useful and get us all something to read during the flight? (*She says this as she looks into a compact mirror and evenly applies lipstick.*) I'm sure the conversation will wear thin long before my next application of lipstick, so—rather than let that happen, let's be prepared. (*Her voice is edged.*) Besides, Lisa needs something to do and I don't want her wasting her mind and time watching some vacuous airplane film.

LISA: (*offers anxiously*) It's okay, Mommy, I've got my diary. I can write during the flight. All I need is a pen. I think I left it at the hotel.

ELIZABETH: (*working on her eyes*) It's okay, Honey. Daddy can buy you a pen at the gift shop. I'm sure you will need something to do besides write in your little book. (*Her voice loses its edge when speaking to her daughter yet feels distant and patronizing.*)

LISA: OK, Mommy. (*She agrees quietly to please ELIZABETH.*)

DARRYL: (*getting up*) The plane leaves soon, so I'd better go and hurry back.

ELIZABETH: While you're at it, pick me up a *Vanity Fair*.

DARRYL: Why? Not enough of your own to go around? (*He says this with sweet sarcasm and leaves before she answers.*)

LISA: (tentatively) Mommy?

ELIZABETH: (now that DARRYL has left she abruptly closes her case and loses interest) Yes? (Her eyes wander around the airport.)

LISA: Can I sit next to the aisle this time? I never got to coming here.

ELIZABETH: We'll see. What difference does it make, Lisa?

LISA: Well, I just thought maybe you and Daddy might want to sit next to each other for awhile.

ELIZABETH: (aHa! sound) Not to worry about that, Kitten. We've had years of that already. Twelve long years.

LISA: (puzzled) What Mommy?

ELIZABETH: (her eyes finally find LISA's, but only for a moment before wandering again, like they're looking for someone to notice her) Oh, nothin' Honey. I just meant when you've been married as long as your father and I have, you don't worry about sitting next to each other as much.

LISA: (her expression solemn) Why not Mommy?

ELIZABETH: Because, we—just get used to each other.

LISA: Well, if you are used to each other, doesn't it feel OK—good to be close—like my Tigger . . .?

ELIZABETH: (angry now, impatiently breaks her off) Tigger is a stuffed toy, Lisa. It's not the same.

LISA: (her fingers grip her book tighter. She begins to look around her—hurt.) I guess not, Mommy.

ELIZABETH: Look, if you really want the aisle seat, I'm sure it's OK with your Daddy.

LISA: (brightens up a little) Thanks!

(DARRYL enters followed by ANGEL. He goes to sit with his family as ANGEL goes over to a seat. His arms are filled with several magazines, a pack of pens and a box of chocolate. He passes the magazines to his wife and gives LISA the pens and chocolate.)

ELIZABETH: Darryl, why did you buy her chocolate? You know how I feel about her eating candy, especially chocolate.

DARRYL: (nasty grin) Because my little girl deserves chocolate. It's been a long time since she's had any, right Precious?

LISA: (she eyes the candy with delight) Forever! Thanks Daddy. (She gives him a big hug. Over his shoulder, LISA sees ELIZABETH seething and lets go of her daddy.) Maybe Mommy's right. All this chocolate . . . (fingering the box nervously)

DARRYL: (angrily, to ELIZABETH) Why don't you let her have fun? Kids love chocolate.

ELIZABETH: Yes, and dentists love kids that love that kind of fun. Look at her teeth. *(She pulls LISA's mouth toward him.)* Perfect. Why? Because I won't let her abuse herself eating what's not good for her. *(Lets go of her mouth. LISA rubs her jaws.)* If you understood the meaning of discipline, you'd understand . . .

DARRYL: *(breaks in)* What the hell do you mean if I understood discipline? It's my discipline that got me where I am and that pays for your spa visits. How is it you always manage to distort a gift into something devious and ugly? *(His voice rises a little. ANGEL, TONYA, the STEWARD and others begin to look at them.)*

ELIZABETH: Don't raise your voice to me. *(Angry whisper)* You know how I feel about feeding Lisa sugar. Why can't you respect that?

DARRYL: Because that would mean respecting you and I haven't found a good reason for doing that lately!

ELIZABETH: You son-of-a . . .

DARRYL: Uh, uh, uh . . . *(looks at Lisa and back at ELIZABETH)*

LISA: *(the whole time she has sat there clutching the chocolates and watching them both with fearful eyes.)* Daddy?

DARRYL: *(tearing his eyes from Elizabeth)* Yes?

LISA: I would rather not, you know, take a chance. Thanks, though—really. *(she gives him back the chocolate.)*

DARRYL: Oh, Lisa, we're just touchy. Enjoy your candy.

LISA: I don't feel like it anymore.

ELIZABETH: *(smoothing out LISA's hair)* You really are very smart, Lisa, for not giving in to temptation. What do you say, if once the plane takes off, after breakfast you have just one chocolate? Then you can brush your teeth immediately afterwards. OK?

DARRYL: *(wanting to help smooth things out)* Yeah, Lisa, one chocolate won't hurt. *(He eyes Elizabeth with contempt.)*

LISA: Sure. OK—one chocolate. *(DARRYL gives her back the candy and she absentmindedly places it on an empty seat next to her.)*

STEWARD: *(voice-over)* Flight #116 to Boulder, Colorado, is now boarding. *(The door to the rear of seats facing the audience opens. It is next to the ticket counter. TONYA has already made her exit to prepare the plane.)* First-class boarding first. *(The Worthingtons pick up their belongings and board. On the seat next to where LISA was sitting remain the chocolates.)*

SCENE 3

Lights up and curtain up to view of LISA and her parents aboard the plane. LISA is seated on the aisle. The flight is under way and DARRYL looks to be sleeping while ELIZABETH flips through a magazine casually. Then, bored,

*closes it and stares out the window. LISA pulls her red book from underneath
her seat. She eyes her parents cautiously and when she is certain they aren't
watching she pulls a key on a chain around her neck from underneath her
blouse. She unlocks her diary and begins to write.*

LISA: *(voice-over)* Dear God, this is my eighth letter to you and things haven't
changed. I hope you're still listening. Mommy and Daddy had another fight
today and it was all my fault again. I know you saw it all. I'm really sorry
God; if it hadn't been for me, Daddy would never have bought those stupid
chocolates and made Mommy angry. I'm trying really hard not to be bad,
but somehow I always make a mistake. *(Voice-over ends. She gets up to go
to center stage, to audience.)* I should have never asked Mommy about the
White House. I just wondered what the president's house looked like and if
she'd ever seen it up close. I didn't think she would make Daddy so mad
that he would take us to see it. I'm glad I got to see it and the other presi-
dents' statues and stuff, but it only made Mommy and Daddy madder at
each other. The whole time they hardly spoke to one another, and when
they did, it was that funny talk that feels like they're sticking knives in one
another.
  One night while we were there Daddy drank too much wine and
punched some man for staring too long at Mommy. Mommy cried and took
me back to our room. She slept in my bed that night because Daddy called
her bad names. I wish I could take back the wish of ever seeing the White
House because maybe if I could they would like each other more. Maybe if
I could sit quieter and not ask too many questions, they would be OK like
they used to be when I was little. They could hug and kiss each other in
front of the TV while Daddy held me on his lap. Please God, don't let
Mommy and Daddy divorce, because if they do, it'll be all my fault. My
fault because Mommy says I need to attend an all-girls school. My fault
because I outgrow my clothes so fast or tear them during recess or because
Mommy says I should always dress for where I'm going not where I am—
whatever that means. It'll be all my fault, God, for not being a boy and
Mommy refusing to have anymore babies because it nearly ruined her
body. I guess I did that too God. It'll be my fault for piano lessons, speech
lessons and violin lessons. I only want them back the way it used to be when
they liked each other and me. I don't care about any of the other stuff—just
us being a family again. I don't mean to be a bore, God, but Mommy says
persistence pays off, so I'm gonna keep writing you until you do something
to help them become friends again, because you know, God, when they're
not so afraid and angry, they're really nice people. Honest they are, you
have to take my word on this one. *(DARRYL stirs in his sleep and ELIZA-*

BETH sees him waking up and pulls out her vanity case to adjust her makeup. Returns to seat. Voice-over begins again.) I gotta go now because I don't want them to know I'm writing you. The last time we went to church was four years ago, Christmas mass, and I don't think they'll understand why I'm writing you instead of seeing a psychi . . . psychia—I can't spell the word. Headshrinker. But, anyway, one day I was sitting downstairs in the basement crying and Sheila, our maid, came down to do the laundry and found me. She asked me what was wrong and I said I couldn't tell her because Daddy says family matters are family matters. She looked at me and smiled and said, "Well, Lisa, if you feel this bad and can't tell anybody, but you need somebody to talk to, then sit down and write God a letter. He'll listen and give it some time because sooner or later He'll answer your letter. You understand, Honey?" She smelled like a fresh bath when she hugged me. I believe in Sheila, God, and because I believe in her, I believe in you too. Love, Lisa. *(Lights fade.)*

ACT II

SCENE 1

Lights up on a campsite at night. ANGEL, her girlfriend CINDY, and two other women, SONYA and MERTYCE. Camping gear is strewn around a makeshift fire. Two logs nearby provide the women with a place to sit. They all hold beer cans and are very animated. It is obvious they have been drinking for a while. They are all dressed in jeans, boots and shirts. MERTYCE, however, is in fashion L. L. Bean gear and matching hat.

CINDY: So there I was locked in this immortal embrace, feeling his strong legs wrapped around me when suddenly I realize I have to fart. And it's not one of those quiet kinds. *(The other women are falling over one another laughing.)* It's one of those kind that kicks at the back door saying—you either let me out or I'll blow the house down. *(Takes a drink.)*

SONYA: So what did you do?

CINDY: Well, real smoothly, I said, "Max, honey, I've gotta leave for a second." "Leave and go where?" he said, looking into my eyes with those sexy eyes of his. "I'll only be a minute—now let go." I pulled myself away from him gently and walked towards the bathroom. I could feel his eyes on me so I tightened my cheeks for him and to keep the unexpected company at the door. Just as I opened the door and closed it behind me, my unwelcome guest spoke—loudly! *(They all laugh and make rude noises.)*

MERTYCE: I can't believe you ordered black beans on a date. Talk about tempting fate.

SONYA: Either that or you weren't expecting that he'd end up sleeping with you.

CINDY: Wait, let me finish. It was so loud that he asked, "Did you say something?" I was terminally embarrassed. I had to think fast, so I said through the door, "Bad news!" "What kind of news?" he asked, "Are you OK?" "Well, yes and no," I answered. I reached beneath the sink and grabbed a box of tampons out of the vanity. I opened the bathroom door and flashed the box at him. *(They laugh.)*

ANGEL: Oh, no! You didn't!

CINDY: Oh, yes I did. The expression on his face was classic. A mixture of Laurel and Hardy. "Well, I guess I'd better go," he said getting out of bed. "I know how you women like to be alone at this time." What he really meant was call me when the Red Tide has passed. He was gone in less than 15 minutes. I spent the rest of the night passing gas alone in my bed.

ANGEL: *(laughing, yet sympathetically)* I'm sorry, Cindy.

SONYA: Yeah, me too. *(They all look at one another and crack up again.)*

ANGEL: Did he ever call?

CINDY: Oh, about a week later. We went out to dinner and had a really nice time. This time our evening was much less eventful. I'm kind of glad it happened the way it did. We both spent the next evening cuddling and watching an old movie.

MERTYCE: *(jokingly)* What did you have for dinner that night?

CINDY: A nice salad. *(They all laugh.)*

MERTYCE: *(stirs up the fire a little)* Well at least you've had dates. I can't seem to find anyone I like well enough to date. I guess I'm just too particular. *(She straightens her hair underneath her red cap.)*

SONYA: *(mocking)* You particular? No?! *(They laugh.)* Mertyce, how many people do you think are out here camping with bottled Perrier?

MERTYCE: Well, I like Perrier! Why should I suffer when I'm out to have a good time? Besides, you never know about these streams.

SONYA: Mertyce, we have tablets to purify the water. Cindy knows what she's doing. She camps year round.

MERTYCE: It's nothing personal, Cindy. I'd just rather not take chances.

SONYA: You're taking a helluva chance with your back carrying all those damn bottles of water up and down the trails. *(Kidding, yet biting)*

MERTYCE: Well, it's my back. *(Angry)*

ANGEL: Ladies! Please—no blood at the campfire. Mertyce, why can't you get a date? You're attractive, professional, independent.

MERTYCE: You just put the nails in the coffin. The men I've dated are either intimidated by me or pretend not to be, waiting for the opportunity to let me know who's boss. I'm from the South, Marietta, Georgia, to be precise.

Men there are still trying to evolve into what I don't know. But what I do know is that they want their women washing their laundry and doing the cooking. I don't like doing my own laundry; why the hell would I do it for anyone else? And the last time I cooked Reagan was in office, and just like him I can't remember what it was. And I'm opinionated. And that usually kills the count of most southern men.

SONYA: Well, don't feel so bad. It's no better in Los Angeles. They eat better there and exercise more, but when it comes to honest discussions or heart-to-heart communications, they sometimes fall short. I dated this guy once for nearly eight months. He was a beautiful hunk. We'd been out several times and I really liked him. He was funny, thoughtful and a good listener. Before we slept together I asked him over dinner if he was serious about any women in his life. He looked straight into my eyes and said no—not until now. We had such fun. (*She sighs.*) I guess I started to feel too comfortable. I stopped over at his place spontaneously one afternoon with a picnic basket and wine. Thinking to myself this should be fun! Well, fun was not the operative word for that surprise visit. I rang the doorbell and waited—no answer. Then I rang again—I could hear voices, I thought. Chad came to the door in his bathrobe at three in the afternoon. He looked tousled and surprised. "Sonya, what are you doing here? I thought our date was for tomorrow," he smiled, not asking me in. I could feel my face redden, my heart was racing. "I thought I'd surprise you and it appears I have," I said. Chad's face was a mixture of embarrassment and amusement. Then behind him I heard a voice, "Chad where's the shower gel?" Then the face of a very attractive Greek-like god peered over his shoulders.

MERTYCE: No! You can't mean . . .

SONYA: Oh, yes I do mean. (*She takes a swig of beer and smiles.*) "Chad," I said, "I asked you if there was anyone you were serious about and you said no." "No," he argued gently smiling, "You asked if there were any women I was serious about, remember?" "Oh, I see," I said. I was stunned and angry, but even worse, I was hurt.

CINDY: (*looks at her with sympathy*) What did you do Sonya?

SONYA: I shoved the basket into his arms, wished them both happiness and left. He followed me to the elevator. He was honestly hurt that I couldn't accept his deceit and still be friends. (*She looks at the campfire with a bitter smile on her face.*)

ANGEL: And I thought my luck was bad.

SONYA: Gee, thanks. That makes me feel a hell of a lot better. (*She laughs.*)

ANGEL: I'm sorry.

SONYA: It's water under the bridge, (*pauses*) or should I say a ferry across the water. (*They all laugh.*)

ANGEL: Where are all the men that make great friends and lovers? (*No one answers.*) I've got an idea. Mertyce, do you have an empty Perrier bottle?

MERTYCE: One half full. (*She holds it up from behind the log.*)

ANGEL: Can I have it?

MERTYCE: Sure, when I finish it.

ANGEL: No, now! Just dump the water out.

MERTYCE: Are you serious? This costs nearly two dollars a bottle.

SONYA: Oh, Mertyce, give it up. It's only water after all.

MERTYCE: Maybe to you, but not to me.

CINDY: Look, let's all have a drink of it, finish it off. Would that make you feel better?

MERTYCE: (*reluctantly*) Well, yes, I guess so. (*She passes the bottle to ANGEL first. They all take turns until the bottle is empty.*)

ANGEL: Now, let's write a letter and put it in the bottle and then toss it into the lake.

SONYA: What kind of letter and why are we putting it in a bottle?

ANGEL: We'll write a letter to the man of our dreams.

MERTYCE: Angel, dreams aren't real; besides, who's going to find a bottle out here in the middle of nowhere?

ANGEL: That's not the object. Of course, I don't expect anyone here to find it. It's an old tale, I think Native American, that if you tell your problems to the waters, then the spirits will help you solve them.

CINDY: You've had too much to drink.

ANGEL: Come on, it'll be fun—different anyway.

SONYA: Different is right, but what the hell. I've got pen and paper. (*She gets up to rummage through her bag.*)

ANGEL: Okay, now just write what's in your heart; try and stay out of your head—it's too busy controlling up there.

MERTYCE: (*bowing to the ground in ANGEL's direction*) Oh, yes, Master, teach this ignorant grasshopper.

ANGEL: (*mocking, in a southern drawl*) Excuse me, but I believe this expression in Marietta is boll weevil. (*They all laugh.*)

CINDY: Angel, since it's your idea, why don't you write the letter and we'll critique it? I'm sure we're all good at that.

ANGEL: Oh, all right. (*She takes the pen and paper from SONYA. The light fades on all the other characters, with only ANGEL seen. She gets up and faces the audience with pen and paper in each hand.*) To whoever finds this, I believe that there is someone out there waiting to find me. Waiting to be a friend to someone who needs one. Waiting just like I am for someone to sit quietly with and never wonder what the other is thinking. Someone who likes to laugh before and after we make love to one another. I believe you wait for me because I wait for you, not willing to settle for less. I can hear your name floating on the air that ripples the waters and ask only that you accept me for who I am. I have faith that your love is not dominating or controlling and that mine won't be either. In compassion, there is clarity and kindness to love beyond judgment, so I keep warm this fire within me as I wait. The arms that gather me will know that we are separate, yet joined in love, will understand that my evolution is as distinct as their own. I give to these waters my faith, hopes and dreams. When they wash upon the shore may they find you, waiting. *(ANGEL goes back to sit down as the light fades. She finishes the letter as the light comes up again on all the characters. She passes the letter and they all read it.)*

ANGEL: Well, any criticism? *(She says wistfully.)*

SONYA: None here. I didn't know you were a poet, Angel. *(Smiles)*

MERTYCE: Good stuff. *(Nodding approval)*

CINDY: My words exactly. *(Puts an arm around MERTYCE)*

ANGEL: Well, pass the bottle, Mertyce.

MERTYCE: *(picks up the bottle and shakes out any stray water)* I've got a baggie here. *(She reaches into pack.)* Let's put the letter in the baggie so it doesn't get water stained.

ANGEL: Oh, it's OK Mertyce. I don't really expect anyone to find this; it's just a ritual after all.

MERTYCE: Hey, *(puts the letter in the baggie)* you never know. Besides I'm a romantic. Mr. Soulmate could be downstream.

ANGEL: *(laughs)* You drank too much of that damn water.

CINDY: I agree with Mertyce.

SONYA: Me too. It could be the beer, but I say we treat the letter like it was going to Federal Express. Wrap it up. *(MERTYCE passes the letter and the bottle to ANGEL.)* Okay, Master, finish it. *(ANGEL puts the letter into the bottle and walks with the others to the river behind the campsite.)*

ANGEL: Here's to fate! *(Holds up bottle.)*

CINDY: To the wind that bears their name.

MERTYCE: To great sex.

SONYA: To good friends. *(ANGEL tosses the bottle. A splash is heard. They stand there watching it disappear into the night. Light fades.)*

SCENE 2

Lights up on the airport terminal waiting area, Gate 8. A group of stewardesses enter from behind the check-in counter. Their flight just landed, and they are all excited about having the next three days off. In uniform and carrying an array of bags they mill around the empty gate area and talk. There are four women and one man.

TOMMY: I'm glad this flight is over. *(He leans on the counter.)* If I had to tell that brat in coach one more time not to kick the seat in front of him I was going to shorten his flight by several thousand feet and every passenger onboard would have given me a standing ovation.

STEWARDESS 1: I still can't believe he was traveling alone. Why would anyone send that kind of terrorist on a flight alone?

JANICE: Maybe that's why he was alone.

TOMMY: *(high-fives her)* Good point!

TONYA: *(laughing)* You should have seen your face, Tommy, when he threw his cottage cheese into the aisle, screaming how much he hated cottage cheese. I was impressed by your restraint.

TOMMY: When that cottage cheese splattered onto my new loafers, all I could see was his face turning blue and my fingers on his chubby little throat. Then, I thought, only four months, Tommy, and you'll have a permanent position on the ground. You'll be escorting dignitaries, VIPs and the disabled to their gates—an ambassador for Blue Skies Airlines. No ten-year-old spoiled spawn of Satan is going to ruin this opportunity.

STEWARDESS 2: When you cleaned up the mess and politely asked him if he'd like some applesauce instead, I thought, now that's class.

TONYA: Yeah, real class. *(Mocking)* Especially when you brought him a glass of milk.

STEWARDESS 1: *(breaks in)* And with a lot of class—

TONYA: *(finishing)* You managed to trip at just the right moment and spill every ounce of it into his surprised little face. *(They all laugh.)*

STEWARDESS 1: You even managed to make it look like you were sorry.

TOMMY: *(mockingly)* But I was—honest I'm sorry. I was aiming for the top of his head. *(He sighs deeply.)* Oh well. *(More laughs)*

STEWARDESS 1: Well, I gotta go. Janice and I are off on a hot date. *(She links arms with Janice.)*

TONYA: With whom?

JANICE: Remember those two hockey players from Canada last week? Well, they remembered us too. They called last week.

STEWARDESS 2: Oh, they were real cute guys.

STEWARDESS 1: Cute and fun. I laughed a lot on that flight. See you all later. *(She and JANICE exit.)*

STEWARDESS 2: *(to TOMMY and TONYA)* See you two in three days. My husband and I are spending time fixing up our new place together.

TONYA: That sounds like work and play! *(She winks.)*

STEWARDESS 2: Guaranteed! See ya. *(Exits)*

TOMMY: So, Ms. T, what about you? Going out this week or are you still clutching that torch for the mystery pen pal? *(He jokes warmly.)* How long has it been now?

TONYA: Just ten years.

TOMMY: Just—ten years. Girl, do you realize how many loves I've had in ten years?

TONYA: Tommy, there's only one other person who's had as many loves as you and she sells perfume and doesn't give a damn what anyone thinks of her.

TOMMY: Oh yes, she's my idol! If only I had her money! *(Wistfully)* Or her men.

TONYA: You are so bad!

TOMMY: Isn't it just spicy? *(He hugs her.)* Tonya, I worry about you. You've got to start having a real love life. Not this Malibu Ken and Barbie stuff. I think it's great that you love this guy, but it is all on paper. Hell, girl, you don't even know what he looks like, except that old photo he sent to you. Tonya, what if the photograph is phony? What if he looks like the Elephant Man?

TONYA: I'll still love him Tommy. He's in here. *(Points to her heart)* Not here. *(Pinches TOMMY's cheek)*

TOMMY: *(weepy)* I just love a good love story. You give me faith.

TONYA: Please Tommy, no tears. Besides, I've got a letter right here. *(She looks through purse.)* From him. *(Pulls out letter)* I've been saving it. Just waiting for some time alone to read it. I'm hoping this is the one I've been waiting for . . .

TOMMY: *(excited)* You think he's going to ask you to marry him by mail? Oh, how pioneer! Do you remember that old western movie about all the women brought to this mining town because there weren't any women only men? And all the women had were letters from their prospective grooms. There was this French actress with large white boobs bursting out of her—

TONYA: Tommy, what are you talking about? *(Laughing)*

TOMMY: Oh, *(He stops his reverie.)* I'm sorry. I do get carried away, don't I?

TONYA: Carried away? Try rocketed away? Anyhow, I've got my letter and I'm expecting he'll propose. It's been long overdue.

TOMMY: Speaking of long overdue—I've gotta go. Do you need a lift?

TONYA: No, thanks, Tommy. I'm going to grab a cab. *(They hug again.)*

TOMMY: Call me if you need me, but not before 10 AM or after 6 PM. My schedule is quite busy. *(He feigns a British accent and pulls on an invisible mustache.)*

TONYA: Bye, Tommy.

TOMMY: See ya, Tonya. *(Exits)*

(TONYA pulls her luggage to the side of a chair and sits down. She looks at the letter, pauses, then opens it and begins to read. TOM is heard reciting the letter out loud for audience.)

TOM: Dear Tonya, It took me awhile to write this letter. I kept starting and stopping, not sure of what to say. Ten years is a long time to know someone either as a friend or lover. You'd think by now I'd be able to tell you anything and usually I can. There are so many things you know about me that no one else does. My feeling about joining the Army, the first time I ever cried when my dog died. You even know when and where I lost my virginity—not even my best friend Jake knows that. He thinks I lost it sneaking into that whorehouse down near RuBer's. I didn't have the heart or the guts to tell him that the prostitute I chose turned me on about as much as he did. You made me feel OK about it though—made me realize that I wanted something more than a cheap ride at the carnival. It meant a lot that you never asked who she was. I could live to be 300 and still not have enough lives to give for the one that is yours. You are and always will be my best friend.

(TONYA stops reading and looks at the audience.)

TONYA: *(flushed, excited)* Maybe I should save this part for later. *(Holds letter to her heart)* You know, over a glass of wine with candles burning. You don't get proposed to often in life—at least I don't intend to. *(Pauses to look at stage in front of her gently)* I do wish it was him, down on his knees right here. He takes my hand and holds it like a flower, looks deep into my eyes and soul *(stops, looks at letter again)* but I'll take what he has to offer because I love him. Besides, I've waited this long—a little longer won't hurt. *(She returns to the letter. The voice continues to read.)*

TOM: That's why this is so difficult because we've been more than friends but only in our hearts—not in the real world. I guess I need to get on with it and quit beating around the bush. Tonya, I'm getting married. *(Tonya's body language shifts. She is holding her center, her space.)* I've met someone who is really wonderful and I've asked her to marry me. Believe me when I say I never planned any of this. It just happened. A whirlwind swept us both off our feet. Please don't hate me for falling in love. I always thought it would be you, but I guess it wasn't meant to be. I'm sorry, Tonya. I know you'll find someone who'll love and appreciate everything you have to offer. If I don't hear from you again, I'll understand. The worst part about this for me is the thought that I could be losing my best friend. I hope someday you'll understand and forgive me. Correy (that's her name) and I will marry two weeks from today, April 1st. If not now, I hope someday in the future, we'll have your blessings. Take care of yourself, and if you ever need me, just write or call. I'm always there for you as a friend. *(The words "as a friend" reverberate over and over again.)*

TONYA: *(crushes letter, crushed, tearful expression, looks to audience and whispers)* As a friend. *(Lights fade.)*

SCENE 3

Lights up on the interior of a very elegant bedroom. A painting is hung over a fireplace in the center of the room and there are two couches facing one another not far from the bed. The bed is large, covered with gold bedding and ornate pillows. A nightstand sits next to the bed with an Elizabethan lamp. A full-length mirror occupies a corner of the room conspicuously with a vanity nearby, lined with cosmetics, brushes and combs. ELIZABETH enters carrying fresh-cut yellow roses and places them on the table between the couches. She fluffs them exaggeratedly and looks pleased with the result. She is wearing a lemon-colored peignoir that flatters her body and matching slippers. She moves to her vanity, sits and begins to brush her hair, staring at her face in the mirror vacantly. With each stroke, she looks less and less there, less animated. Mid-stroke she pauses and sets the brush down. She gets up and checks her figure, turns, running her hands over her body, as though she is looking for faults. The light is now focused on her and the mirror.

ELIZABETH: Daddy always said I was the belle of Ballton County. That I could have anything I wanted. Mama said to always look and act like a lady, but never give an inch to any man. Mama taught me control. All those beauty pageants paid off. I got an education, and a rich husband at the same time. *(She pauses to run her hand over her belly, looking at herself from side to side. Frowns at the pseudo bulge.)* Darryl was my knight in shining armor. He came from good stock and played sports. He was popular and on the Dean's List every semester. He was majoring in law. *(Her expression has changed from the critical to one of tenderness, wistful.)* He made me laugh. And he always complimented me on how I dressed, told me how pretty I was. Bragged about his beautiful southern belle. *(ELIZABETH faces the audience and goes to the edge of the stage—the lights follow her.)* What did I do wrong? *(Hurt, bitter voice)* I gave him one child. It was a difficult labor. The pain was so great I thought I'd die. *(She covers her space, her center.)* Then they cut me to get her out. I nearly bled to death because of something called DIC. I lay in that hospital for a month, only seeing my baby every once in awhile because I was too weak to nurse her. It took me months to recover—to get my body back the way it was—(*She pauses to look at herself.*) the way he liked me. This was my ticket into this world, my ticket out of the small town I grew up in. (*She touches her face.*) This face stopped him midsentence at a freshman sock hop. I saw him stumble over his feet trying to get to me. (*She laughs lightly, like a schoolgirl.*) He looked at me then as though I was the finish line. (*She pauses, bitterness returns to her voice.*) After Lisa was born, I put my foot down—no more babies. Then he changed, became a kind of monster, said he wanted sons to follow in his footsteps—as though I was a kind of machine built to produce male Worthingtons. Even threatened to divorce me if I did not concede. Well, I fixed his wagon. (*She laughs menacingly and walks to other end of the stage.*) I told him I was going to see my parents. And I did. But while I was gone, Mama and I talked. When I returned to Darryl a week later, I told him my tubes were tied. It was a lie, but Mama backed me up and it worked. (*Her expression turns to pity.*) I'll never forget the look on his face when I told him. He'd just passed the bar and was like a big puppy dog, all excited and giddy. He came home that night a little tipsy and wanted to celebrate. I was all for that too. Then he ruined it by bringing up the subject. He thought I'd been off the pill. He didn't know I was sneaking them when he wasn't looking. He wanted to know why I hadn't gotten pregnant yet. Then I told him. Told him I could never have another child. That I'd gotten my tubes tied. He looked like he'd been punched in the gut unexpectedly. He got up off the bed and went over to the couch. Then he did what I'd never seen him do before. He put his face in his hands and cried. (*She strolls to the middle of the stage.*) I sat in the middle of the bed and watched and waited. When he was through he got up and left the room. I didn't see him again for a month. His parents called and told me in a number of creative ways what they thought of me, but I had Mama's support. (*Her posture becomes upright, restrained. Her voice artificial.*) When he came home we talked, decided to not break up Lisa's family. After all she was only a year old. So I've done my job. I'm a good mother, a joiner of charities and committees. (*She goes back to mirror taking light with her.*) I keep this body and this face attractive, even though he hardly touches me anymore. (*Bitter yet nostalgic*) He has his extracurricular women and I have security. (*Fear creeps into her voice.*) Now Lisa's getting older and unfortunately so am I. I can feel his impatience—his final blow. He's ready to cut the proverbial cord. But, I've kept my ducks in a row. If he wants out, fine! I'll get what's due me and Lisa. There's not a judge in town that isn't aware of his sexual exploits, and if there are, my detectives will fill them in. (*She is bitter again. Then her face softens and her voice does also. As she looks in the mirror.*)

Sometimes I miss knowing him the way I did—the way he was when he approached me the very first time. Wish I could wish away the pain between us. I'd like to be that finish line again.

(Lights fade. DARRYL enters. Unlike ELIZABETH, he is dressed as though he is going out for the evening. He goes to a bureau drawer filled with ties as ELIZABETH places herself on the couch. She picks up a magazine and casually flips the pages. DARRYL selects two or three ties and walks to the full-length mirror. He compares each with the suit he has on.)

Big night out again tonight?

DARRYL: I'm meeting a few associates downtown. I'll probably be out late, so don't wait up for me. *(He selects a tie and puts it on.)*

ELIZABETH: I never do.

DARRYL: *(He knots tie.)* Don't forget the benefit dinner tomorrow night at the Moore's. Get a sitter lined up for Lisa.

ELIZABETH: Already done Captain. *(Edge in her voice)*

DARRYL: Do you think you can refrain *(coming to edge of couch)* from embarrassing me with your flirting this time? You're getting a little too old for it to be taken as cute anymore.

ELIZABETH: *(flares at the word "old")* Who the hell are you calling old? *(Flings the magazine to the side.)*

DARRYL: *(walks over to check his appearance in the mirror.)* Well, if the shoe fits. *(He smiles.)*

ELIZABETH: It isn't my hairbrush that is filled with tons of hair every morning. *(She smiles back in defiance as DARRYL unconsciously touches his hair.)*

DARRYL: *(He turns from the mirror in a fighter's stance.)* I've always lost a little hair—it being so thick and . . . *(He stammers.)*

ELIZABETH: *(getting up to face him off)* Well, it's starting to show, Old Man. *(She goes to the door to exit and turns back to DARRYL.)* I'll make a deal with you; you ignore my harmless flirtations, which by the way I know make you jealous, and I'll ignore the hairs in your brush—like I've always done. *(She leaves. DARRYL stands in the middle of the room with his hands curled in fists. LISA enters dressed for bed. She plops down on the couch.)*

LISA: Are you going out Daddy?

DARRYL: *(Goes over to sit next to her. Puts his arm around her.)* Yes, Honey, just for a little while. *(He kisses the top of her head gently.)*

LISA: Is Mama going too?

DARRYL: No, Mama's staying here, I've got a business meeting to attend.

LISA: *(snuggles up against DARRYL)* Daddy? Do you believe in God?

DARRYL: *(looks surprised and puzzled. Looks into Lisa's face.)* Why do you ask that question Lisa?

LISA: Well, do you or don't you? (*She looks at him expectantly, quizzically, waiting for an answer.*)

DARRYL: (*looks as though he's unsure*) I guess so Lisa. There must be someone up there looking out for us poor fools, helping us clean up the messes we sometimes make of our lives. (*He looks reflective, sad.*)

LISA: (*seeing the expression on his face*) What kind of messes Daddy?

DARRYL: (*realizing he's said too much*) Oh nothing, Lisa. I just meant (*puts his arm around her and she hugs it*) that it's nice to know there's something bigger out there that watches over us all. Even when we sometimes forget. (*He appears gentle and aware of his love for LISA.*)

LISA: Do you think Mama believes?

DARRYL: (*visibly bristles, gets up and goes to mirror to adjust tie*) Honey if your mama and God ever met, I'd take odds on your mama being the next in line to take charge if God called in sick. (*He turns to look at Lisa and they both laugh. Lights fade.*)

ACT III

SCENE 1

Lights up at a busy airport terminal, ticket counter at Gate 10. TONYA arrives, enters from right of stage. People are seated, waiting to board. A sign above the counter reads "Flight #129—New York." Behind the counter is a woman ticket agent scanning the computer in front of her. TONYA puts the baggage cart down and checks in.

TONYA: Any changes?

AGENT: No, on schedule.

TONYA: Good, this is my last leg and I can't wait to check into my hotel room, put my feet up and call it a week. (*Over the intercom a voice is heard.*)

INTERCOM VOICE: (*voice-over only*) Paging Sergeant T. Williams. Sergeant T. Williams please report to the Paging Desk. Sergeant T. Williams, please report to the Paging Desk.

TONYA: (*Her eyes look about the room as though she is expecting Sergeant T. Williams to materialize.*) Did you hear that?

TICKET AGENT: (*caught up in her duties, casually*) Yeah, it sounded like a page for Williams.

TONYA: (*excited*) Would you watch this please? I've got to check on something. (*She bulldozes the bag behind the counter and takes off.*)

AGENT: You've only got ten minutes. You can't leave now. (*She yells to TONYA's back and the lights fade.*)

SCENE 2

Lights up on the paging desk. A man is behind the counter. He picks up a mike and pages.

PAGING DESK AGENT: Sergeant T. Williams, paging Sergeant T. Williams to the Paging Desk. *(TONYA enters at a quick pace. She is breathless. Noticing TONYA's uniform)* Are you meeting someone here, miss?

TONYA: Yes, I guess you could say that. *(She is still trying to catch her breath. A woman in an Army uniform with sergeant's stripes walks up to the desk.)*

TOM: Excuse me, did you page a Sergeant T. Williams? *(Doesn't see TONYA)*

PAGING DESK AGENT: Yes. Is that you? *(He looks a little surprised.)*

TOM: Yes, I'm Sergeant Williams.

PAGING DESK AGENT: Oh, I have a message from your unit in Germany. *(He picks up a slip of paper and gives it to her. TONYA is watching with a surprised and confused expression on her face.)* Sorry, but I assumed you were a man.

TONYA: So did I. *(She says out loud, unconsciously)* Sergeant T. Williams? *(Tonya looks incredulous.)*

TOM: Yes. *(She stammers a little)* It's Tomasina. Tomasina Williams. *(They stare at one another as the light fades.)*

SCENE 3

Lights up at the airport Gate 139. The sign above the gate reads "Gate 139—New York." Angel is dressed in a business suit and is seated to the left, reading a book. A man in his 40s enters wearing a suit and tie. He has a sling bag over one shoulder. He sits to the right. He rummages through his bag and pulls out a baggie; inside there is a letter. He reads it, smiling the entire time. He puts the letter back into the baggie reverently and puts it away in the bag. He takes out a pen and a pad. As he begins to write, his voice is heard in a voice-over. He gets up, goes center stage and faces the audience, leaving the pad and pen on the chair. The light in the background fades as a spotlight is focused on JOSH.

JOSH: Dear Mom, by the time this letter reaches you I'll be back behind my desk in New York and far away from Colorado. I had a great time with the guys. We camped and hiked, told a few lies and probably drank too much. It was good to get away, get a different perspective on my life. It has been nearly four years since Karen died, so making the trip back here without her this time was easier, but she'll always be a part of the Colorado Rockies for me. *(Pauses)* I'm doing well and still trying to date, but things are so different now. People seem to have changed or maybe I have. All the women I've dated have left me either cold or confused. A lot of them seem to have a checklist they run by you before they consider you date material. Makes me feel like some kind of commodity on the stock exchange. It's so hard after Karen. She didn't care what I did for a living. If she had, she would have never bothered dating a guy pumping gas. I remember telling her on our first date about my trying to earn a degree in Finance at New York University. (*Smiles*) She was no more impressed than if I'd said I like vanilla ice cream. That's the kind of woman she was. She only saw me, not my future office on Wall Street. (*Sighs and puts his hands in his pockets*) Enough of that though.

The strangest thing happened while I was out camping. It was early, the sun had just crested the mountains and I wandered into the woods to (*pauses*) to put it delicately—to relieve myself. I was walking back along a stream and saw a Perrier bottle wedged between a few rocks. The sight of the bottle littering the stream disgusted me so I leaned out into the water and grabbed it. After pulling it out of the water, I noticed there was something inside—folded up like a letter. (*Here Josh removes his hands and demonstrates his retrieval of the letter.*) I was curious, so I tried using my finger at first to get it out. When that didn't work, I tried a stick—too tricky. So finally I just broke it against a large rock. I pulled it out and sure enough, folded inside in a Ziploc baggie, was a letter. (*Looks amused*) Must have been someone pretty anal that thought of the baggie. Anyway, I took the letter out, still dry, and read it. (*Soft expression*) Mom, it was the sweetest letter. Like some poor soul lost at sea looking for a soul mate. (*He looks a little forlorn.*) I kept the letter for no particular reason; (*pauses*) maybe it reminds me of Karen. Who knows? I've had my soul mate this lifetime and I guess we only get one. I hope whoever wrote this letter finds what they're looking for—we all deserve to be loved, well, at least once in a lifetime. (*He smiles, recovers*) Well, gotta go. Give my love to Dad and I'll see ya soon. Love, Josh.

(*He goes back to chair and picks up the pad and pen and signs off. He puts the pad and pen away. He pulls out the letter again, smiles sadly. He walks over to the garbage can near ANGEL and throws it away. On his way back to his seat, just as he's about to pass ANGEL, he trips over ANGEL's feet, catches himself with Angel's help.*)

Excuse me. I'm really sorry.

ANGEL: No. I shouldn't have stuck my feet out like that. Are you OK? (*She smiles at him and he looks at her and returns the smile. There is an immediate attraction between the two.*)

JOSH: (*standing with a boyish grin, facing Angel*) Believe me, it's not the first time I've stumbled. Usually it's my tongue—not my feet.

ANGEL: Well, maybe given an opportunity *(she flirts)* there might still be a chance of that happening.

JOSH: *(laughs)* Are you on your way back to New York too?

ANGEL: Yeah, gotta get back to the routine on Monday.

JOSH: Me too! *(He pauses—searching for a way to ask if he can join her.)* Uh, Miss, uh . . .

ANGEL: Angel. The name's Angel Henderson. *(She extends her hand.)*

JOSH: *(beams)* Angel, that's a real pretty name. *(A subtle recognition crosses his face.)*

ANGEL: Thanks. *(He holds her hand a little too long and then lets it go.)*

JOSH: Angel, would you mind if I sat with you while we wait?

ANGEL: Yeah, sure, but only if you tell me what your name is—that is—unless you want to keep it a secret.

JOSH: *(laughs)* Oh, it's Josh. Josh Jacobs.

ANGEL: It'll be nice to have company.

JOSH: I'll get my bag and be right back. *(He begins to walk away and turns back to Angel, smiling.)* You know this is the first time I've ever flown with an angel. *(Lights fade.)*

SCENE 4

Lights up on the same area, same ticket counter. ELIZABETH and LISA enter from stage right. ELIZABETH looks a bit harried, not her usual well-coifed look. LISA, in tow, is holding her journal and looks unhappy. ELIZABETH goes to the ticket counter and gives the agent her tickets. She gets their seat assignments and goes to sit in the seat vacated by JOSH with LISA.

ELIZABETH: We'll be in New York by ten. That should give me plenty of time to get things in order. *(She speaks not really to LISA, but around her. She pulls out a compact and begins to apply a light touch.)*

LISA: What things, Mama? *(LISA looks afraid of the answer.)*

ELIZABETH: *(looks at her smiling, real this time)* Nothing, honey. I just thought this would be the perfect opportunity to get some shopping done. You know how much I love catching the sales in New York.

LISA: Daddy didn't look so good when we left. *(She fingers the clasp on the locked journal.)*

ELIZABETH: No, uh, he's not real happy about my spending his money. *(Lying edged with bitterness)*

LISA: When will we go back home, Mama?

ELIZABETH: Oh, in a couple of days. Don't worry. You'll be back in time for school Monday. *(She is edgy and deep in thought. LISA watches her, all the while picking at the clasp on her journal.)*

LISA: Mama, I need to go to the bathroom.

ELIZABETH: *(looks up from staring at her hands)* OK, you can go alone. It's right there. I can watch you from here.

LISA: OK. *(Lisa gets up and puts her journal on the chair. She exits left as ELIZABETH smiles after her, waving to her, assuring her that she's watching until she goes into the bathroom. Once she's inside, ELIZABETH's smile disappears. Her face softens in sadness. She reaches into her purse, rummaging for something.)*

ELIZABETH: Where in he hell did I put that attorney's card? *(She mumbles to herself.)* Oh, well, I'll call information when I get there.

(She decides to put her purse on LISA's chair, and as she does the journal is accidentally knocked to the floor. She reaches down, picks it up, and just as she is about to put it back on the chair she realizes it has opened. She looks for a second toward the bathroom, then opens the journal to the last entry and reads. LISA's voice-over is heard as the light focuses on ELIZABETH.)

LISA: *(voice-over)* Dear God I had an idea that I thought maybe you could help me with. I think it might help Mama and Daddy to like each other again. What if Mama got pregnant again God? I mean you can make that happen can't you—like you did with me? I know Mama and Daddy have to be there too. I'm not that young anymore. I understand sex a little. I just think that if Mama got pregnant then Daddy would feel better about things. I remember how he loved tossing me up on his shoulders when I was a baby. He read me stories and made the funny parts funnier. When he took me to the playground, he'd take turns pushing all the kids that were along on their swings. I watch him sometimes staring at the kids down the street out the window—he looks kinda lonely, God, like he'd like to play too. The best day of my life was the day Mama and Daddy took me to King's Park. We stayed all day, riding rides until it was dark out. I remember falling asleep on Mama's lap and Daddy touching my hair. Just as I fell asleep he looked at Mama and said, "She's worth all the blood, sweat and tears life has to offer." I could feel Mama hold me closer and her hand reach over to hold Daddy's. Please God, help Mama get pregnant again. I know she loves Daddy, but she's too stubborn about something to show it. She was softer when I was little. Maybe another baby will soften her again and help her remember that no matter how old she gets or looks, that I love her and Daddy loves her too. He's just lonely for another baby because he really likes kids a lot. I've heard that women worry about their clocks not ticking when they reach a certain age, but I don't think that applies to Mama 'cause last night while Daddy was tucking me into bed, I asked him if he thought Mama was beautiful and he said, "Honey, your mama will always be the flower of my youth." (*ELIZABETH is visibly touched now by all she has read and she reaches up to touch her cheek gently.*) So I guess that means her clock is still on for him. I know I've written a lot of these to you lately. Fifteen to be exact. But Mama says persistence pays off. Please God, help me because I think time is running out for this family. Love, Lisa.

(*ELIZABETH flips back through the other entries with a look of pain and warmth at all the letters. She hurries to close the journal, securing the clasp and puts the book back on LISA's chair. Just as she does, the light goes up and LISA enters and picks up her journal and sits down. ELIZABETH spontaneously and tearfully hugs LISA. LISA returns the hug, surprised, and speaks live.*)

Mama, are you all right?

ELIZABETH: Yes, honey. (*She says gently, in a whisper. She pulls LISA out to look her in the face.*) What do you say we forget about this trip to New York and go home? We could do some shopping and surprise Daddy with a gourmet dinner and dessert.

LISA: (*She beams.*) OK!

ELIZABETH: I need to make a phone call first. (*She gathers up her things.*) Come on.

LISA: (*stops for a second*) Mama?

ELIZABETH: (*quizzical look*) Yes, Lisa, what is it?

LISA: Is your clock ticking?

ELIZABETH: (*quizzically*) What?!

LISA: (*She stammers a little.*) You know, the big clock that, uh . . .

ELIZABETH: (*She laughs and hugs her again.*) Yes, Lisa. My clock is up and running again. (*Lights fade.*)

SCENE 5

Lights up on TONYA, seated at an empty gate. She looks wounded. She turns a letter in her hand over and over as though studying its exterior. The stage lights darken, leaving only her with the letter visible. She holds the letter up for the audience members to see and addresses them.

TONYA: (*speaking with irony, sad*) She, he, (*laughs bitterly*) Tom said she was going to mail this to me airmail. Well, there you have it! (*She holds it up like a torch, then pulls her arm slowly downward.*) I don't know which is worse, having fallen in love by mail without ever having seen my lover's face or the face of my lover on the body of a woman. But maybe the worst is (*turns the letter in her hands*) getting a Dear John letter from a Jane pretending to be a John. (*She smiles reluctantly. She looks at the audience.*)

Should I open it? *(Pleading)* How much opera can my life stand? *(She goes back to sit down, tears the letter open. As she does a voice-over of TOM is heard.)*

TOM: Dear Tonya, by the time this letter reaches you, I'll be home again in South Dakota. I hope back here in the wide-open spaces I'm able to find peace again. I haven't slept much since my last letter to you. Thinking of all the pain I've caused you by my lies torments me now. I don't know what to say—or how to tell you the truth. So maybe the best way is to just blurt it all out and be done with it. For starters, I'm not a man. I'm a woman. *(TONYA breathes in deeply here, gripping the letter.)* The pen pal letter started out as a desperate means to an end. I was lonely and wanted someone to want me. I don't expect you to understand or even accept what I've done. I'm only trying to explain why I did what I did. I've known I was attracted to women since I was 12. Growing up in a little town like White Springs, South Dakota, is like living in a fishbowl. By the time I was an adolescent, I craved what could never be expressed or shown to others without fear of abuse and alienation. So I decided to camouflage my gender as a pen pal and become what I wasn't. In other words, live a lie. The worst part of it was that I was living a lie pretending to be heterosexual for my family and living a lie with you by pretending to be a man—another heterosexual charade. All the time wishing I could just be who I was.

It started out harmlessly enough. You lived miles away, we were kids, but then *(a pause)* I started to really look forward to your letters. You became real to me—flesh and blood without the body. Your words carried me through many dark nights when I just wanted off this planet. You were my light at the end of the tunnel. I fell in love with you Tonya. I don't even know which letter did it for me—it happened gradually, like the last light a candle gives before dying. And I know that is as it should be between us now. I'm sorry—so very sorry for betraying you, for betraying love. I told you I was getting married to avoid the truth. I knew it would hurt you, but not nearly as much as this probably does. I won't insult you further by asking for your forgiveness for this charade. I only ask that you forget.

Thanks for all the years of loving the part of me that was written out on the pages of those letters. I will treasure and take all you gave so freely in your letters. Flesh or no flesh, gender or no gender, my love for you was created out of your soul and in some measure so was your love for me. Have a good life Tonya Blake. P.S. The photo was my brother. He was always the most photogenic in the family.

(TONYA folds the letter slowly and places it back inside the envelope. Lights are up now. The gate begins to fill—an agent sets up behind the counter. Two

passengers drift in, and walk over to the counter. She walks over to a phone near the desk, dials.)

TONYA: Yes, Operator, *(looks at the letter in her hand)* could you connect me to White Springs, South Dakota? Yes, . . . I'll wait. *(She smiles a "what-the-hell" smile as the lights fade.)*

END OF PLAY

Ola Nä Iwi
(The Bones Live)

VICTORIA NALANI KNEUBUHL

Foreword

Ola Nä Iwi was first produced by Kumu Kahua Theatre at the Merchant Street Theatre in Honolulu on November 11, 1994. The production was directed by John H.Y. Wat, with the following cast:

Kawehi: Lyla Bonnie Berg
Erik: Jack Boyle
Mina: Karen Kaulana
Fatu: Ron Encarnacion
Gustav: Andy Mennick
Pua: Venus Kapuaala
Nanea: Kehaunani M. Hunt
Deidre: Laura Louise Bach
Player 1: Pamela Sterling
Player 2: Craig Howes & Peter Knapman
Player 3: Jon Hamblin

Set Design: Joseph D. Dodd
Lighting Design: Gerald Kawaoka
Costume Design: Yvette La Fontaine

The play was commissioned by Kumu Kahua Theatre, whose activities are partially funded by the State Foundation on Culture and the Arts, State of Hawai'i.

Characters
Kawehi (part Hawaiian)
Erik (Caucasian)
Mina (part Hawaiian)
Fatu (part Samoan)

Gustav (German)
Pua (part Hawaiian)
Liliha (Hawaiian)
Deidre (Caucasian)

The Players
Player 1: Female,
Mrs. Mahler, Waitress, Miss Ida, Camilla, Clown

Player 2: Male,
Customs Inspector, Southerner, Nineteenth-Century Phrenologist, Warren K.
    Moorehead, Clown, Dorsey

Player 3: Male,
Nineteenth-Century Professor 1, Nineteenth-Century Professor 2, Grave Rob-
    ber, Clown, Franz Boas, Nineteenth-Century Physician

The Set
KAWEHI'S HOUSE is a Polynesian-looking living room with a small rattan sofa,
two chairs and a coffee table. Two exits lead to a bedroom and to the outside. In
A PLAYING AREA DOWNSTAGE are other locations, to be suggested by minimal, moveable furniture and props, and lighting.

Time and Place
The play is set in Berlin and Honolulu. The time is the present, except for brief
historical interludes.

ACT I

SCENE 1

*(Honolulu. A CUSTOMS INSPECTOR stands behind a table. Enter KAWEHI.
She places two bags on the table and hands him her papers.)*

INSPECTOR: Where are you traveling from, ma'am?
KAWEHI: Berlin.
INSPECTOR *(Looking in passport)* Berlin?
KAWEHI: London. Sorry, I spent the night in London. I must be really tired.
INSPECTOR: How long were you in Germany?
KAWEHI: Two weeks.
INSPECTOR: Vacation?
KAWEHI: Half a vacation. I was with the 'Aulama Theatre at the Berliner The-
    atre Festival.

INSPECTOR: Did I read about that somewhere?

KAWEHI: Yeah, we did *Hamlet*.

INSPECTOR: No food items, plants, nothing to declare?

KAWEHI: Nope, just clothes and some props.

INSPECTOR: Are you an actress?

KAWEHI: I was just a stagehand, and a kind of consultant.

INSPECTOR: Consultant? Could you open your bags please?

KAWEHI: Sure. (*Unzips bags*) A cultural consultant.

INSPECTOR: Where do you work?

KAWEHI: Oh, I'm a teacher.

INSPECTOR: Teacher?

KAWEHI: I'm on sabbatical.

INSPECTOR: (*Pulls out a Hawaiian pūloʻuloʻu stick*) This doesn't look German.

KAWEHI: The play was set in pre-contact Hawaiʻi. I helped research and supervise the reproduction of artifacts. Looks real, doesn't it?

(*THE INSPECTOR brings out a skull.*)

INSPECTOR: Alas, poor Yorick?

KAWEHI: That's poor Keaka. You like Shakespeare?

INSPECTOR: I played Laertes in high school.

KAWEHI: Did you go to high school here in Honolulu? Maybe I saw you.

INSPECTOR: No, Annandale, Virginia. This looks so real.

KAWEHI: We had a whole set of bones made just for the show. I had to pack it in my clothes to protect it. Careful! They cost a small fortune.

INSPECTOR: (*Carefully wrapping it up*) You sure you don't act?

KAWEHI: (*Smiling*) Well, every once and a while.

INSPECTOR: I was thinking about getting back into it.

KAWEHI: (*Taking the skull from his hands*) Oh, you should. You really should. It's a great release. I bet this job can be stressful.

INSPECTOR: Don't I know it. You can't believe what people try to smuggle in their bags. Just the other day there was a guy with a tarantula.

KAWEHI: A tarantula?

INSPECTOR: Yeah, just running around in his suitcase, not even in a jar or any-thing.

KAWEHI: Are mine okay?

INSPECTOR: Huh?

KAWEHI: My bags, I mean.

INSPECTOR: (*Gives back her passport*) Oh, sure. Just follow the green line out. Maybe I'll see you on the stage.

KAWEHI: I hope I see *you* there.

INSPECTOR: Have a nice day.

SCENE 2

(An office, Berlin. ERIK JAMISON, an American, and MRS. MAHLER, a German woman.)

ERIK: No, I don't know anyone like that, Mrs. Mahler.

MRS. MAHLER: You are sure?

ERIK: I haven't even run into anyone here in Berlin from the south.

MRS. MAHLER: That is what she told Dr. Heinrich at the museum. An anthropologist from the south. He said she had, how do you say it? A charming southern drool.

ERIK: That's drawl, southern drawl.

MRS. MAHLER: Drawl. But maybe it's an imitation.

ERIK: I don't understand what the police think this has to do with our production.

MRS. MAHLER: It is because of the nature of the missing items.

ERIK: What's that?

MRS. MAHLER: Valuable archaeological specimens.

ERIK: What was it? Jewelry, sculpture?

MRS. MAHLER: Human remains.

ERIK: Bones?

MRS. MAHLER: Hawaiian.

ERIK: Oh.

MRS. MAHLER: So, you see, you were a large group from Hawai'i.

ERIK: Naturally. When did this happen?

MRS. MAHLER: Two nights ago, Tuesday.

ERIK: The cast left Berlin on Sunday. I've just been resting.

MRS. MAHLER: Here is the artist's drawing. You are sure you've not met such a woman?

ERIK: Positive.

MRS. MAHLER: The museum is most anxious. It doesn't want, well, ideas to spread.

ERIK: Ideas?

MRS. MAHLER: The museum holds things from many countries and cultures. What would we do if everyone wanted everything back?

ERIK: I see. Whose were they?

MRS. MAHLER: Pardon?

ERIK: The bones?

MRS. MAHLER: Some native specimen. Well over 100 years old.

ERIK: Kept for?

MRS. MAHLER: Research and exhibit Mr. Jamison. That is what we do, research and exhibit.

ERIK: Look, we just came to do a play at the festival. I don't know anything about this person or the incident.

MRS. MAHLER: Not an incident, a *theft*, Mr. Jamison.

ERIK: I know nothing about it.

MRS. MAHLER: You will be in Germany long?

ERIK: I leave tomorrow.

MRS. MAHLER: You will leave information, in case we need to contact you?

ERIK: Certainly, but I don't imagine I could be of any help. *(Short pause)* If that's all, I'd like to be going, Mrs. Mahler. I have some business at the theatre, and I need to pack, say goodbye to friends, you know.

MRS. MAHLER: Of course, I understand, Mr. Jamison. Thank you for your time.

ERIK: *(Exiting)* Good day.

MRS. MAHLER: Good day. *(After a pause)* You can come now, Gustav.

(Enter GUSTAV)

MRS. MAHLER: What do you think?

GUSTAV: Could be he's telling the truth. Could be he's lying. Who knows, he's in the theatre.

MRS. MAHLER: I used to do some theatrical work.

GUSTAV: You gave it up?

MRS. MAHLER: When I married. My husband is very conservative. He enjoys watching, but feels that participating invites promiscuity.

GUSTAV: I see.

MRS. MAHLER: He's a liar, of course.

GUSTAV: Your husband?

MRS. MAHLER: No, no, this Jamison fellow! Someone at the theatre has seen him with the woman.

GUSTAV: Why did you—

MRS. MAHLER: We need to find *her*. *She* has the artifacts. I'm afraid this means you will have to follow him.

GUSTAV: You mean, in the middle of winter you want me to leave Berlin and—

MRS. MAHLER: Yes! Go to Hawai'i!

GUSTAV: *Ach du meine Gote!*

MRS. MAHLER: And no publicity. If this were made public, it would only create sympathy for the other side.

GUSTAV: How will I manage if I can't use the police? I know no one there.

MRS. MAHLER: We have help for you. Scotland Yard owes us for—well they owe us. They've asked an inspector on leave to help us, someone with native blood, who understands the islands.

GUSTAV: *(Jokes)* Who is it? Charlie Chan?

MRS. MAHLER: He'll contact you in Honolulu. His name is Mr., Mr., *(She puzzles over it, has trouble pronouncing it)* Fat-you!

SCENE 3

(Playing area. A Nineteenth-Century PROFESSOR.)

PROFESSOR: Doubts, there are those who raise doubts to the fact that the human species is descended from a single pair. In most instances, these objectors point to the weak intellects and savage customs of barbarous peoples. But with the dawning of the new 19th century comes the enlightened explanation to these doubts. Through modern scientific thought, we now recognize the astounding effects of the *environment* on the development of the human species. Environments determine not only our physical appearance, but our character, customs, and intellect as well. Our own advanced civilization abounds with innumerable stimuli of a civilized, scientific, educational and religious nature. The weak intellect of the savage is due to the want of these stimuli. Our studies positively conclude that through the manipulation of environmental influences it is possible to mold the savage into an acceptable civilized form. And these practices are underway right now with the missions to the heathens. Yes! With teachings of our enlightened civilization, we *can* actually change them culturally and physically! Isn't it wonderful?

(Playing area. A Nineteenth-Century SOUTHERNER.)

SOUTHERNER: All very well in theory sir, you and your Philosophical Society are all very well in theory sir, but let us look toward the facts. Could anyone possibly think that the whole human race is descended from a single pair? Do we, gentlemen, at all resemble the dark and savage races which inhabit the remote areas of the globe? Now, it might be nice to think that we could raise up the barbarians of the world to a state of Christian civilization, but the fact is they were born into a low mental state, and they will die that way. Whether we expose them to all the benefits of civilization or not, we cannot change their essential nature. Take as an example, if you will, the child-like African, who has shown only slight progress under slavery and after over 100 years. The American Indian does not flower under civilization. On the contrary, he withers up and dies. The truth is that non-white races are inferior in every way, and will never advance. They must either be kept in slavery, or allowed to become extinct in order to make way for progress.

SCENE 4

(Kawehi's house. KAWEHI and ERIK.)

KAWEHI: *(With a fake southern accent)* And so I said, "I so admire your progressive paper Dr.Heinrich, 'Measurement Variations in the Rocker Jaw of Pre-Contact Hawaiians between 1720 and 1721' and I've heard you have the most fascinating bone collection here!"

ERIK: Why did you do it, Kawehi?

KAWEHI: I don't know Erik. One thing just led to another. Maybe I was tired, tired of all the *talk* about things being returned to us. Who knows? I just did it, and now it's done.

ERIK: You know, I think maybe somebody's watching us!

KAWEHI: What?

ERIK: I heard noises outside the window a while ago.

KAWEHI: Did you *see* anybody?

ERIK: I thought I saw some shadows.

KAWEHI: Maybe you should go upstairs to your place and try to get some sleep. I think you've got jet lag.

ERIK: Will you come with me?

KAWEHI: No.

ERIK: Why not?

KAWEHI: Because I have to figure out what to do with the, you know, my little parcel.

ERIK: Where are they?

KAWEHI: Under the bed.

ERIK: Ugh.

KAWEHI: What do you mean, ugh?

ERIK: Well, I guess it's perfectly normal for you to have a strange skeleton under your bed. I should just shut up.

KAWEHI: Don't get weird just because I'm not going to sleep with you tonight.

ERIK: Hey, you were the one who told me those creepy stories about spirits hanging around their bones.

KAWEHI: Come on, Erik, I need to take it somewhere, give it a decent burial. That person was Hawaiian. Some asshole grave robber stole those bones. They couldn't even leave us alone after we were dead. Those kūpuna *(elders)* should all come home, every single one of them.

ERIK: I know how *you* feel about it love, but international robbery and skeletons under the bed make *me* a little nervous.

KAWEHI: Are the prop bones safe?

ERIK: They were shipped with the set. I have them at the theatre.

(A loud sound from the outside. KAWEHI and ERIK both jump.)

ERIK: Oh shit. I told you someone's out there.

KAWEHI: Go look!

ERIK: Me? You go look. They might not want to hurt a woman.

(KAWEHI makes a face and tiptoes over to the window and looks out.)

KAWEHI: There's nothing but the neighbor's cat.

ERIK: Maybe you could give them to that group that takes care of reburial.

KAWEHI: Maybe.

ERIK: When?

KAWEHI: When I want to.

ERIK: Kawehi—

KAWEHI: I said I would.

ERIK: But when?

KAWEHI: I just want to keep them for a while.

ERIK: Why?

KAWEHI: I don't know. I took a big risk for them.

ERIK: Taking, you're *taking* a big risk. I told you those museum people want them back pretty bad. They've got people looking for you.

KAWEHI: So? You told them you didn't know me.

ERIK: Maybe they believed me, maybe they didn't. You know I'm taking a big risk too. It's called withholding evidence.

KAWEHI: I saw that box, and I *had* to do it.

ERIK: You know, I think you just need to take a break, Kawehi. You've plowed through the last ten years like a steamroller, your mother just died. Look, you don't *have* to work for awhile. Couldn't you just take some time off?

KAWEHI: I don't really have a job to go back to anyway.

ERIK: What?

KAWEHI: While I was away, Pua's made a few changes. She's terminated four out of the five positions in our department, redefined them, and we all have to reapply. It's called restructuring.

ERIK: You've been there twice as long. You were offered her job.

KAWEHI: I hate administrative work. I want to work on exhibits.

ERIK: She's too much.

KAWEHI: You're telling me. I have to talk to her this week, and it might not be pretty.

ERIK: *(Getting up to leave)* Yeah, so won't you come up and spend the night with me?

KAWEHI: When I want to sleep with you every night, I'll marry you, okay?

ERIK: Promise?

KAWEHI: Maybe.

ERIK: Try to relax and have a peaceful night.

(ERIK kisses KAWEHI. Exit ERIK. KAWEHI starts to straighten up and hears a noise like a voice. She stops, listens, and continues. She hears the noise again. There is a soft tapping and a female voice.)

VOICE: Please, let me in.

KAWEHI: Who's there?

VOICE: Please let me in. I'm so cold.

(KAWEHI moves to the door.)

KAWEHI: Who is it?

VOICE: So cold out here. Please help me.

(Silence. KAWEHI hesitates, pulls open the door.)

KAWEHI: Oh, my god!

(KAWEHI exits.)

KAWEHI: *(Off stage)* You're like ice.

(KAWEHI enters with NANEA. NANEA is shivering and cold, with torn clothes. KAWEHI steers her to the sofa.)

KAWEHI: Are you crazy? You can't wander around like this.

NANEA: Please, I'm so cold.

KAWEHI: What happened?

NANEA: Everything. They took everything and left me.

KAWEHI: Who?

NANEA: Somehow I got back. I just came back. I don't know, don't know anyone.

(KAWEHI gets a blanket and puts it over her.)

KAWEHI: Are you hurt? Did they hurt you? Maybe I should call an ambulance.

NANEA: What?

KAWEHI: A doctor.

NANEA: No, please, no doctor.

KAWEHI: But I think you're ill.

NANEA: Doctor, ambulance, maybe police. No, I don't think you'd like police either.

KAWEHI: Why do you say that?

NANEA: Why do you think?

KAWEHI: What are you doing here?

NANEA: You have something, don't you?

KAWEHI: What do you mean?

NANEA: It's under your bed.

KAWEHI: Who are you?

NANEA: Call me Nanea.

SCENE 5

(A Waikīkī hotel bar. FATU and GUSTAV.)

FATU: My name's pronounced "Fah-Too" not "Fat-You."

GUSTAV: Sorry, Fatu, these Hawaiian words are difficult for me.

FATU: Samoan, my father was half-Samoan.

GUSTAV: I was under the impression you were born *here*.

FATU: No, Apia, Western Samoa. I work now in London.

GUSTAV: You're a long way from home.

FATU: My mother's from London. She was an anthropologist for the British Museum.

GUSTAV: Ah, then you understand the value of the missing artifacts.

FATU: I know why you want them back, yes. Germany holds quite a collection of Polynesian remains and artifacts.

(Enter a WAITRESS in a raffia hula skirt and sequined bra-top.)

WAITRESS: Good evening, welcome to our Aloha Nui Lounge, can I take your order?

GUSTAV: I think I will try this "Planter's Punch."

FATU: Glenlivet, neat, please.

GUSTAV: *(To WAITRESS)* Is this a native costume you are wearing?

FATU: It's a costume, my friend, not native to anything.

WAITRESS: Don't you like it?

FATU: *(Embarrassed)* Well, to tell you the truth, no, I don't.

WAITRESS: Why don't you complain to the management about it? I don't like it either.

GUSTAV: Why wear it?

WAITRESS: Well sir, all I have right now is a high school diploma. If you could find me a politically correct job that pays this much I'd be happy to take *that*, but in the meantime this "costume" supports two kids.

(Exit WAITRESS. Enter MINA. She is dressed tastefully.)

FATU: Ah, Mina, welcome.

MINA: *(Kisses him on the cheek)* Tālofa lava, Fatu.

FATU: Mina, this is Gustav, whom we'll be assisting. Gustav, this is the private investigator I've engaged to work on your behalf, Mina Beckley. I've worked with Mina many times before. As I told you, she is extremely good.

MINA: Besides, I'm his second, or is it third cousin?

GUSTAV: Inspector Fatu has told you how we will rely on your utmost discretion.

MINA: I couldn't afford to be in this business if I wasn't discrete. I've located Jamison.

GUSTAV: So soon?

MINA: If you're interested in theatre, you know him. He's one of the only innovative directors on the island.

FATU: *(Slightly flirtatious)* Are you interested?

MINA: Umm-Hmm.

FATU: My grandfather wrote several plays.

MINA: The famous Inspector Fatu wrote plays?

FATU: As opposed to his undistinguished grandson?

MINA: Sorry, Fatu.

FATU: They were never produced. He hid them away, but I've read them. I think they're quite good.

MINA: Could I read them sometime? I know a small theatre, always looking for new scripts.

GUSTAV: *(Trying to interrupt)* Could we please? Oh—

(WAITRESS enters with two drinks.)

WAITRESS: There you are.

GUSTAV: Ah ha! Very fancy.

FATU: *(To WAITRESS)* I hope I haven't offended you. I was very insensitive.

WAITRESS: It's okay. Forget it. Ma'am, can I get you something?

MINA: I'd like an Old-Fashioned please.

(Exit WAITRESS)

GUSTAV: So you've located Jamison?

MINA: Yes, and there's a woman living in the flat just underneath his—

FATU: Girlfriend?

MINA: I think so.

GUSTAV: Is it her?

MINA: Could be.

GUSTAV: Good, let's talk to her.

FATU: Now, slow down. You know Gustav, Hawaiians often work together very closely. If she suspects—

MINA: It might not even be her. All we have is the artist's drawing.

FATU: If she suspects—

MINA: And even if it *is* her, the bones might not be there.

FATU: If she suspects, she could dispose of them like that, and you'd never see them.

(WAITRESS returns with MINA's drink and exits.)

MINA: I think we should get in there some other way, make friends and—

FATU: Yes, Mina is right. I agree, gather more information.

GUSTAV: *(Trying an American accent)* Size them up, buster!

MINA: Let Fatu and I check things out. You could have a little vacation in the meantime. There's a party at the theatre next week which I'm sure they'll be at. We'll all go to that.

GUSTAV: I think it's better they don't see me.

MINA: They won't see any of us. It's a costume party.

FATU: Mina, you're wonderful.

GUSTAV: Perhaps I will go on a historical walking tour. There are several of them I would like to see.

MINA: Those "Take You Back in Time" walks?

GUSTAV: Yes, and I would like to go swimming in the Pacific Ocean while I am here. I might never get another opportunity.

MINA: The beach is quite nice right in front of the hotel here.

FATU: We can finish talking at dinner. You have a swim, and we'll meet you in the lobby at seven.

GUSTAV: Yes, yes, you've read my mind exactly. Thank you, yes I will go now, and we will talk more at dinner. Charmed to meet you, Miss Mina.

(Exit GUSTAV.)

FATU: I told you he wouldn't be much trouble.

MINA: So far.

FATU: Have you made contact with the woman?

MINA: Not yet. There's a complication.

FATU: Someone else has shown up?

MINA: I think so. Your mother said something like this might happen.

FATU: That was awfully fast.

MINA: This is way more complicated than those other artifacts. We'll have to keep Gustav away until we're sure. He could mess things up.

FATU: Do you want me to call mother in now?

MINA: Not now, but I want to know who that is and what's going on.

FATU: I'll ask her. *(Pause, amused)* Are we really going to a costume party?

MINA: It's characters from Shakespeare, in honor of the Berlin performance.

FATU: Great, Gustav can go in drag as Ophelia.
MINA: Don't be mean. I'll have a costume for you too.

(*WAITRESS comes in.*)

WAITRESS: Would anyone care for another drink?
FATU: (*Looks at WAITRESS*) I have to wear a costume too?
WAITRESS: You can borrow mine.

SCENE 6

(*Kawehi's house. KAWEHI and ERIK.*)

ERIK: Wait a minute. First she tells you she's been away for a long time, and now you're saying she's landed a job in two days?
KAWEHI: Yep. She has a costume and everything. Some kind of historic tour downtown.
ERIK: How does she explain showing up naked and knowing about the bones?
KAWEHI: I don't want to pressure her. She seems a little mixed up.
ERIK: Great, now there's a crazed woman *and* a skeleton.
KAWEHI: (*Defensive*) You haven't even met her. She's not crazy. She's had some kind of trauma. She's . . . just vulnerable, that's all.
ERIK: (*Accusing*) You *like* her.
KAWEHI: I want to be compassionate.
ERIK: That doesn't mean foolish.
KAWEHI: Besides, we have to be nice to her. She *knows*.
ERIK: Better find out what her game is—fast.

(*Enter NANEA with a shopping bag.*)

NANEA: Aloha awakea (*good afternoon*), Kawehi.
KAWEHI: Aloha nö (*greetings*). Where have you been?
NANEA: Out. I used your clothes again. I hope you don't mind. I'll have my own soon.
KAWEHI: Nanea, this is my friend, Erik.
NANEA: How nice to meet a friend of Kawehi's. Look, I have all this food, beer, and I got this packet of 'awa (*kava*), all ground up. Isn't it clever? Let's eat.

(*NANEA takes out all kinds of Hawaiian food and beer. ERIK watches her.*)

NANEA: Here, have a beer. (*Pause*) What a kind face you have, Erik.
ERIK: (*Embarrassed*) Well, thank you. Thank you.
KAWEHI: Erik is the artistic director for the 'Aulama Theatre.

NANEA: I love plays. Once when I was a girl, this wild Englishman built this theatre set in—where I was living—and he made this forest and a castle out of kapa (bark cloth) that was cut and dyed. He even made a bamboo cannon, and in one scene that was supposed to be a battle, he fired the little cannon but it missed its mark, and set the kapa castle and forest on fire. We laughed so much.

ERIK: That sounds dangerous.

KAWEHI: Where was this?

NANEA: Oh, it was so long ago . . . Eat, eat . . .

KAWEHI: Nanea, how did you pay for this?

NANEA: The man just gave it to me.

ERIK: You're kidding.

NANEA: No, he and I spent a long time speaking in Hawaiian. He loved the way I talk, and I loved talking to him. You know, it's been a long time . . .

(NANEA stops and stares as if far away.)

KAWEHI: Since?

NANEA: What?

KAWEHI: It's been a long time since—

NANEA: *(Sadly)* Since, well, since I've had anyone to speak with.

(Pause. ERIK and KAWEHI look at her and each other.)

KAWEHI: *(Moving to comfort her)* Hey, it's all right. We all feel a terrible loss. It's one of the things that bind us together.

NANEA: Loss, that must be it. All that loss, and then to be home.

KAWEHI: I don't know what you've been through, but if you're in any trouble, I'll help you.

NANEA: Kind, you're so kind.

KAWEHI: Erik will too. *(Pause)* Won't you Erik?

ERIK: Sure, sure I will.

SCENE 7

(Playing area. Enter a nineteenth-century PROFESSOR.)

PROFESSOR: Now, with the modern scientific research of the 1850's into the questions of racial origins and differences, modern investigators conclude that the comparison of *crania* is a principal requisite to such inquiries. Mr. Camper, the renowned anatomist, asserts that some races are closer to primates. His theory rests on the facial angle that measures the degree to which the lower jaw protrudes from the face. This protrusion is more pro-

nounced in apes and non-white races alike, and stands as scientific evidence
that such races are, indeed, closer to primates and hence, more primitive.
Furthermore, there are certain important points, gentlemen, that we must
remember in our investigations. One, that each race possesses a uniquely
shaped skull; two, that skulls do not reflect environmental influences, and
therefore provide a more accurate index of racial capabilities; three, that
cranial measurements indicate brain size and therefore intelligence; four,
that we will have to acquire for our study numerous skulls for the advance-
ment of this new and most important science, craniology.

SCENE 8

(An office. KAWEHI puts files in a box. Enter PUA.)

PUA: Packing?

KAWEHI: That's right, Pua.

PUA: I got your application.

KAWEHI: Good.

PUA: To tell you the truth, I didn't like your exhibit on the Wailele site. In fact,
I'm taking it down from the gallery.

KAWEHI: I did an exhibit based on archaeological evidence and oral history.

PUA: Flimsy archeological evidence.

KAWEHI: Oral history is valid evidence.

PUA: You have absolutely no proof there was a heiau *(temple)* there.

KAWEHI: That history was meticulously handed down for hundreds of years.
More than one chant names that place as the site of a luakini heiau.

PUA: And you drew too much attention to human sacrifice.

KAWEHI: I *explained* it. Pretending we were pristine and perfect makes us look
foolish.

PUA: Our culture was great. I guess you don't think that, Kawehi.

KAWEHI: You know I do. I just don't have to pretend it was perfect to love it.

PUA: Well, you can apply for the position if you want, but I should warn you,
you'll have some competition. And I'm carefully considering everyone's attitude.

KAWEHI: The Wailele site is on the verge of resort development.

PUA: Attitude, I don't want anyone with a racist attitude.

KAWEHI: What are you talking about?

PUA: As a native Hawaiian in this position, I have to make sure that Hawaiian
history is portrayed correctly and accurately by people who care.

KAWEHI: By you and a House of Un-Hawaiian Activities.

PUA: It's not un-Hawaiian to protect the culture from misinformation.

(Pause. KAWEHI stares at PUA.)

KAWEHI: It's true, isn't it? *(Pause)* You're in bed with the developers.

PUA: My only concern is for the Hawaiian people.

KAWEHI: Don't do it, Pua.

PUA: Development brings money and jobs to a community.

KAWEHI: *(Sarcastic)* Right Pua, and Waikīkī's made Hawaiians into million-aires. *(Pause)* You're afraid my research will get in the way.

PUA: You are a nobody. I've been a leader in the Hawaiian movement from the very beginning!

KAWEHI: And you're making sure it pays off.

PUA: *(Threatening)* Don't talk to me like that.

KAWEHI: I don't want to talk to you at all.

PUA: Good, because you're never going to work here again.

KAWEHI: I could go to the Board of Directors about this.

PUA: I've already had a talk with them.

KAWEHI: About donations from the developer?

PUA: They're smart.

KAWEHI: I could go to the press.

PUA: I could too.

KAWEHI: You don't speak for everybody.

PUA: But when I talk, more people listen.

KAWEHI: That's because you talk out of both sides of your mouth.

(Blackout)

SCENE 9

(A nineteenth-century PHRENOLOGIST and his assistant MISS IDA enter the Playing Area.)

PHRENOLOGIST: Welcome, welcome, welcome to all you good gentlemen of Pinhead. I am the good Reverend, Dr. Pinchbottom, and here's my lovely assistant, Miss Ida. I come before you today, gentlemen, to testify to you, that just as the feathers identify the bird, just as the flowers foretell the fruit, just as the map reveals the lay of the land, I tell you today, good gentlemen of the town of Pinhead, that phrenology, that's p-h-r / e-n-o / l-o-g-y, phrenology, has been given to mankind to unfold the mysteries of life. I swear to you truly, on my soul, on my honor, on my deep love of God, this marvelous new science holds the key to a better life—free of sickness, free of crime, free of pain, personal calamity, bad choices, bad marriages, bad business, bad crops, and bad breath. Miss Ida, please. *(MISS IDA rolls down a phrenonolgy chart)* Now as we see here, the brain is simply a big muscle, and like a muscle, those parts which we exercise become larger, as a muscle would become larger through frequent exercising. And as you can all see by this scientific chart, different muscles of the brain control different traits. Note here the areas of intelligence, health, conviviality, and criminality. Now sir, step up here for a moment, and let Miss Ida roll up your sleeve. That's it, now would you be so kind as to flex that arm for Miss Ida. Now Miss Ida, I want you to feel those muscles on the gentleman's arm. Can you feel them? Now, just as Miss Ida can feel those rippling muscles, so can I, by examining the lumps, the bumps, and the organic contours of your head, so can I reveal to you your true nature, according to the muscles of your brain which you have, and have not, given to exercise. I can read your tendencies, your flagrancies, your miseries, and your jealousies. I can tell your good habits, bad habits, and habits you wish you had, your strong parts, weak parts, and your parts unknown. I can even help you to find true love, or just a little you-know-what, through my modern scientific training in the marvelous, miracle science of phrenology. Remember now, the finger of divine providence may point the way to your golden opportunities, but it is up to you to follow. Now who'll be the first to line right up for only one dollar and receive the light of new knowledge? I should add, that this dollar includes, unique to the Pinchbottom method of phrenology only, the Universal Current Enhancing Phrenology Massage, by the lovely Miss Ida—guaranteed to bring out the best in your potential. Now don't push, gentlemen, and start lining up right here. I said, don't push!

(Blackout, then lights up to half.)

PHRENOLOGIST: *(quieter)* Oh yes, I almost forgot. In order to advance this wonderful study of phrenology, there are many, many, scholars in need of skulls for their scientific investigations, especially skulls from the various heathen tribes. All those interested in the financial rewards of promoting this worthy science by providing specimens please see me—tonight.

SCENE 10

(Mina's house. MINA AND FATU sprinkle themselves with a ti leaf and salt water.)

MINA: Quit whining, Fatu.
FATU: It drives me crazy when my mother wants me to do this weird stuff.
MINA: Don't be a wimp, a little salt water won't hurt you.
FATU: If we were in my father's village, Mina, you'd be more respectful.

MINA: Cooperate or I'll tell your mother.

FATU: She's so—superstitious.

MINA: What!?

FATU: Tulou lava *(excuse me)*, traditional. And that fax she sent—bones, chiefess, high rank, such inefficient communication.

MINA: You're quite the fussy pälagi *(Caucasian)* these days.

FATU: O a'u Samoa *(I'm Samoan)*.

MINA: Then just do what she says—anytime we go near the house or anyone that comes in and out of it. And she said to keep a ti leaf on us too.

FATU: Okaoka *(oh my)*, these primitive rituals!

MINA: Still remember how to tail someone?

FATU: Can I tail you?

MINA: I *am* going to tell your mother.

FATU: I can't help it. You island women just make my hot Polynesian blood boil.

MINA: Shut up, Fatu.

SCENE 11

(Playing area. NANEA in a 19th-century dress. GUSTAV stands as if part of an audience. MINA and FATU watch from a distance.)

NANEA: Here we are at Kawaiaha'o church, symbol of the new religion of Christianity in nineteenth-century Hawai'i. Many of the chiefs joined the church and attended services here. But some of the chiefs felt oppressed by the new laws, Christianity, and the casting off of all that was sacred. When the chief Boki decided to show his allegiance to Kauikeaouli, Kamehameha the Third, in the old way, he gave him all his Hilo lands to divide up as he saw fit. It angered Ka'ahumanu and the other Christian chiefs, for she took it as a sign that Boki rebelled against *her* authority. When she announced that the government would assume the sandalwood debts of all chiefs, she excluded Boki and insulted him by making him the only chief responsible for his own debt. Then, Ka'ahumanu did a thing which Boki could never forgive or forget. A thing which, whenever he thought of it, plagued his heart and tore at him from the inside. In January of the year 1829, to prove her loyalty to the Christian faith, and to assert her authority, Ka'ahumanu went, accompanied by some of the missionaries, to Hale o Keawe where the sacred bones of our chiefs lay. Some of the bones she gathered up and moved to the caves in the cliffs above Ka'awaloa. The rest she burned. Many peopled heaped her name with abuse for this supreme insult to the bones of departed chiefs. "The bones of our chiefs should be well cared for," shouted Boki, "Instead, she breaks down Hale o Keawe, shows the hidden bones of the chiefs in public, and burns the others." "Perhaps," he cried, "if she knew where Kamehameha's bones lay, she would show them in public too."

(Lights to half on MINA and FATU.)

FATU: I've seen that face before.
MINA: She's absolutely magnetic.
FATU: I'm telling you, I know I've seen her face before.

(Lights fade on MINA and FATU.)

NANEA: And Boki heard there was sandalwood in the New Hebrides. He dreamt of cutting enough sandalwood to clear his debt. The trees came crashing down in his dreams, log after log, enough to erase the entire debt of the nation. In his dreams, he returned wrapped in the sweet scent of sandalwood and foreign money—a hero, a chief greater than Kaʻahumanu. He placed his land and authority in the hands of his wife, Liliha, and to the laments and pleas of those who loved him, he sailed away with his dream. *(Pause)* Liliha never saw him again. His bones would be lost, never to return to rest in his homeland.

(GUSTAV claps and approaches NANEA.)

GUSTAV: Excuse me, I wish to ask why was it so upsetting to burn these bones?
NANEA: We believe that the spirit, the essence, the mana *(spiritual power)* resides in the bones. If not properly hidden or cared for in the old way, the spirit of the departed one is forced to wander, unhappy and restless, never finding its way to the ao ʻaumākua, the realm of the ancestors, never finding home. No peace.
GUSTAV: I see. I have learned so much about your history tonight, and I wish to tell you, you were, how do you say in English, enchanting?
NANEA: Yes, enchanting.
GUSTAV: *Sprechen sie deutsch?*
NANEA: *Ja, ein bisschen.*
GUSTAV: It's lucky for me they picked you for this job.
NANEA: I'm glad you think so.
GUSTAV: History is a fascinating study, and all the things connected with it. So important.
NANEA: German history is very interesting too.
GUSTAV: *Vielleicht könnten wir zusammen kaffee trinken gehen und etwas plaudern?*
NANEA: *Ja, jetzt.*

(Exit NANEA and GUSTAV.)

MINA: Did you hear that?

FATU: What's going on here?

MINA: So you thought Gustav was harmless and easy to handle?

FATU: I don't know. Maybe she just speaks German.

MINA: "Lucky for me they picked you for this job"?

SCENE 12

(Kawehi's house. ERIK and KAWEHI.)

ERIK: And there she was, drinking coffee with this German guy and chatting away.

KAWEHI: So?

ERIK: In German.

KAWEHI: So she speaks German.

ERIK: You have this blind trust. How do you know what she's getting us into?

KAWEHI: I don't want to hear this.

ERIK: Wake up Kawehi. You take those, those, you know—

KAWEHI: They're called bones.

ERIK: You take those bones from Berlin. You know they're looking for you. She appears a few days later, knows about them, and just happens to speak German.

KAWEHI: I just don't think she's like that.

ERIK: Look, if you don't care about being caught and arrested for your noble cause, fine. But I don't want to be entrapped.

KAWEHI: What do you want me to do?

ERIK: *(Escalating)* I want you to see what's going on. I want you to be a little more suspicious. I want you to be a little more cautious. I want you to develop some kind of awareness of the position she's putting us in.

KAWEHI: *(Yelling)* If she's what you say, why hasn't she just had me arrested?

ERIK: I don't know! You're risking everything for some bones. That person is dead and gone. I'm trying to be patient. I'm trying to understand, but I just don't.

KAWEHI: Maybe you can't because—

ERIK: Because? Because? Go ahead and say it. Because I'm not Hawaiian?

(Exit ERIK. Lights out.)

SCENE 13

(Playing area. A GRAVEROBBER steps into light.)

GRAVEROBBER: You ask about my manner of collecting? Their burial places are in plain sight of many Indian houses not far from the fort, and very near frequented roads. I wait until the dead of night, when not even the dogs are stirring. After securing a skull, I then have to pass the Indian sentry at the stockade gate, so I never enter with more than one at a time underneath my coat. The male skull of the old Indian I send you died at the fort on January 7th, 1869. I secured his head the night of the day he was buried. He was laid to rest in his blankets and furs in the usual place, about a half a mile from the fort. Now there is a growing suspicion among them about me, and I knew that it was their intention to watch over the body. Believing probably that I would never steal his head before he was cold in his grave, they did not keep watch the first night, and thus myself and my two hospital attendants easily secured this fine specimen for you. Perhaps you might decide sometime to honor me as a collector and display it.

SCENE 14

(*Kawehi's house. Soft lights. A roll of sennit cord on the table. NANEA is mixing awa in a bowl.*)

KAWEHI: What's the sennit for?

NANEA: We need to weave a kāʻai, a casket for the bones.

KAWEHI: No one knows how to make those.

NANEA: I do.

KAWEHI: How?

NANEA: Watching the kūpuna (*elders*).

KAWEHI: What kūpuna?

NANEA: My kūpuna. It's a family secret.

KAWEHI: Is it going to take a long time to make?

NANEA: Would that bother you?

KAWEHI: (*Uncertain, uncomfortable*) I'm just asking how—

NANEA: You want to just do what Erik says and give them to—

KAWEHI: No! I don't want to. Do you?

NANEA: I want to make a kāʻai.

KAWEHI: And then?

NANEA: What were *you* going to do?

KAWEHI: Find a quiet place—a cave, cool and dry, hidden away.

NANEA: That sounds like a plan for her.

KAWEHI: How do you know it's a her?

NANEA: Because I know. In a woman, the skull is smoother and smaller, the bones of the hands are smaller, and so is the jaw. But the biggest difference is in the pelvic structure. The pelvic girdle is wider and the surrounding bones more delicate—lighter and slender. If you held the pelvic bones of a woman up to the sky, you would see more blue encircled by a softer whiteness, or more stars framed by their curving arch.

KAWEHI: You've studied anatomy?

NANEA: I know a lot about bones.

KAWEHI: From?

NANEA: Mostly listening.

KAWEHI: Are you sure we can do this?

NANEA: Yes, but we shouldn't tell anyone, not even Erik.

KAWEHI: He's mad at me anyway.

NANEA: Why?

KAWEHI: Nothing.

NANEA: Can't be nothing.

KAWEHI: It's the bones.

NANEA: Oh.

KAWEHI: I don't want to talk about it. How shall we start?

NANEA: With 'awa.

(NANEA stirs the bowl for a moment and looks at KAWEHI.)

KAWEHI: We're in this together, aren't we?

NANEA: Of course.

KAWEHI: Then you'll swear it as we drink this 'awa that we'll do anything to protect those bones, to make sure they'll rest forever here, where they belong?

NANEA: Do you know what you're—

KAWEHI: *(Raising her voice)* Will you or not?

NANEA: *(Softly, looking right at her)* I will.

(They drink from the 'awa cup, serving each other. Pause.)

NANEA: Remember, Kawehi, it was you who bound us together.

KAWEHI: How does it start?

NANEA: Here, at the very beginning, at the bottom of things, at the piko, at the center, the vertical strands radiate out while the horizontal thread makes a continuous spiral, turning over and under, over and under. Can you see? Can you see the center?

KAWEHI: *(Slowly remembering)* You, I saw you. You were in Berlin somewhere. I saw you there.

NANEA: *(Helping herself to 'awa)* It's amazing how 'awa clears the mind, isn't it?

SCENE 15

(Playing area. GUSTAV is picking up papers he has dropped on the floor. Enter PUA in the path of the spilled papers. She stops and looks intently at one of them.)

GUSTAV: Excuse me. I am so clumsy.
PUA: Let me help you.

(PUA picks up the particular paper and looks at it.)

PUA: What is this?
GUSTAV: *(Taking it from her)* These are not for . . . Do you know this woman?
PUA: I'm not sure.
GUSTAV: *(Giving paper back to her)* Look again.
PUA: *(Cagey)* It's possible.
GUSTAV: Really?
PUA: She does look like someone who worked here, maybe.
GUSTAV: Who?
PUA: Why do you want to know?
GUSTAV: Do you work here?
PUA: I'm the assistant director.
GUSTAV: It's a serious matter. Perhaps I should speak to the director first.
PUA: Do you have an appointment?
GUSTAV: No, not yet, I—
PUA: Let me take you to his office. I'm sure if I drew his attention to this, we could see him right away.
GUSTAV: He is a discreet man?
PUA: Sometimes, but he's very careful, and he's into red tape.
GUSTAV: Red tape?
PUA: He never makes any important decisions unless he has at least twenty consultations.
GUSTAV: But this needs immediate action. Very confidential action.
PUA: Maybe you'd like to meet with me first about this in my office.
GUSTAV: I don't know if your authority—
PUA: *(Forcefully)* That woman used to be part of my staff. Do you want to talk to me or not?

SCENE 16

(MINA's house. MINA looks at a fax and some books.)

MINA: See page sixty-two, *Portraits of 19th Century Hawaiian Chiefs. (Opens book to page.)* Oh my God! *(Looks back at the fax.)* See *Ruling Chiefs,* page 297. *(Opens another book and reads as FATU enters.)*

FATU: (*At the same time*) Mina, you won't believe—
MINA: (*At the same time*) This is incredible—

(*Short Pause.*)

MINA: You first.
FATU: I just saw Gustav, and he's met some woman at the museum. He told her everything. She told him about Kawehi, her address—she painted a very bad picture of her, and even agreed to snoop around for him.
MINA: Snoop around? Does that mean going to her house?
FATU: I don't know what it means.
MINA: What's this woman's name?
FATU: Pua Ho'olale.
MINA: Brooks.
FATU: What?
MINA: I know her. She was Kelly Brooks. She changed her name.
FATU: (*Perplexed*) Kelly Brooks?
MINA: She's my cousin—distantly, thank god. Like you.
FATU: Thanks Mina.
MINA: Come on, you know I didn't mean it like that.
FATU: Isn't it interesting how we always end up related?
MINA: With her, it's not interesting.
FATU: Sounds like she's got it in for Kawehi. Know why?
MINA: She's probably in Pua's way.
FATU: (*Sniffing*) Is that power politics I smell?
MINA: She screams about injustices done to the Hawaiians, but she'd just as soon bulldoze over a Hawaiian as anybody else if they got in her way.
FATU: One of a growing number. What do you think she'll do?
MINA: She's capable of anything, and she's smart.
FATU: If the other woman was really working with him, why would he need Pua?
MINA: Good point. Speaking of the other woman, your mother sent us another fax.
FATU: More instructions from the great beyond?
MINA: References, page numbers. Here, just look at this picture.
FATU: She's the living image!
MINA: There's more about her in here, a whole chapter and more.
FATU: Kuini Liliha.
MINA: Apparently she was poisoned by a relative.
FATU: Why?
MINA: Doesn't say. But it does say that the people loved her immensely, and

that if she wanted to, she could have easily rallied them and overthrown the stranglehold of the Christian chiefs.

FATU: She's lovely, isn't she?

MINA: She's absolutely magnetic.

FATU: You said that before about—

MINA: I did!

FATU: Do you think she—

MINA: You mean do I think it could be—

FATU: No, no—

MINA: That's crazy—

FATU: Never.

MINA: Maybe that salt water and the ti leaves—

FATU: Stop it, Mina. Don't even think it!

MINA: We're getting out of control.

FATU: That's it! It's time for action.

MINA: Right.

FATU: We'll take the bones ourselves as soon as we can.

(*Lights out.*)

SCENE 17

(*Kawehi's house. Night. ERIK sits on the couch, moving around some miniature figures on the table. NANEA enters quietly.*)

NANEA: Erik.

ERIK: That's me.

NANEA: You're waiting for Kawehi?

ERIK: Where is she? Do you know?

NANEA: She went out with someone I've never seen before.

ERIK: She does that when she's upset with me.

NANEA: Why is she upset with you?

ERIK: Maybe because I'm not Hawaiian.

NANEA: I don't think so.

ERIK: No?

NANEA: It's just things you don't understand yet. (*Looking at figures*) What is that?

ERIK: Nothing.

NANEA: Looks like something.

ERIK: If these were real people, I would be telling them where and when to move around on the stage.

NANEA: That's the director's job. Arranging the bodies.

ERIK: You make it sound morbid.

NANEA: I used to watch them in Germany.

ERIK: So you've lived in Germany?

NANEA: Yes and I liked to watch rehearsals. I know that's not the only thing you do.

ERIK: Really?

NANEA: You interpret the script, figure out what's going on in every scene, what the whole play adds up to.

ERIK: That's us.

NANEA: *(Sitting by his knees, touching figures)* So what's going on here, Erik?

ERIK: More than it looks like, I think.

NANEA: They say the sub-text gives things depth.

ERIK: They say.

NANEA: You fight about me.

ERIK: Yes.

NANEA: You don't feel comfortable with me.

ERIK: No.

NANEA: And you know why, don't you?

ERIK: Because I find myself drawn to you, like you're pulling at me and I can't stop moving toward you.

NANEA: And what is it in the through line of action, propelling things forward?

ERIK: They're under the bed.

(NANEA rests her head on ERIK's knee.)

NANEA: You will help me, won't you? It's urgent.

ERIK: What is it?

NANEA: And it's not just for me.

ERIK: What do you want?

NANEA: I want you to take the bones to a safe place.

ERIK: It's not safe here, is it?

NANEA: Not anymore. You will, won't you?

(Pause.)

ERIK: We'll exchange them.

NANEA: Yes, that's it.

ERIK: I'll take them to the theatre and put the prop bones under the bed. Kawehi won't know.

NANEA: And she won't be endangered. One more important thing.

ERIK: What?

NANEA: Copy the identification number from the bones on the exact spot on the prop.

ERIK: Where is it?

NANEA: Left femur. Black numbers written on the bone. That's what they do, assign numbers for the objects.

ERIK: (*Starts for the bedroom*) I'm going.

NANEA: (*Gets up*) I'll go too Erik, so you don't have to be alone.

ERIK: Thank you.

NANEA: But you, you have to carry them yourself.

(*Lights out.*)

End ACT I

ACT II

SCENE 1

(*Kawehi's house. MINA and FATU, pretending to be journalists, interview KAWEHI.*)

FATU: Right, the *Pacific Performance Journal* is a new scholarly publication.

MINA: Our circulation will be almost exclusively in the Pacific. You know, Hawai'i, New Zealand, Australia, Fiji.

KAWEHI: Sounds great.

FATU: Your role in the production was really unique.

MINA: One we hope other productions will adopt.

FATU: Accurate reproductions, not "props."

KAWEHI: It costs a lot.

MINA: You researched the costumes too, didn't you?

KAWEHI: I did. Of course, we couldn't ask the women to dress authentically.

MINA: You did come close, using body suits.

KAWEHI: Right, and Tahitian camouflage.

FATU: Pardon me?

MINA: Long hair, over the chest area. Get it?

FATU: Got it.

MINA: Good. Now what *about* hair?

KAWEHI: (*Showing them some pictures*) Well, most people have this image of the lovely Hawaiian maiden with long flowing hair, but the earliest artists' drawings we have show women with very short hair and a white kind of lime combed in around the hairline. We couldn't ask actresses to cut their hair so—

(Enter NANEA.)

KAWEHI: Aloha, you're back.

NANEA: Aloha kākou.

KAWEHI: This is Anthony and Kaleinani. My friend, Nanea.

FATU: Hi.

MINA: Hi.

NANEA: Anthony and Kaleinani?

KAWEHI: They're from the *Pacific Performance Journal,* doing a piece about Erik's production in Berlin.

NANEA: Is Erik here?

MINA: We'll be interviewing him this afternoon at the theatre.

FATU: When we have a look at the reproductions.

MINA: We heard about the bones.

KAWEHI: Bones?

FATU: Complete set, isn't it?

(Pause.)

KAWEHI: Ask Erik, at the theatre. He'd be glad to show them to you.

NANEA: They're not there.

KAWEHI: What?

NANEA: Didn't Erik tell you? He brought them here last night.

KAWEHI: Upstairs?

NANEA: No, right here. He couldn't find room at his place—you know what a pack rat he is—so he put them under your bed for now.

(NANEA exits.)

MINA: Who made them?

KAWEHI: They were specially ordered from somewhere in Washington, D.C., and very expensive.

FATU: Authenticity comes at a price these days.

(Enter NANEA with a bone.)

NANEA: *(Waving it around, gives it to FATU)* See? Aren't they wonderful?

FATU: Like the real thing.

NANEA: The product of science and art.

MINA: Perfectly aged.

NANEA: Distressed, that's what they say in theatre, distressed.

FATU: Look, there's some sort of number here.

MINA: I see.

KAWEHI: *(Thinking fast)* It's a prop code for storage.

NANEA: Like artifacts.

KAWEHI: They're being very careful with the reproductions.

NANEA: Erik's going to pack them up to mail to another theatre.

FATU: What play will they be in next?

NANEA: *(Twirling the bone around)* It's a mystery. *Skeletons in the Closet.*

KAWEHI: *(Inappropriate anger)* Don't do that! You could break it!

MINA: *(Awkward pause)* Well, thank you, I think that's it for today.

FATU: Yes, we're very grateful for the time you've given us.

MINA: Very.

FATU: And I must say, those bones are a very good reproduction.

MINA: Excellent.

FATU: We'll have another chance to talk when we meet with Erik.

MINA: Yes, thank you, good-bye.

(Exit MINA and FATU. NANEA enters.)

KAWEHI: How could you do that!??

NANEA: It's what they wanted.

SCENE 2

(CAMILLA, a refined nineteenth-century woman, enters the playing area. She spreads a lace tablecloth over one of the tables and places on it a vase with a single rose. She turns to the audience.)

CAMILLA: January, 1893. My dear Flora, I write to tell you the most thrilling news. I was escorted last evening to the Bennington Charity Ball by none other than Mr. Warren K. Moorehead—

(Enter to one side a nineteenth-century gentleman, WARREN K. MOORE-HEAD, attending to his appearance.)

CAMILLA: —the famous collector of artifacts and antiquities for the Peabody Museum and Harvard University. What a dashing figure he cut when I first met him, engaged in serious conversation with Father in the study. I was immediately struck by his dark moustache, his intense eyes, which pierced me to the bone, and his general countenance, which oozes adventure, travel, and far off places from every pore. Imagine my surprise when the very next day Father informed me that Mr. Moorehead had requested the honor of escorting me to the charity ball!

(MOOREHEAD approaches the table.)

CAMILLA: He has the most gallant manner, and is ever so modest about his occupation.

MOOREHEAD: I am of course largely self-taught, and the fact is, the selling of antiquities is very tiresome to me—but necessary to support my great passion. Which is fieldwork—the discovery and collection of the objects themselves!

CAMILLA: Mr. Moorehead, I said—

MOOREHEAD: Call me Warren.

CAMILLA: I've read with great interest of your dig in the Ohio Valley for the Chicago Exposition.

MOOREHEAD: Shall we dance?

CAMILLA: He smiled engagingly and swept me away.

MOOREHEAD: Ah, yes, the Ohio Valley. I directed a force of men to open graves and village sites along the river, sometimes 300 feet down. I secured at least thirty-five good crania from that site.

CAMILLA: Thirty-five! Imagine!

MOOREHEAD: But at the next site, I really hit pay dirt, as they say. Seventy-nine skeletons!

CAMILLA: Over one hundred all together!

MOOREHEAD: And one remarkably preserved child of six or eight years old!

CAMILLA: What a great contribution to the World Exposition!

MOOREHEAD: *(He leads her back to her seat and stands beside her.)* I suppose.

CAMILLA: You're disappointed?

MOOREHEAD: No, it's just. . . . I'm sure I should be gratified by my contributions. But you see my dear, as I said, my greatest rewards are in the field— the strange lure and promise of it all—my joy and drive always boundlessly
- aroused by what might lie underground. What I might dig up, discover, unbury and expose to the shining light of day—what ancient secrets the earth might yield to me!

(Exit MOOREHEAD.)

CAMILLA: So you see, dear friend, I have quite fallen under the spell of a man of science. Tell me truly, my Flora, do you think I should have any hope of securing the affection of such a brilliant star? Do write me, please do, hurry. All my love, Camilla.

SCENE 3

(Kawehi's house. KAWEHI sits. PUA enters slowly, taking in the place.)

PUA: I see you still go in for tacky exotic.

KAWEHI: You're not welcome here.

PUA: I think you better listen to me.

KAWEHI: Say what you have to say and get out.

PUA: I met a man from Germany.

KAWEHI: Good for you.

PUA: He told me about the bones.

KAWEHI: I don't know what you're talking about.

PUA: It's no good playing dumb. Have you got them here?

KAWEHI: I'd never tell you what I had here or anywhere else.

PUA: If you don't want any trouble, leave them at the museum for me, and no one will ask any further questions.

KAWEHI: Even if I did have such a thing, which I don't, what makes you think I'd give them to you?

PUA: I'm doing you a favor. I'm helping by negotiating a peaceful settlement.

KAWEHI: Looking for a screen for your other activities?

PUA: There is nothing wrong with my other activities. You make me out to be a monster, but I use my position to help the general welfare of Hawaiians— not some remnants of the past.

KAWEHI: Listen to yourself!

PUA: We can't eat stones, Kawehi!

KAWEHI: Can't we?

PUA: You better think about what you've done. If you're no descendant to those remains, you have no spiritual right to them. I'm a leader in the Hawaiian community. I should take charge of them and—

KAWEHI: And?

PUA: And as a cultural authority I can help determine the spiritually correct procedure.

KAWEHI: Your career, your position—assumed, hired, elected—that doesn't make you a spiritual leader.

PUA: This is your last chance.

KAWEHI: That authority comes from another source, Pua.

PUA: You'll be sorry.

KAWEHI: Get out of my house.

(*Exit PUA*)

SCENE 4

(*Mina's house. MINA and FATU enter.*)

FATU: (*Tired*) So now we have about fifty pictures of reproduction artifacts and grubby actors.

MINA: Give them a break. They're in rehearsal.

FATU: No excuse for slovenly dress, not to mention manners.

MINA: *(To herself)* Positively medieval.

FATU: Did you find the fake bones?

MINA: It was easy. I enraptured a stagehand. We'll get them tomorrow night at the costume party.

FATU: Is it tomorrow? I forgot.

(MINA fusses with the contents of a box.)

MINA: I didn't. I found a costume for you.

FATU: That was pretty silly of us to think that Nanea person could have been— well, who we thought.

MINA: It was late. We were tired.

FATU: Did you see the way she tossed those bones around?

MINA: No class.

FATU: And that story about the prop code. That's a museum accession number if I ever saw one.

MINA: Right down to the year of accession.

FATU: They must think we're real fools.

MINA: Well Fatu, by tomorrow night you will be.

(MINA pulls out a jester's cap out and jingles the bells at FATU.)

FATU: *(Groans)* I think I hate detective work.

MINA: *(Teasing)* Fatu the fool and his bag of bones.

FATU: Now, now, Mina. "Mend your speech a little, Lest you may mar your fortunes."

MINA: You don't have any fortune.

FATU: Maybe we should go to Kawehi's and switch the bones on the same night.

MINA: Perfect, they'll all be at the party! You know, you should be very grateful I'm letting your wear this costume.

FATU: Don't tell me, you were going to make me the ass from *Midsummer Night's Dream.*

MINA: *(Pulls out a donkey head mask)* No! Not you! That part's for Gustav!

SCENE 5

(Kawehi's house. KAWEHI is in an Elizabethan dress. NANEA is dressed like Cleopatra. NANEA pins flowers in KAWEHI'S hair.)

NANEA: Pass me another pin.

KAWEHI: I'm not looking forward to this.

NANEA: Why are you going?

KAWEHI: I was part of the crew. It would look funny if I didn't. You know, for Erik—

NANEA: *(Indulgently)* Oh, Erik.

KAWEHI: *(after a pause)* Do you like him?

NANEA: Yes, I like Erik.

KAWEHI: He likes you.

NANEA: Is that so?

KAWEHI: He didn't before.

NANEA: No?

KAWEHI: He didn't want you staying in my house.

NANEA: I guess he changed his mind.

KAWEHI: He can do what ever he wants.

NANEA: That's right.

KAWEHI: You can do whatever you want.

NANEA: I will.

(Long pause.)

KAWEHI: It's all going wrong!

NANEA: What is?

KAWEHI: Everything. Maybe I shouldn't have taken them. Maybe I should give them to the museum. Then everything would be all right.

NANEA: Would it?

KAWEHI: We'd all be safe.

NANEA: Except the one who would sit on the shelf.

KAWEHI: Who?

NANEA: The person whose spirit is left to wander. 'A'ole maluhia ka wahine *(The woman is not at peace).*

KAWEHI: But Pua's right. I'm not related. I have no authority.

NANEA: You don't?

KAWEHI: You know that.

NANEA: Maybe you have the highest authority. *(Long pause)* Think back, just think back a little, Kawehi, back to a cold night. It's raining and there's coffee on your breath. You're with Heinrich in the room. You've tricked him, and the thrill of getting away with it is making your heart pound. He leaves the room to get the camera you say you left in his office. You're all alone now, in that room.

KAWEHI: Yes, I'm all alone and I'm thinking how dark and cold it is all of a sudden. I look around me at the rows and rows of gray steel storage shelves. Aisle after aisle of bones and bones and the words rushing out of nowhere: kupuna käne, kupuna wahine, nä hulu mamo, nä lei hiwahiwa *(grandfather, grandmother, esteemed elders, precious ones)*, and I feel so lonely, and sad, so isolated in all this chill and gray with the sharp smell of metal and cold, shiny concrete floors. And I'm thinking, how can this be? How can this be real? I look over at one shelf all by itself, with one and only one box on it, and there you are standing next to it, with your arms opened out to me, weeping.

NANEA: Yes.

KAWEHI: And when you put it like that, how could I ever refuse?

NANEA: There was a time when I would have expected more: ritual, veneration, and ceremony. But time goes by and we learn to ask for less. Just a quiet place, cool and dry and smelling of the earth, just a peaceful place to lie, undisturbed, in my own native land. What human right denies us this final resting place?

KAWEHI: After every other insult—

NANEA: What human heart?

KAWEHI: Who are you?

(NANEA whispers in KAWEHI'S ear.)

SCENE 6

(Playing area, a costume party. NANEA is Cleopatra. FATU is a jester and carries a bag. GUSTAV is in a donkey mask. A WOMAN is dressed as a witch. KAWEHI, ERIK, PUA, and MINA are in Elizabethan garb. All are masked. They dance and talk in small groups. The party members freeze as three PLAYERS enter dressed as Elizabethan clowns.)

PLAYER 1: What and who have we here?

PLAYER 2: Judging by their costume, they judge themselves to be fine ladies and gentlemen.

PLAYER 3: Except the one who perceives himself to be an ass.

PLAYER 1: A fool.

PLAYER 2: And she that sees within herself a witch.

PLAYER 3: What purpose makes them so?

PLAYER 1: Know not thy betters?

PLAYER 2: The lords and ladies of this world?

PLAYER 3: No.

PLAYER 1: They are actors, Humblebee!

PLAYER 2: Except when they're asses, witches, or fools.

PLAYER 1: Which they're known to be with frequency.

PLAYER 3: What a muddle-brain I am, in this very realm where they "strut and fret their hour."

PLAYER 1: It is a pity.

PLAYER 2: Indeed, a pity.

PLAYER 1: 'Tis only an hour.

PLAYER 3: They seem to know it not.

PLAYER 1: They must *not* know it, else they would cease to be real!

PLAYER 3: But they are actors—

PLAYER 2: So *we* told *thee,* Humblebee.

PLAYER 3: So you did, so you did. But when their hour is done?

PLAYER 1: It's off to the bone yard—

PLAYER 2: Every one.

(The music comes up quickly as the party continues. PLAYERS join the party. MINA and FATU dance while PUA and GUSTAV are at a table. The others are engaged in party business.)

PUA: Shakespeare was such a racist.

GUSTAV: White, English, middle class, born around 1564, most likely you are right. But perhaps that's not all he was.

PUA: Do you have to wear that donkey head?

GUSTAV: No one must see me.

PUA: So it's Mina you work with.

GUSTAV: You know her?

PUA: We're related, distantly.

GUSTAV: Everyone here seems to be related.

PUA: I'm glad to see she's with a local man. No offense to you.

GUSTAV: He is Samoan.

PUA: Really?

GUSTAV: Can I get you a drink?

PUA: Please.

MINA: *(Joining PUA)* Pua, I see you've met our friend.

PUA: Mina, how nice to see you.

MINA: How are you?

PUA: Fine. I've been promoted. Yourself? Other than dating Samoans, I mean.

MINA: Fatu is a close colleague of mine, but I wouldn't hesitate to "date" him.

PUA: Still no sense of humor?

MINA: Not like you, coming with a donkey.

(FATU comes to the table.)

MINA: Pua, this is Anthony Lemanatele Fatu. Fatu, this is Pua Ho'olale.

FATU: Hi.

PUA: Aloha käua.

MINA: I think I'll help Gustav.

PUA: Mina tells me you're Samoan.

FATU: Um-Hm.

PUA: You know, it's just wonderful how many scholarships there are available now for Pacific Islanders. Especially if you're interested in athletics.

FATU: Umm-Hmm.

PUA: Are you?

FATU: Hmm?

PUA: Did you ever play football?

FATU: Well, I played some cricket at Oxford, but when I went to Cambridge, I gave it up. A bit bored, I guess.

(MINA and GUSTAV return with drinks.)

GUSTAV: Here we are.

MINA: *(Toasting)* Manuia.

FATU: Soifua.

GUSTAV: Your father, Fatu, did you say he was Inspector Fatu, *the* Inspector Fatu?

MINA: His grandfather.

GUSTAV: I should have remembered the name when I first heard it. Some of his cases were written up. I read them long ago.

MINA: I love them.

FATU: Those accounts were a little romanticized.

GUSTAV: But the logic, so precise, and such an uncanny understanding of human motives.

PUA: Does that surprise you?

GUSTAV: I beg your pardon?

PUA: Because he was Polynesian?

GUSTAV: No, I simply admire his work.

FATU: Come Pua, would you like to dance?

PUA: It's been a long time.

FATU: Come on. A lovely woman like you should dance more often.

GUSTAV: Did I say something wrong?

MINA: Poor Pua, all she knows is how to attack or defend.

GUSTAV: Listening to those history talks—I can understand why many of you are angry.

MINA: Yes, a healthy anger can help us to make changes, but . . .

GUSTAV: But?

MINA: But somewhere along the way Pua started to—love the taste of her own anger, and it's poisoning her. Will you excuse me?

GUSTAV: Certainly.

(MINA exits with FATU'S bag. FATU and PUA return.)

FATU: Gustav, you have to dance!
GUSTAV: I could try.

(GUSTAV'S donkey head nearly hits FATU.)

PUA: Just keep looking to one side.

(GUSTAV looks, and nearly hits PUA.)

GUSTAV: Oh yes I see, so I don't hit you.

(NANEA walks up to FATU.)

NANEA: Anthony, isn't it?
FATU: Antony I'm wishing now, to fair Cleopatra.
NANEA: Having a good time?
FATU: Very.
NANEA: I'm going to dance with a beggar.

(NANEA dances with a PLAYER. THE WITCH pokes FATU with her broomstick.)

WITCH: Don't slouch, boy. A jester should be peppy.

(FATU stares at the WITCH. KAWEHI walks up to him and gives him a small nosegay.)

KAWEHI: And pansies, that's for thoughts.
FATU: And what do you think?
KAWEHI: About what?
FATU: Anything.
KAWEHI: I think, I think I've crossed the line where what I think doesn't count
for much.
FATU: *(Takes her hand)* I want you to know I—

(The music gets louder and MINA is at FATU's side with the bag, whispering in his ear. FATU waves at KAWEHI as he and MINA leave. KAWEHI watches and turns away. THE WITCH has been watching also and follows them. ERIK whisks KAWEHI up to dance as lights fade to black.)

SCENE 7

(Kawehi's house. The lights are very dim, almost black. Enter MINA with a flashlight. FATU follows with the bag. They are still in their costumes.)

FATU: I don't like carrying these.

MINA: They're not real, Fatu.

FATU: I don't care. Did you hear something?

MINA: No. Come on. She said they were under the bed.

(MINA and FATU exit through the bedroom door. THE WITCH enters with a flashlight, looks around quickly, and goes into the bedroom. FATU screams and runs out followed by the WITCH. MINA pauses in the doorway. THE WITCH shines her light in FATU's and MINA's faces.)

WITCH: *(Lifting off her mask a little)* I knew what you were going to do.

FATU: God damn it! I've told you a thousand times, never sneak up on me!

MINA: *(Kissing her)* Deidre. Not a very warm way to greet your mother, Fatu.

FATU: Sorry, Mother, but you know—

DEIDRE: Save it for later, dear. I'll keep watch. You two finish what you came here for.

(MINA and FATU exit through the bedroom door. They quickly return.)

DEIDRE: Let's go that way.

(DEIDRE leads toward the other exit. All of a sudden the flashlights go out and everything is pitch black. NANEA, unseen by the other three, switches the bones.)

DEIDRE: They both went out at once. Did you see that?

MINA: I can't see a thing.

FATU: I don't like this.

DEIDRE: We need to get out of here.

FATU: I can't get it to work.

DEIDRE: Just feel your way.

FATU: I can't find the bones.

DEIDRE: What?

FATU: I just put them here.

MINA: Ouch, Fatu, you kicked me.

FATU: No I didn't.

DEIDRE: Hurry up.

FATU: I can't find—you didn't have to shove them at me, Mina.

MINA: What?

FATU: God, your hands are cold.

MINA: I didn't even touch you.

(Flashlights go back on)

DEIDRE: You two just get your bums out of here fast!

(Exit FATU, MINA, and DEIDRE. NANEA sticks her head out of the bedroom doorway and smiles, then retreats. Blackout.)

SCENE 8

(Two pools of light in the playing area. Two 19th-century GENTLEMEN step out.)

DORSEY: Mr. Franz Boas over there is simply sour about me being named Curator of Anthropology at the Field Museum instead of him. Because of this, he began this personal war with the museum and our department of anthropology, accusing me of things that—

BOAS: *(Germanic accent)* Hardly a war, Mr. Dorsey. As the Curator of Anthropology at the American Museum of Natural History, I would hardly say my actions constitute a war. I was simply saying in that interview that as a collector and an anthropologist, you should hardly presume to put yourself in my league.

DORSEY: Listen, Boas, I have recently collected myself, in the field, two skeletons of the Kootenay tribe, which you could never get because they watch their cemeteries very carefully now. And, I have one complete skeleton of a Tlingit shaman, which is practically unknown, as the Tlingit prefer cremation.

BOAS: Dorsey, I had already collected and sold many remains to Washington, to Berlin, to important museums throughout Europe before you could even say "anthropological dig," and furthermore, over one hundred and seventy specimens in your own collection are the result of my ingenuity.

DORSEY: Your ingenuity? You mean the Sutton Brothers, to whom you paid $5 a skull and $20 a skeleton.

BOAS: At least they're circumspect. Your paid man Newcombe only knows rip and plunder, chasing epidemics or waiting until villages are out on a hunt to rob their burial grounds.

DORSEY: Oh, *you've* never done anything of the sort, have you, Boas?

BOAS: At least I have never *angered* the Indians.

DORSEY: No you let the Suttons do that.

BOAS: You, on the other hand, have actually been arrested for grave desecration.

DORSEY: At least I haven't run a bone brokerage! You're just jealous because your museum's collection will never equal ours!

BOAS: Our collection will equal and outnumber yours.

DORSEY: Not as long as I'm curator of the Field.

BOAS: Better start digging Dorsey—if you want to keep playing with the big boys.

SCENE 9

(NANEA in her Living History costume in the playing area. Separately, DEI-DRE and GUSTAV watch.)

NANEA: Boki left Liliha to be his successor in the care of the young king, Kauikeaouli. The boy's attachment to her was very strong, but the Christian chiefs were determined to keep him away from her. They took the king and embarked on a tour of the outer islands to spread the word of God. But taking the boy was not enough. Kaheiheimālie came back to Oʻahu and insulted Liliha in public. As the harsh words fell from her mouth, there arose an uproar among the common people who loved Liliha, and were tired of the tyrannical yoke of the Christian chiefs. Talk of rebellion spread, preparations were made for war. Liliha's followers held the port of Honolulu and refused entry to any of the Christian chiefs on the penalty of death. But they tricked her. They sent the one they knew she would never harm—her own father, Hoapili. He persuaded her to stop, and then, to his shame, he watched as those who had sent him, stripped her of all land and power. She died sometime later. Poisoned, perhaps by one of her own family. *(Pause)* Few chiefs were ever so loved, were ever shown such affection by the common people. It is said that never has there been, or never shall there be, such lamentations as the night of her death. The river of Kīkīhale was stamped dry by the throngs of Hawaiians coming to mourn her in the city. Her body was taken to Lahaina to rest.

(GUSTAV approaches, clapping.)

GUSTAV: Thank you. Thank you. I was very much affected. Do you have time tonight?
NANEA: I'll meet you at the cafe. There's someone I have to talk to first.
GUSTAV: Then, I wait for you. Tonight was very special.

(GUSTAV exits. NANEA approaches DEIDRE.)

NANEA: I thought perhaps you might come.
DEIDRE: I'm Deidre McIntyre.
NANEA: You mean Deidre Fatu?
DEIDRE: Not professionally.
NANEA: They talk about you all the time in Berlin.
DEIDRE: Really?
NANEA: Mahler hates you. She'd like to see you arrested. She'd die if she found out Fatu was your son.
DEIDRE: I'm careful about that. *(Short pause)* If I had known it would be like this, I would have come sooner.

NANEA: I didn't know myself, until that night when Kawehi came into the room.

DEIDRE: How long do you think it will be?

NANEA: Not much longer I think.

DEIDRE: Is it hard for you?

NANEA: It should be, shouldn't it? But it's not. I've been watching everything for so long.

DEIDRE: Will you be sorry when . . .

NANEA: No, you see, I'm very tired.

DEIDRE: I understand.

NANEA: Waiting so long.

DEIDRE: I know.

NANEA: I'm worried about her. She's done so much.

DEIDRE: I'll do everything I can for her. That's why we're here. To help her, and you.

NANEA: And the others? There are so many others.

DEIDRE: We're doing everything we can.

NANEA: Tell me, why do you do this?

DEIDRE: I was an anthropologist for a long time. I don't know. I married an islander. My son is Samoan. After a good many years, I just began to see things in a different way. It helps me to sleep at night.

NANEA: I'm grateful.

DEIDRE: Could you tell me how it happened?

NANEA: Well, supposing a person suspected that someone was trying to kill them. Supposing it came to them that they might not have much longer to live, and supposing the one thing that was abhorrent to them was that their bones might lie on the grounds of those who caused them pain and suffering, perhaps even death. Suppose they could not bear to lie on the ground of a Christian god who would never be hers. (Pause) There was an old man who greatly loved her and served her, a common man who promised if something happened he would take her away. After her death, he opened the unburied wooden box, and with the help of others who also held her dear he traded the bodies and nailed it back up. Off he went in his canoe with his beloved ali'i (chief) to a lonely place, where the only voices are in the sea and the birds and the owl at night. There he performed his loving task, cleaning the bones of mortal flesh and oiling them carefully, always in silence but—Auē! Aloha piha 'o ia (Oh! He was full of love). He hid them in a cave and left. No one ever saw him again. They lay there for so long, until one day, foreign men found them by accident. They wrapped them up, took them out, and exchanged them for so much money.

DEIDRE: Then you are whom I thought.

NANEA: How did you know?

DEIDRE: I dreamed of the bones. In the dream a young woman sailed for a far off place in a feather cape. Waving goodbye were crowds. They called out her name.

NANEA: Which was?

DEIDRE: Kuini Liliha.

SCENE 10

(MINA, FATU, PUA and GUSTAV meet in the playing area.)

MINA: I just don't want to be the one who breaks and enters.

GUSTAV: I understand. You two have done so much already.

PUA: You know for sure they're in the house?

FATU: We know exactly where they are in the house.

MINA: And we have a foolproof plan to confuse them.

PUA: Them? I thought they wouldn't be there.

FATU: We're fairly sure she's only part of a larger group, and we think there's a very good chance they're watching the house.

PUA: Highly probable.

MINA: *(To GUSTAV)* Now, Pua drives you to the corner.

FATU: She let's you off here and drives away.

MINA: You enter the house.

FATU: They'll be with us at the theatre doing an interview.

MINA: But make sure the friend isn't there.

GUSTAV: Friend?

MINA: Just make sure no one's there before you go in.

FATU: Take the bones—you'll find them bundled under the bed.

PUA: How do you know?

MINA: We *know.*

FATU: Take them to the big empty lot out back.

MINA: It's overgrown and people have dumped trash there.

FATU: You'll see an old blue Ford.

MINA: Go to the car, and you'll see this red sports bag and this bundle in the back seat, identical in size to the bones you took from the house.

FATU: Listen, now this is very important. Put the bones you have on the floor and then put the bundle that was already in the car into the red sports bag. Lock the car up and leave.

MINA: Pua will pick you up again at the corner.

GUSTAV: Clever. Anyone watching will think I have the bones and be led away from the real thing.

MINA: We wait and retrieve the bones the next day.

GUSTAV: Excellent, excellent.

FATU: Then it's over.

GUSTAV: *(Dejected)* Yes, yes and back to Germany.

PUA: How are you going to get the bones back through customs to Germany?

GUSTAV: Mahler will arrange it all through the consulates.

MINA: What's the matter?

GUSTAV: I don't know. It's those history walks. The way she has been explaining everything. I begin to feel very bad about things. *(Pause)* But I suppose I must do my duty.

(GUSTAV stands to exit. PUA gets ready to go.)

FATU: If anything is strange just stop and abandon the plan.

GUSTAV: Until 5 this evening.

PUA: See you then.

(Exit PUA and GUSTAV.)

MINA: Is the car fixed up?

FATU: Yes.

MINA: I hate that part.

FATU: I'm very careful. I won't detonate unless I know it's safe.

MINA: If anyone got hurt.

FATU: There's always a risk, but it's small.

MINA: I never told you Fatu, but . . . I don't know how to tell you. . . . I really admire you for doing this—these jobs.

FATU: You do them too.

MINA: When we have the opportunity, we have the obligation.

SCENE 11

(Kawehi's house. KAWEHI and LILIHA.)

LILIHA: *(Folding up sennit kāʻai)* It's finished.

KAWEHI: You did it so quickly.

LILIHA: We did it.

KAWEHI: I just watched.

LILIHA: You helped too.

KAWEHI: Will it fit?

LILIHA: Perfectly. But you'll have to finish this one part the way I showed you.

KAWEHI: Why?

LILIHA: *(A little nervous)* I have to leave now.

KAWEHI: When?

LILIHA: Now.

KAWEHI: Now!?

LILIHA: Now—

KAWEHI: But you can't leave. You have to help me. You have to be here to tell me—

LILIHA: No.

KAWEHI: Who will?

LILIHA: You'll have help.

KAWEHI: Please, I want you to be here.

LILIHA: Don't pull on me like that.

KAWEHI: I'm not.

LILIHA: With your feelings. It hurts.

KAWEHI: I just don't want you to go now.

LILIHA: When then?

KAWEHI: I don't know.

LILIHA: You see, the bond is already too strong. It's dangerous.

KAWEHI: For you?

LILIHA: For us both. Listen now, and be strong. The ones that were taken keep crying out for home and find no rest. In turn, the islands themselves weep for their return. It's up to you, the living. You carry the past and the future.

(*KAWEHI and LILIHA embrace.*)

LILIHA: Bring us all together and bind us as one, just like we wove the threads together, you and I. Don't cry, and don't fail me. Look what we made. (*Pause*) Here, you should put it away where it's safe.

(*KAWEHI takes the kāʻai and exits through the bedroom door.*)

LILIHA: Don't cry, kuʻulei (*my darling*). I'll never be far away.

(*Exit LILIHA. Enter KAWEHI. She looks around and sits sadly. Enter ERIK.*)

ERIK: Kawehi? What's wrong? I just saw her rush out like the wind.

KAWEHI: Yes, like the wind.

SCENE 12

(*Mina's house. MINA enters with interview equipment and begins putting things away. PUA enters with red sports bag.*)

MINA: Pua, did everything go smoothly?

PUA: Like butter.

(Gives her the bag.)

MINA: No problems?

PUA: No. But there's about to be one.

MINA: What's that?

PUA: Yours, not mine.

MINA: Skip the bait, just say it.

PUA: You didn't think I was just going to let that guy take the real bones back to Germany, did you?

MINA: What?

PUA: And you, what kind of Hawaiian are you, selling out your own ancestors.

MINA: This is my job, the way I make a living.

PUA: Well it's pretty scuzzy.

MINA: Your place of employment holds a large collection of human remains.

PUA: This is different.

MINA: What do you want?

PUA: By 11:00 tomorrow morning, I want those bones dropped off in a box at the museum addressed to me.

MINA: You let us find them, get them to a safe place, and then take them for yourself?

PUA: I helped.

MINA: What about Gustav?

PUA: Tell him if he doesn't comply, phones will ring—customs, immigration, police, newspapers, Hawaiian groups . . .

MINA: I've got the picture.

PUA: Good.

MINA: And what do you intend to do with them?

PUA: First, I'll hold a press conference. Then, I think it would be appropriate to set up a committee to decide what the most correct procedure is spiritually and culturally. We'll decide who should have authority.

MINA: That could take a long time.

PUA: What's the rush, once they're back in the proper hands.

MINA: Germany could press its legal rights.

PUA: Public legal battles get publicity for issues—

MINA: And people.

PUA: *(Exiting)* Just have them there.

(FATU enters.)

FATU: She's not carrying the sunshine is she?

MINA: Why does she have to be my cousin?

FATU: Well, did she—

MINA: Right on cue, almost exactly like we thought.

FATU: Like *you* thought.

MINA: She'll probably show about 11:30.

FATU: I'll be ready.

MINA: Gustav?

FATU: I guess he should be there too. I'll have him drop me off, and tell him to wait down the block. That should be close enough.

SCENE 13

(A NINETEENTH-CENTURY PHYSICIAN enters.)

PHYSICIAN:My dear fellow doctor. When I parted with you a month ago, I told you I would send you a present. Well, here it is! A skull, a genuine skull of a Sandwich Islander. It has served my purpose, and now I turn it over to you for, I hope, a place in your outcoming work on crania—a work which I believe will be on the shelf of every man of science for years to come. I give you a brief history of my man Friday. He was about twenty-seven or so, and he declared himself a member of a royal line. He had gone out one day on a fishing excursion and was driven by a storm far out to sea. There he languished many days, when finally he was rescued by a whaling ship and landed near Panama. From there he found his way to New Orleans, and then on to our city, where he fell ill, entered the hospital, and as providence would have it, was placed in my care. He died of nervous exhaustion, and nostalgia. I knew him very well, attended him up to the end, and as he had no means of payment, I made his *head* responsible for his medical bill. I now place it, a native offering, as they say, on the altar of science—a testament of my belief in the path which I love to follow. Truly, Dr. M.

SCENE 14

(Kawehi's house. KAWEHI and ERIK.)

KAWEHI: *(Distressed)* They were here yesterday!

ERIK: When we got home?

KAWEHI: Before we left. I don't check every minute.

(Knocking on door.)

MINA: Hello. Hello. Are you there?

KAWEHI: We're busy!

MINA: It's Mina. Kaleinani. Please-

ERIK: We can't talk now! Go away!

MINA: I know what's missing!

(*KAWEHI opens the door. MINA enters.*)

KAWEHI: What is this, Kaleinani, Mina, whatever your name is?

MINA: Mina, Mina Kaleinani Beckley. I'm helping some people that recover things, unofficially.

ERIK: (*To himself*) Oh, shit.

MINA: Don't worry. They're safe, everything's okay. We have them. Fatu, that's Anthony, and I work with his mother on certain cases, like this one, to retrieve things. Things that should go back to their proper places, different things.

KAWEHI: You didn't have to interfere.

MINA: Be serious! Germany knew exactly who you were. They would have found you and the bones eventually. We stepped in, because we wanted to get them and other *interested parties*—

KAWEHI: You mean Pua?

MINA: —exactly—off the trail forever. Things that don't exist aren't looked for anymore.

KAWEHI: If it doesn't exist, it's gone, destroyed.

MINA: No, no they just *think* it's destroyed, gone, vanished, up in smoke. We took that set of fake bones that Erik locked in the trunk at the theatre—gee Erik, you'd have thought Houdini was in there—and we switched them with the real bones under your bed.

ERIK: Oh shit!

MINA: Then, we had Pua and Gustav steal the fake bones from you and hide them in the car we planted in the empty lot.

KAWEHI: Why?

MINA: Because in about one minute, that car is going up in smoke and they'll think the bones are lost forever.

ERIK: No, no you can't do that!

MINA: It's too late. I know they're expensive props, but—

ERIK: NO! NO! YOU DON'T UNDERSTAND!!! She wanted me, she asked me, she made me—I switched the real bones from under the bed with the prop bones days ago, and now you switched them back! Those are the real bones out there!!!

KAWEHI: No, please, no.

(*KAWEHI runs out the door with ERIK and MINA after her.*)

MINA: Stop! Stop her!

ERIK: Kawehi, no—
FATU: (Off stage) Get back! Get away!

(The sound of an explosion. Flashing lights. Blackout. Lights come up on
KAWEHI huddled in the playing area.)

KAWEHI: I don't know exactly how to tell you what happened. It was like
    watching—just like watching myself in a movie. I was running for the car
    and she came, like a fast blurry image out of nowhere. She grabbed on to
    my shoulders and turned me around and pushed me. I fell forward as if I
    had been slammed by some incredible force.

(Lights suggest explosion and fire, no sound.)

KAWEHI: And then I felt a second push, a lighter shove of air and heat, and in
    the corners of my eyes the brilliant flash of orange and yellow light, and her
    body coming over me like a dark wave from behind and falling and the
    blackness surrounding me curling and covering me like a deep warm blan-
    ket, and things falling all around, hot metal things rushing by.

(Pause. Enter ERIK)

KAWEHI: The next thing I know Erik is there, pulling me away.
ERIK: Are you all right?
KAWEHI: Nanea, is she . . . ? Where is she? Did she?
ERIK: She's not here, love. Just be quiet.
KAWEHI: I saw her. She saved me.
ERIK: She's not here, love. She left yesterday morning. Don't you remember?
KAWEHI: I saw her. I did. She saved me.

SCENE 15

(Kawehi's house. FATU, MINA, and ERIK.)

FATU: It's my fault.
MINA: No, I'm responsible.
ERIK: I shouldn't have done it.

(Enter DEIDRE)

DEIDRE: This looks like the tomb of gloom. What's the matter? Gustav and
    Pua weren't convinced?
FATU: Oh, they're convinced.
MINA: Thoroughly.
FATU: The trouble is—

ERIK: So are we.

DEIDRE: Could someone translate for me?

MINA: Deidre, I'm sorry, we blew it.

ERIK: Literally.

FATU: We torched the real bones by mistake.

ERIK: I switched, you switched, and then—

FATU: Poof!

MINA: The ones you have, the ones we got that night, weren't the real ones.

DEIDRE: Yes they were.

FATU: No, mother, we just explained it to you. They're fake.

DEIDRE: You become increasingly insolent with age, my dear boy. Your mother was an anthropologist in the field for over 30 years. I've worked with bones from New Guinea to China the long way round and back, and I know a human bone from a fake one, thank you.

MINA: What?

FATU: Are you sure?

DEIDRE: Of course I'm sure.

ERIK: But how did they get back?

DEIDRE: That I can't tell you.

MINA: There was something strange that night when we came here. Fatu, you said some weird things.

FATU: I just told you you didn't have to shove the bones at me—

MINA: But I didn't. I didn't touch any bones or you. In fact, I thought you pushed me.

FATU: (Slowly) And those hands were so cold.

DEIDRE: HMM. Well, it wasn't me.

ERIK: Do you think she—I mean who else—

MINA: She must have known—

(Pause)

FATU: Let's not talk about it.

DEIDRE: He has a complex about the supernatural, like Freud.

FATU: (To MINA) If I have any complexes, I'm sure they're due to my eccentric upbringing.

DEIDRE: Where is she? Kawehi? The poor child must think—

ERIK: Now I see why, why she did everything—the through line of action. And Kawehi, I didn't know why she was doing what she was doing until I picked up the bones, until I had to carry them myself.

DEIDRE: Where is Kawehi?

ERIK: She's taking it pretty hard.

DEIDRE: Well don't just sit there, go and tell her!

SCENE 16

(Mina's house. GUSTAV waits. FATU and MINA enter.)

MINA: Gustav.

GUSTAV: I came to say goodbye. You weren't here, so I just . . .

MINA: I'm glad you waited.

FATU: Sorry things didn't work out, Gustav.

MINA: The police say kids hang around the lot, but they don't have any suspects.

GUSTAV: Did you see how fast Pua ran away?

MINA: I'm sure she's praying no one saw her there.

GUSTAV: Mahler will not be pleased with me.

FATU: I hope she doesn't make it hard for you. I'll write her a report myself.

GUSTAV: You know, in a way I'm glad I didn't have to take those bones away. I mean, I'm sorry for the loss, but after learning a little, I'm glad I didn't have to do it.

MINA: What would you have done with them?

GUSTAV: I think, hmm, I think I would entrust them to somebody. Perhaps a woman I met. She gives a history tour in a costume, something I will never forget. In fact, I have her name written here. I was wondering, could you do me the favor of contacting her and saying goodbye for me? She was so kind, and we had many wonderful talks. I won't have time. You could do this?

MINA: I'll do it myself.

GUSTAV: Yes, I would give them to her. *(Short pause)* Well, goodbye. You have both been very kind. Aloha, as you say.

MINA: *Auf wiedersehen.*

FATU: Safe journey, my friend.

(Exit GUSTAV. Silence.)

FATU: Feel a little guilty?

MINA: *(Nods yes)* Umm-Hmm.

FATU: After we finish, would you like to come to London for a couple of weeks?

MINA: *(Nods no)* Uh-Uh.

FATU: Apia?

MINA: *(Nods yes)* Umm-Hmm.

SCENE 17

(Playing area. KAWEHI.)

KAWEHI: Deidre, Mina, Fatu, and Erik all helped me to choose a place for her. We picked a night that was bright and beautiful with moonlight, just as she was in life. Together we took her to the home she had waited for, for all these years. Then, we all made a pact of silence. Fatu and his mother returned to London, but pass through here frequently. We agreed not even to discuss things among ourselves, feeling that giving voice to it would somehow be one step toward exposing, would betray that which should be hidden and concealed in the womb of the ʻāina *(land)*. But on certain nights, just before I fall asleep, sometimes my room is filled with the unexplainable fragrance of soft blooming flowers, or the fresh smell of the upland forest. I think about her then, to the sound of my own quiet breathing. I think about her resting, and the world gives way to a sleep of peace.

(Playing area. LILIHA.)

LILIHA: Carefully, carefully the sennit net draws round to a close. Now carry me far, far up into the hills, and when the air turns sweet, find a place, a small place, clean and dry, inside the cool earth. Lay me there on a bed of green ferns, of palapalai and lauaʻe, and maybe a bit of maile you found along the way. Hide the resting place with rocks and branches, hide it so only the birds know where I am, and then leave me. Leave me in the breathing, beating heart of my beloved ʻāina. I will lie there quietly in the darkness, and in the darkness I will hear them coming. I will hear the long slow sound of the conch, the steady beat of the pahu *(drum)*, and then creaking of the mānele *(palanquin)*, swaying back and forth and back and forth. I will feel their footsteps shaking the air, and stretching out, I will see the endless, winding procession of torches, and then the faces of every loved one gone before me. And one will leave the great line and slowly come toward me, and bending over so softly she calls back, "Stop and wait, for here is one of our own, come home to us at last."

(Blackout.)

CURTAIN.

Strength of Indian Women

VERA MANUEL

Characters

Sousette, an elder, the peacemaker
Suzie, her thirteen-year-old granddaughter
Eva, Sousette's daughter, in her mid-thirties
Lucy, an elder, dark skinned, strong and cantankerous
Agnes, an elder, a flashy dresser, lively personality
Mariah, an elder, light skinned, shy and nervous

Setting

All scenes take place in the living room of a house on a reserve.
Act I
    Scene 1: Dawn
    Scene 2: Late afternoon, the same day
    Scene 3: Evening of the second day
Act II
    Scene 1: Late afternoon, the next day
    Scene 2: Evening of the same day

Kootenai words used in the play
Napika—the spirits
Titti—grandmother

ACT I

SCENE 1

Music fades into a darkened stage. Scenes of residential school are reflected in slides off the back wall. The room is simple, with a couch, two armchairs, a coffee table, kitchen table and two kitchen chairs. Someone is sleeping on the couch. During the last slide, SOUSETTE enters the room. She is wearing a nightdress and has just woken up.

It is early morning, just before dawn. SOUSETTE, an elder of the Kootnai people, always wakes early. Hers is the first light that goes on in the window of the houses in this small British Columbia reserve. But first she putters around her front room in the dark. This is her favorite time of day, before anyone else is awake. She knows every inch of her beloved home by heart; she doesn't need the light to see. She is trying to be quiet though, so as not to wake her granddaughter who is asleep on the couch. She is searching for something, digging through tins and bags beside the couch, searching among the books and magazines under the coffee table.

SUZIE: What're you looking for, Granny?

SOUSETTE: Oh, no, don't wake up. I'm trying to be quiet. I'm looking for pictures . . . of some girls I used to know.

SUZIE: It's still dark. What time is it? *(She puts on light. Yawns, stretches.)* I'll help you look, Granny.

SOUSETTE: You go back to sleep. Ah, here they are.

(SUZIE, a tall, awkward thirteen-year-old wanders off, dragging her blanket behind her. She is at that age of almost being a young woman, but in many ways still a child. SOUSETTE sets her picture aside and from her crouched position by the coffee table she gazes lovingly after her grandchild. SUZIE almost bumps into her mother, EVA, who is a stern, serious woman in her mid-thirties.)

EVA: I hope you're not going back to bed. It's time to get up.

SUZIE: Ah, Mom . . .

EVA: *(sternly)* You should get some wood in, and help me start getting breakfast.

SOUSETTE: Eva, let her sleep a little bit longer. *(Suzie exits into bedroom.)*

EVA: *(with slight animosity)* That's not what you used to tell me when you used to chase me out of bed in the middle of the night.

SOUSETTE: *(surprised at her outburst)* She's going on a fast for two days. She'll need her strength and all our love. *(EVA is a bit ashamed of her emotions.)*

EVA: I'll get some wood.

SOUSETTE: I brought a whole pile in last night.

EVA: You should let Suzie do those things, she's young.

SOUSETTE: Well, that's how I stay young. Here are those pictures I was looking for. *(She motions to EVA to come sit beside her and hands her a picture.)* I can't see without my glasses. *(SOUSETTE searches in her bag for her glasses, while EVA describes the pictures to her.)*

EVA: It's a bunch of little girls. Lots of them, standing in front of a big grey building. There's a priest and a nun standing there with them. *(SOUSETTE puts her glasses on and takes the picture.)*

SOUSETTE: That's the school, that's the one I was telling you about, St. Eugene Residential School. That building's still there. All our cheap DIA houses falling down, but that building still stands there, reminding us. How old do you think these girls are?

EVA: They look younger than Suzie; they're about eight, or nine. A few of them look older.

SOUSETTE: I was looking all over for this picture. I wanted you to see it. You were asking me about Lucy, see, there's Lucy there.

EVA: Wow, she sure was pretty; she doesn't look anything like that today. She has beautiful eyes, but still she looks sad.

SOUSETTE: She don't look like that anymore because of Joe Sam. He nearly poked her eye out, and he broke her arm so many times it would never lie straight anymore. He was so mean, and so jealous.

EVA: Wasn't there a story she had a baby in the residential school?

SOUSETTE: Still that never gave Joe the right to do what he did to her.

EVA: Of course not. He beat her pretty bad, huh?

SOUSETTE: He'd be in jail today if he was still alive. Every time he got drunk, he beat her. I don't know what made that man so mean except he never would let her forget about that one baby that wasn't his.

EVA: Whose baby was it?

(The silence is broken by a loud bang, the sound of a bucket and some tools being dropped. EVA is startled, but SOUSETTE is used to these interruptions and grand entrances. LUCY, an elder who looks very strong and fit in her gum boots and work clothes, enters very loudly. Her voice is startling in the early morning quiet.)

LUCY: I stopped by to see if you wanted to go cross the road with me. I'm gonna fix up that little bit of fence that's falling down by Joe's grave. Huh. You got company. I better get to work before it gets too late. *(LUCY begins to hurry away.)*

SOUSETTE: Lucy, I told you Eva and Suzie are staying for a few days. Lucy, come back here, I'm talking to you. We're having Suzie's "coming of age" celebration; she's going to become a young woman. You come back later today. You are going to help, aren't you?

LUCY: Yeah, yeah, yeah. I've got lots of work to do. I'll come back tomorrow.

SOUSETTE: No, Lucy, you come back today. You help us with Suzie; she'll be real disappointed if you're not here.

LUCY: I have to go now, it's getting late. I've got lots of work to do.

SOUSETTE: She doesn't have anything to do; she's just pretending she's busy. She spends all her time in that graveyard visiting her babies . . . and Joe.

EVA: She scared me, sneaking up on us like that. Do you think she heard? *(SOUSETTE silences her with a motion.)*

SOUSETTE: She says she's deaf. *(SOUSETTE sits back down and picks up the picture again.)*

SOUSETTE: I've thought about it a long time, and I talked to the others. We decided that you need to know everything, about the school, and about us. You need to know because of Suzie. It's her history, too. *(EVA is grave, and respectfully silent, listening.)* Everybody suspected it was the priest who did that to Lucy. Not just Lucy; other girls had babies, too . . . lots of babies buried behind the school, buried in the schoolyard. She never would talk about it though. That baby died anyway, same as all her other ones. She had 14 babies, all of them by Joe, except for that one baby. Her daughter Angeline was the one who got killed in that car accident last winter. She was the last one. There's no one left, just us. We're all the family she's got.

EVA: Oh Mom, that's sad. Why did she marry Joe, when he was so mean to her?

SOUSETTE: She had no choice. It was arranged by her people. He was a widower with small children, and she was pregnant with no husband. It wasn't easy in those days for a woman to get by on her own. Joe never had an easy life either. His parents died when he was a baby, and he was passed from relative to relative, nobody really wanting him. Musta been someone hurt him real bad when he was little. The way they used to beat those boys in that school, it's a wonder they didn't all turn out mean. *(SOUSETTE focuses her attention back to the picture.)*

SOUSETTE: Can you pick out which is me? Right there. The pretty one.

EVA: The one with the nice haircut, eh?

SOUSETTE: That's my bowl cut. I still wear my hair like that sometimes, when I get tired of braiding it. *(Both women laugh.)* And this other picture here is of me in that white buckskin dress.

EVA: Mom, you were so beautiful. Is that the dress Suzie's going to wear for her feast?

SOUSETTE: That's the one. The deer hides were brought from the hunt by my grandfather, and tanned and sewn together with beads and shells by my grandmother. I was a girl like Suzie when this first dress first came to me. I can still see my grandmother. "I made this special for you," she said, and she slipped it over my head. It was so soft. She took me outside to show grandpa. He told me a story about the hunt, that the deer just stood and waited for him . . . like they knew they were offering up their lives for something special. They made me feel special. *(SOUSETTE is far away as she speaks, as though she has gone back to that time. EVA is very quiet and still. She doesn't want to break her mother's concentration. SOUSETTE picks up the picture of the girls again and continues on. As she speaks, the lights fade, and a slide of the picture of the girls in the school lights up on the back wall. Mother and daughter talk quietly in the background.)* You know, out of all these girls there must only be a handful of us still alive. Most of them died, pretty violent too . . . alcohol, suicide . . . murder. This one here, her name was Annie. She got murdered in the city. She was Agnes' friend, and Agnes was my best friend. Here's Agnes here.

EVA: That's Auntie Agnes? Yes, she still looks like that. She's got a bowl cut too.

(The women laugh. Blackout.)

SCENE 2

Late afternoon of the same day. SUZIE and SOUSETTE sit on the couch unpacking the white buckskin dress that SUZIE will wear at her celebration feast after her fast. SUZIE is dressed in a long flowing ribbon dress and moccasins. She has special paint on her face. She is waiting for her aunties to take her to the lodge. She is excited about her fast, and especially about the celebration feast. EVA is on the floor packing a small bundle for SUZIE, consisting of her medicine, smudge, cup for water, a towel and a light blanket.

SUZIE: Granny, it's so beautiful.

SOUSETTE: We have to be careful with it. Some of these beads may be loose. I'll get your mom to repair it before you put it on. *(She holds the dress up to SUZIE to see the fit.)*

SUZIE: How old is this dress if it was made by my great-great-grandmother?

SOUSETTE: I was 9 when I first wore this dress, and I'm 67 now.

EVA: That would make it 58 years old, and if we take good care of it, your daughter will wear it to her feast.

SUZIE: Did you wear this dress, Mom, at your feast?

EVA: *(sharply)* No, I didn't have one.

SUZIE: But how come?

SOUSETTE: I suppose that was my fault. We quit having puberty ceremonies when your mom was a girl. People were afraid of the Indian ways back then.

SUZIE: Was that sad for you, Mom?

EVA: No, I didn't know about those things then, so I didn't miss it. *(EVA softens.)* But I always wanted this for you. You'll make up for the feast I never had.

(A soft knock on the door. SOUSETTE answers it.)

SOUSETTE: Why Mariah, come in. What have you got there? Let me help you; that box looks heavy. Suzie, the aunties are here, they're just pulling up. You better hurry. Don't forget your bundle. Come and give me a big hug.

(SOUSETTE sets the box on the coffee table and gives SUZIE a hug.)

SUZIE: I'll see you in two days.

SOUSETTE: I'll be down to visit you later. You listen to the aunties and do everything they tell you.

SUZIE: I will. *(SUZIE gives MARIAH a hug. MARIAH stiffens slightly. She is not used to touches and hugs, but she loves SUZIE, and she pats her on the cheek.)* Hi, Granny Mariah. Bye. Will you come later, too? *(MARIAH nods.)*

EVA: I'll be down there as soon as I can too. Don't worry about anything, the aunties will take good care of you, and if you need to know anything, you just ask. They can tell you everything you need to know. Are you excited? *(EVA and SUZIE'S eyes glisten with tears and excitement.)*

SUZIE: Yes, yes, yes.

EVA: Hurry, hurry, hurry. You better go.

(EVA goes to the table and sits down to make bread. She is silent and unobtrusive, dutiful and listening.)

SOUSETTE: Isn't this wonderful, Mariah? Our little baby girl is all grown up.

MARIAH: I brought jars of canned peaches for Suzie's feast. I canned them in the summertime. I was hoping we could talk. I haven't been sleeping very good again. Every time I close my eyes, I see something. I was hoping you could give me more of that medicine.

SOUSETTE: Oh, I've been so worried about you. Why don't you let me take you to that medicine person I was telling you about? This medicine I got here, all it will do is help you to sleep. It can't take care of the real problem. It can't take care of what's troubling you in your heart. *(Mariah nervously tugs at a gold cross that hangs from a chain around her neck.)*

MARIAH: I can't. I can't go there, Sousette. I can't go against the church like that.

SOUSETTE: Mariah, it's not going against the church. This person I'm telling you about is a very spiritual person too, and I can't believe the things she does is anything against the church. She's a very respectful and very kind and loving person. She knows about dreams, Mariah. She knows about those kinds of dreams that haunt you. I wish you would trust me on that. You know I'd never do anything to hurt you.

(While SOUSETTE and MARIAH talk, EVA is working. LUCY enters, silently this time. MARIAH'S back is to her, so she can't see her.)

MARIAH: I know, Sousette. Maybe if I pray on it, I'll know what to do. I'll leave it up to the Lord. He'll tell me what to do.

(LUCY is suddenly dramatic and loud. Startled, MARIAH tries to hide behind Sousette.)

LUCY: Oh Lord! What is the Lord going to do now?

(LUCY chuckles to herself and mocks MARIAH. MARIAH tries to stay as far away from her as she can. SOUSETTE attempts to calm MARIAH, while coaxing her not to leave.)

SOUSETTE: Lucy, quit that now. Mariah, come back, at least wait until I get your medicine. It'll only take me a few minutes to prepare.

LUCY: Why you wasting good Indian medicine on her for? You know she don't believe in it. Besides the Lord might get upset, and heaven knows what he might do to you, he might strike you dead.

(MARIAH is at the door by this time and crosses herself. She is horrified at what appears to be a blasphemous comment by LUCY. LUCY, pleased with herself and the reaction that she's getting out of MARIAH, snickers and chuckles all the way to the couch, where she continues to carry on, mocking MARIAH's sign of the cross.)

SOUSETTE: Lucy, will you just sit down and be quiet; this conversation has got nothing to do with you.

(SOUSETTE speaks soothingly to MARIAH. As she speaks, LUCY sneaks up to MARIAH behind SOUSETTE's back and yanks at her skirt, then hurries back to the couch. This last action on LUCY's part totally unnerves MARIAH, who promptly heads for the door. SOUSETTE follows her.)

SOUSETTE: Come back later. I'll have your medicine ready for you by then. And don't mind what Lucy says. Honestly, I don't know what gets into that woman sometimes, but you've got to stand up to her. If you raised your voice to her once, she'd leave you alone.

MARIAH: I'll come back later, after she's gone. Do you think she'll be gone by then?

SOUSETTE: You come back whether she's here or not. You stop *running* from her. Maybe she'll leave early, although it's hard to get her out of here once she gets started.

(MARIAH exits. LUCY is still chuckling to herself. She's had great fun at MARIAH's expense, and this basically sums up LUCY's character. There are not many people that can get close to her or who are not intimidated by her.)

SOUSETTE: Why can't you leave her alone? You just do that because you know she's timid, and you make fun of her religion because you know it's something she cares deeply about.

LUCY: I'm just getting back at her for the residential school.

SOUSETTE: And you think it wasn't hard for her in there too? If you only knew.

LUCY: Oh, yeah, it must have been really hard "being the favorite." You should hear the way she talks about the place sometimes; you'd think it was the Newcastle Hotel and we were royalty, the way she describes it. Well, that's probably the way it was for her, but it sure wasn't that way for us black Indians.

SOUSETTE: Oh, Lucy, your bitterness is going to eat a hole right through you. Be quiet a minute. I've got to prepare this medicine, and you know I must have only good thoughts while I'm doing it. Sing with me that song that we always sing so well. It's a good strong medicine song.

LUCY: One more thing about that medicine. Do you think it's a good idea to be giving it to Mariah?

SOUSETTE: Lucy, good thoughts, and I really want to hear that song. Think of something happy, Lucy, it always sounds so much better when we're happy. Think of Suzie in the lodge, and all the things she's learning to become a strong young woman.

LUCY: Okay, you fix the medicine, and I'll help you sing.

(As SOUSETTE and LUCY sing, all the grief seems to drain from LUCY's face. She becomes calm and peaceful. When the song finishes, they are silent, lost in their happy thoughts until LUCY spots the picture of the girls in residential school on the coffee table in front of her. Immediately, her agitation is renewed.)

What is this? Who are all these kids?

SOUSETTE: That's us in the residential school. Eva, come and show her which ones we picked out. She hasn't got her glasses so you have to point them out for her.

(EVA approaches cautiously, bringing a tray with a pot of tea, cups, milk and sugar.)

EVA: This is mom, and this one here is Agnes, and that's you, I think.

LUCY: That's not Agnes. She didn't look like that. I don't think I'm in this picture.

SOUSETTE: Sure, Lucy, that's Agnes. She's standing right next to me, and Annie's standing on the other side of her, and you're standing down here.

LUCY: Huh? Maybe it is, I don't know. Here.

(LUCY hands the picture to SOUSETTE, who props it up on the table. She *ignores EVA's attempt to serve her tea and starts poking around at the other things on the table.)*

EVA: I brought you a cup of tea, Lucy. What would you like in it?

(EVA looks helplessly at SOUSETTE, and sets the tea down, careful not to get too close to LUCY.)

SOUSETTE: You have to talk really loud when you talk to her. Sometimes she pretends she's deaf, especially when she's not wearing her glasses. She uses lots of cream, like me, and put four spoons of sugar in there.

EVA: Do you need anything else here? If you don't, I'm going to work on my beading. I want to get Suzie's moccasins done before Agnes gets here. She's bringing a cape, so I want to make sure everything is ready for Suzie's feast.

SOUSETTE: You go ahead, Eva, we'll drink our tea and visit.

(EVA sets her beading supplies out and begins to work. She always keeps herself busy, the way she was taught. LUCY is upset, and makes like she's going to leave.)

LUCY: What? What? Did she say Agnes is coming? Is that what she said? I don't want to be here when she gets here. Agnes! Huh!

SOUSETTE: Sit down, Lucy, she's not going to be here for some time. Stay and visit. Besides, you two should bury the hatchet. Try to get along.

LUCY: You know where I'd like to bury that hatchet.

(SOUSETTE is skilled at soothing LUCY's ruffled feathers. She coaxes LUCY to stay by tempting her with EVA's bread. LUCY is still standing and is not going to give in too easily.)

SOUSETTE: Hush now, Lucy, come sit back down and relax. Eva is going to cook some bannock. She could even make some fry bread with strawberry jam. You'd like that, wouldn't you?

LUCY: Well, okay, I could eat some fry bread. I'm not very hungry, though, but I guess I could eat something. *(LUCY is almost lulled into forgetting about AGNES, but suddenly she remembers some real or imagined slight and she becomes agitated all over again. She jumps out of her chair and begins her harangue.)* Just as long as that Agnes don't start telling me what kind of an Indian I should be, when she comes, like she's some kind of expert or something. Talking about First Nations, and what was that other one, aboriginal. Just because she travels around the country doesn't mean she knows everything. *(LUCY sits down close to SOUSETTE and speaks in a conspiratorial tone.)* I wonder if those people she talks to know she used to be an alcoholic, and a prostitute? Used to live down there on skid row. If it hadn't been for us who took her in, she'd still be down there.

SOUSETTE: Hush, Lucy, what makes you so hateful? You know Agnes has worked hard for what she's got, and she deserves to have a good life. She's never said a mean word to you, or about you, and I'm sure if you wanted to travel around, she could set it up for you. She's always been generous that way. Anyway, she's never tried to hide what's in her past, and people love and respect her for that. (*LUCY turns abruptly away. She hates it when SOUSETTE defends AGNES.*) Come on now, Lucy. Let's talk about something else. My daughter Eva, she goes to college and she's doing some studying about Indians. She's gathering lots of material and I told her that the best person she could talk to in the area was you. That you know everything about the history around here.

(*LUCY begins to puff with pride, her interest piqued.*)

LUCY: Well, I guess I do know the history probably better'n anyone. I probably could travel around too and talk about the history. I'm probably the only one who never left from around here. I've lived here all my life you know. I never went off to the city, not once.

SOUSETTE: That's what I told Eva. The best person for you to talk to would be Lucy Sam. Hey, Eva, isn't that right?

(*EVA sets her beading aside, and pulls out a notepad she always keeps close by. She sits attentively, respectfully.*)

LUCY: Your daughter, she doesn't speak Indian though, huh? I couldn't tell it to her all in English. It's too bad she doesn't speak Indian.

SOUSETTE: I know, but I could interpret for her, and she does understand some.

LUCY: I guess I could sit down with her someday, if she tells me what it is she wants to know.

EVA: I'm really interested in anything about the residential school.

(*LUCY stiffens, and moves closer to SOUSETTE.*)

LUCY: Did she say the residential school? I could tell her some things about that, but she can't write it down, not all of it. (*She turns her attention back to EVA.*) There's some things that you shouldn't write down. There's some things that I shouldn't tell you.

(*EVA puts her notepad away.*)

SOUSETTE: But we agreed that we have to tell them sometime, Lucy. That's their history; they have a right to know.

LUCY: Hmmmm, what're they gonna do with it? Sell it?

(*EVA flinches. SOUSETTE is dismayed.*)

SOUSETTE: Lucy! It's her birthright, and it's part of her education. She's been going to school and coming back here every summer for a long time, to get an education. You have to give her credit for that.

(LUCY whispers conspiratorially to SOUSETTE.)

LUCY: You want to tell them everything? What about the priest? What about what he done? You want that they should know that?

SOUSETTE: They know more than we think they do, and we made a promise that we were going to tell them everything. I know it's hard, Lucy, but we must.

(When EVA speaks, they both jump—as though they'd forgotten that she was there, and her words are harsh. She is young and impatient.)

EVA: Tell me what? What is it that you're afraid to tell me? That he molested little girls?

(The old ladies cover their eyes, and LUCY turns away, her back to SOUSETTE. SOUSETTE approaches her cautiously, weighing every word. EVA sits very still, drawing in every word, and rocks gently, cushioning them softly against her heart. These words, she knows, are sacred. Flute music begins.)

SOUSETTE: You know, Lucy, in your heart, you know why Agnes went off to the city, and became what she did. She didn't have any people to go home to; they all died of smallpox, or else they were drinking. She had no one but us, and we weren't much for helpin' one another back then. I remember the day she and Annie left. I went down there and saw them off at the Greyhound. I already had two babies, and all I had was five bucks. I slipped it into Agnes' hand and I made her promise to write to me everyday. She didn't want to take the money, but I wouldn't let her give it back. She cried, and she said I was the only family she had. Annie, she was just anxious to get on the bus, and get out of town before her uncles discovered she was gone. It must have been hard for Annie, being the only girl in that family of men . . . and all that drinking. I stood there and watched the bus 'til it was out of sight. I was thinking I'd never see those girls again, and it was like losing a piece of myself. If it wasn't for them, I don't think I could have survived that school. Agnes was my big sister.

LUCY: I was one of those girls who got caught with Agnes when she ran away. It was her fault we got caught. She was too soft-hearted. One of the other girls, Monika, she went and fell down and hurt herself, and Agnes wouldn't leave her behind. Nobody wanted to go on without Agnes, so we all waited there until they caught up with us. I've always blamed her for that beating. (*Gregorian chant begins.*) If it wasn't for that priest, I wouldn't have even run away. It was the first time he ever got me alone. The older girls always warned me never to be alone with him, but I was on dorm duty, and Sister sent me to get sheets from the storage room, and he was waiting there. He scared me. He rubbed his tongue all over my mouth before he let me go. (*Gregorian chant ends.*) Agnes found me throwing up behind the stairs. She cleaned me up, then she told me she was gonna run. She said some others were gonna go with her, and if I wanted to I could go along. It didn't take me long to decide to go along. We almost made it over the mountains when they caught us. Our own people brought us back.

SOUSETTE: They made us clear away the tables and chairs in the cafeteria. There was Mariah, Julia, Helen, Molly, and me. We didn't know for sure what was going on, but we heard somebody saying they caught the runaways and they were going to punish them. They sounded the bell and called us girls to stand in a circle in the cafeteria. I saw the Sisters bringing you in one at a time, holding you down so you couldn't get away. I heard your screams, and cries, and I heard that whip slicing through the air, cutting through your flesh. We tried to close our eyes, but those Sisters standing among us forced us to open them and look. The whole top of my dress was soaked with tears.

(*On "sounded the bell," a bell rings and flute music begins.*)

LUCY: They took turns whipping us. When one of them would get tired, another would step in. They were harder on Agnes because they said she was the ringleader, and because she wouldn't cry. I wanted to tell her to cry, so they would stop, but she wouldn't cry. The priest was yelling to her, "Cry! Cry! Cry!" but she wouldn't. Then I noticed a trickle of blood running down her leg, and when she fell, it smeared on the floor. She had started on her period, started bleeding, and still they wouldn't stop. They broke her that day.

(*Light begins to fade, and slide of girls in school comes on. The women continue to speak as the stage fades to black.*)

SOUSETTE: They broke her body, they broke her heart, but they never broke her spirit. Agnes' spirit lives inside each one of us.

LUCY: It was my cousin Julia who told me Agnes was on the skids. She hit the skids real hard after Annie was murdered.

(*Blackout*)

SCENE 3

Evening of the second day of SUZIE's feast, and everyone has gone down to be with her. The elder, AGNES, is sitting at the kitchen table with her feet propped up, sipping a cup of tea and reading the newspaper. She has EVA's beadwork in her lap, and every once in a while she stops to look at it. Her bags are all around her on the floor and on the couch. She has made herself right at home. A noise outside signals that the others are getting home. SOUSETTE enters first, followed by LUCY, and then by EVA. LUCY almost bumps into SOUSETTE, as SOUSETTE stops abruptly, surprised to see AGNES at her kitchen table.

SOUSETTE: Well, are you a sight for sore eyes. Look at you, you look great. *(EVA is trying to struggle by LUCY, who has stopped dead in her tracks and refuses to budge another inch.)* I didn't see your car, I had no idea you were here. Lucy, look who's here.

(SOUSETTE firmly moves LUCY out of the way and pushes her towards the couch. LUCY stares in disgust at AGNES's bags on the couch. EVA finally makes her way over to AGNES.)

EVA: Aunt Agnes, you're finally here. I was beginning to worry you wouldn't make it. We just came from making an offering at Suzie's lodge, an offering for her fire.

AGNES: I wondered where you were. My car broke down, but I woulda gotten here even if I'd had to hitchhike. Lucy, just push those things out of your way.

(LUCY bends down and sweeps everything into a heap on the floor and practically steps on them as she sits down. SOUSETTE shakes her head.)

EVA: Auntie, are you hungry? I'm cooking your favorite stew.

AGNES: And I smell bannock. You know your auntie always shows up here hungry. Let me get out of your way so you can do your stuff. The moccasins look great. Let me move over here and settle down beside Lucy.

(AGNES moves over to the couch, bringing her newspaper, the moccasins, and a few of the bags from the floor. LUCY does not want AGNES to sit beside her, so she spreads herself across the middle of the couch.)

Aow!

(SOUSETTE starts to get up to give AGNES her chair.)

AGNES: Now don't get up Sousette, I'll just settle here beside Lucy.

(AGNES squeezes herself in beside LUCY, who is forced to move over, disgruntled.)

EVA: I'll bring your tea. What do you want in it?

AGNES: Just a tiny bit of sugar, Eva. I'm trying to cut down, and no cream please, I have to watch my figure.

LUCY: I'll have another cup of tea too, Eva, double cream and five sugars.

SOUSETTE: That must have been you, with your car, broken down by the Band office. Lucy said she thought that she saw your car over there earlier.

AGNES: Can't sneak nothing by Lucy. She did see me, or pretended not to see me. I was waving away. Didn't you see me waving at you?

LUCY: Now I can't be noticing everything that is going on, now can I? Lots of people wave at me, that I'm too busy to notice.

AGNES: Anyway that was me. This tea is good Eva. It's Labrador tea, isn't it? I tasted this when I was up in the north.

(LUCY raises her cup in mock salute to thank EVA.)

SOUSETTE: Where were you this time?

AGNES: I just got back from two weeks in South Dakota. *(AGNES is a flashy dresser, and she shows SOUSETTE her turquoise jewelry. LUCY studies her in disdain.)* And three weeks in the territories. My, I sure have been gone a long time. But tell me, how's our little girl doing?

SOUSETTE: Suzie? This is her second night; she's doing good. You'll be proud of her.

AGNES: I always am. I'll go down at sunrise, so she'll know I'm here. I brought her the most beautiful cape, it'll go well with Eva's moccasins. By the way, when I came in earlier, it was pretty dark and I saw someone sitting on your back porch. I called out, but whoever it was left in a hurry. I couldn't tell who it was in the dark.

(LUCY makes a mocking motion of the sign of the cross, indicating that it was probably MARIAH.)

SOUSETTE: That must be Mariah. She always comes to visit me late at night, but I doubt that she'll come in with so many visitors. She usually only comes when I'm here by myself.

LUCY: That Mariah, she's always sneaking around like that. She's never sociable. She won't even talk to me. *(LUCY gets up and noisily crosses over to the table to get more tea.)* If you ask me, I think she's crazy.

SOUSETTE: Oh, nobody asked you, Lucy. I've heard the way you taunt her.

LUCY: She still thinks she's better than us.

(LUCY hates it when SOUSETTE defends someone; she takes it as a personal affront. Noisily, she throws sugar cubes into her cup, pokes around EVA's cooking, and stirs her tea loudly. No one pays attention.)

AGNES: It's funny, I never thought she'd come back here to settle. I thought she'd stay her whole life in the city. If she doesn't get along with Indians, it sure must get pretty lonely for her here.

SOUSETTE: She had her grandma's place left to her, that's where she grew up, until they shipped her off to school. That place sat empty for a long time. She sure fixed it up nice, but yeah, she does get lonely. *(SOUSETTE glances at LUCY.)* Some people are pretty unfriendly around here.

LUCY: She don't really belong here.

SOUSETTE: Oh, she belongs here. She belongs here every bit as much as you and I do. You'd be surprised at how much knowledge that woman has. Her grandmother taught her good.

AGNES: Wasn't her grandmother a medicine woman?

SOUSETTE: Yes, and she was a strong woman. I have a feeling that Mariah inherited that strength, and someday she's going to find that out. I think Napika (the spirits) guided her back here. I think she came back to teach us something.

(LUCY returns to her seat noisily. Before she sits down, she retorts.)

LUCY: Well, she can't teach me nothin'.

SOUSETTE: Yeah, that probably would be hard to do. Vow, Eva, you'll keep an eye out for her. She probably won't come tonight, but she will come tomorrow, when Suzie finishes her fast. She promised. Take her this medicine, and ask her as a special favor to Suzie, and me, if she would come in and sit with us, so that she's here when Suzie comes out. Suzie asked that all her grandmothers be here to help her dress for her celebration.

(EVA takes the medicine and carefully puts it in a pouch at her waist.)

EVA: I'll keep it close to me, so I'll have it when I see her.

(EVA returns to the table and continues beading.)

AGNES: I wouldn't mind getting to know her. I remember her from school, but we were never friends. The sisters never allowed us to have too much to do with her. I wonder why that was?

LUCY: She didn't have too much to do with anybody, being a pet like she was. Anyway, if her grandmother was a medicine woman, how come she had a half-white granddaughter?

SOUSETTE: Being Indian, Lucy, is more than just the color of your skin. There were reasons why Mariah was kept separate. I pray that she finds the courage to talk about it someday.

LUCY: What? What is it? I know everything that went on in that school. I never heard nothing.

SOUSETTE: You didn't know everything, Lucy. Maybe there is something that Mariah can teach you.

(*As LUCY and SOUSETTE talk, AGNES's attention is taken by the picture on the table.*)

AGNES: Now, what is this picture here? Sousette, you kept this picture after all these years? I can't believe this is how we used to look. Let me see if I can recognize who these other girls are. There's Lucy, that's me, and Sousette is that really you? You must have just got your hair cut; it looks like you have a bowl on your head. And who is that other one there?

(*LUCY pokes her finger at the picture and gloats.*)

LUCY: That's your friend, Annie.

AGNES: Yes, it is, isn't it? Look at her just smiling away, looking like she didn't have a care in the world. Annie, she was always smiling; no matter how rough things got, she always had that big smile on her face.

LUCY: I'll bet she's not smiling now.

AGNES: Oh, I don't know, I'll bet she is. At least, that's the way I want to · remember her. That's exactly how she looked the last time I saw her, all sparkly and bubbly, in her red dress that kinda hung offa her shoulder, with sequins and glitter all across the front. Annie was real pretty you know, even without all that glitz . . . but she sure liked to dress. (*AGNES is far away in another time, and another place.*) We were hanging around the Zanzibar that night, trying to make some money offa these loggers that just pulled into town.

(*LUCY draws away from AGNES abruptly, like she's afraid she's going to catch something. She is visibly shocked and disgusted.*)

LUCY: Agnes, how can you talk about that? Don't it make you shamed?

(*SOUSETTE, always fascinated with AGNES's life, brushes LUCY away like she is an annoying fly.*)

SOUSETTE: Hush, Lucy, be quiet. (*SOUSETTE turns her full attention back to AGNES.*)

AGNES: Ashamed of what, Lucy, that we made best use of the only assets that we had? Annie and me, we didn't know any better and we were just trying to survive. We left here with just that little bit of money in our pockets. We thought we'd find work, but nobody wanted two Indian girls fresh off the rez, at least nobody who would pay an honest wage. You try makin' it in the city when you got nothin' and nobody to back you up. When you're hungry, or thirsty, you just sell whatever you can just to get that few bucks. Annie and me, all we had was each other. I'd have done anything for her, and I did. She was sick, real sick, and they wouldn't let her in the hospital. I thought she was gonna die. I went down the corner to see old man Bill. I knew he was sweet on me, always givin' me the eye when his wife wasn't lookin'. I told him my friend was dyin' and I needed help. He promised me he would, if I let him. It wasn't hard. I just closed my eyes and did what he said, and didn't think about it. It wasn't much different from those times at school with Father. After the first time, it just got easier, to close my eyes and think about how I was gonna spend all that money. I'd moan, groan and then pretend I was havin' a good time . . . just like that, it was over. Bill kept his word. Annie got better, and she and I took to the streets and bars together. Mr. Bill, he was my best customer. He was still there for me when Annie got killed. That was such a long time ago but I remember it like it was yesterday.

(AGNES gets up and moves to front center of the stage, into the spotlight, as though she is back there standing under a streetlight.)

That night at the Zanzibar was hookers' convention night. That's what we called it when those loggers got to town. We'd been waitin' all week, and by the time Saturday night rolled around we barely had enough money for a cheap bottle of wine to keep our heads together. We knew we were lookin' good. I had on my long black dress, the one with the slit up the side, and Annie, of course she wore her red dress. We came strolling into the Zanzibar that night, turnin' heads all the way, and we knew we were going' to be real busy. By midnight I'd already made close to a thousand bucks, but I was pretty tanked up. This great big man was trying to get me to go with him, but I didn't want to go anymore, and he started gettin' crazy on me. He was all up in my face when Annie came along. When she told him to leave me alone, he got real mean, talkin' about how he'd already spent lots of money on me, buyin' me drinks and all, and how I owed it to him. She tried to calm him down, then she said she would go with him. I tried to argue with her, but she called her friend over and told him to get me home in a cab. You know, the last thing she said to me was, "Agnes, you can have the money. I just don't want you to get hurt. I can handle him. You go home, I'll see you in the morning." She was just tryin' to look out for me. They didn't find Annie for a whole week. I went crazy day and night lookin' for her. She just never came home. When they found her, she was all beat up. You couldn't even recognize her, except for that red sequined dress. I stayed drunk after that. I can't remember a time when I ever felt so alone, or so sad as that time. I know Bill called you, Sousette, and you came to get me. *(The lights begin to rise as SOUSETTE rises and goes to AGNES.)* I know you all chipped in to send Sousette to get me, and I thank you for that. You all saved my life back then.

(SOUSETTE gently leads AGNES back to the couch.)

SOUSETTE: And today you have a beautiful granddaughter who is about to become a woman in a very special way.

(SOUSETTE gently helps AGNES come back to herself. EVA brings a fresh cup of tea, and LUCY is quiet for once.)

AGNES: You know, sometimes when I'm traveling in the city, I still see young Indian girls, just like Annie and me, standing round street corners, hitchhiking, jumping into stranger's cars, and it breaks my heart to think of what must have happened to those little girls. You know the Creator left me alive for one reason. It could just as easily have been me that got killed. Somebody has to talk about it. Somebody has to tell the truth about what happened to all those little girls. I figure the Creator saved me because he knew my big mouth would come in handy someday. Still, it's hard to talk about the things that people are so afraid to hear.

LUCY: We didn't all turn out like that though. Nobody told you two to go runnin' off to the city.

AGNES: And did stayin' here make your life any easier, Lucy?

LUCY: At least I wasn't a prostitute.

AGNES: You were just a battered wife. I wouldn't have traded my life for a life with Joe Sam.

LUCY: If I were you I'd be careful of how I speak about the dead.

SOUSETTE: Now come on, settle down you two, don't fight. Let's have some of Eva's stew. Eva, bring Lucy a piece of that fry bread, and some stew. Agnes and I, we'll help ourselves.

(EVA gets busy serving up some food. SOUSETTE stands up, and picks the picture up. The lights begin to dim.)

There isn't a single one of us in this picture who has had an easy life.

LUCY: Except maybe Mariah, and Sophie, and Joannie, all those teacher pets with their light skin.

(Blackout)

ACT II

SCENE 1

It is late afternoon of the next day, the day that SUZIE is to finish her fast and the ceremony and celebration will begin. There is an air of excitement. SOUSETTE, AGNES and LUCY are bringing all the pieces of SUZIE'S outfit together and making sure everything is ready. SOUSETTE lays the dress out across the chair, AGNES brings the cape, and LUCY holds the moccasins and hair ties.

AGNES: Sousette, that dress is so beautiful. That's the one that was made by your grandmother? The one you wore when you were a girl.

SOUSETTE: The same one. I dreamed about this day before Suzie was even born, and Suzie dreamed about it when she was just a girl. She said, "I'll be wearing that dress and all my grannies will be here, in this house," me, you Agnes, you Lucy, and Mariah. But Mariah's not here, and soon Suzie will come and Mariah won't be here. *(SOUSETTE is clearly disturbed.)*

AGNES: There's still time; maybe Eva will convince her to come.

SOUSETTE: She won't come with so many people in my house.

(EVA appears at the door holding MARIAH by the arm. MARIAH looks like she is still about to flee but EVA has a firm hold of her. SOUSETTE quickly clears off the chair and offers it to MARIAH, while waving AGNES, and especially LUCY, back to the couch. AGNES moves herself so that she is sitting between LUCY and MARIAH. When MARIAH is seated, EVA takes the dress and accessories from SOUSETTE to the kitchen table.)

SOUSETTE: I'm so glad you've come, my friend. This is a special day for all of us, and it will be even more special for Suzie now that you're here. Can I get you anything?

MARIAH: No, Sousette, I've come to talk. I want to thank you for the medicine and thank you for sending Eva to invite me in. You know I have a hard time with so many people, but I know you've been waiting a long time to hear me say what I am going to say here today. Perhaps you would like to sit?

SOUSETTE: Yes, I think I will. Do you remember Agnes?

(MARIAH nods to AGNES but won't look at LUCY.)

MARIAH: I get afraid to talk, all my life people tell me, "Be quiet, shut up, don't say nothin'." Even the old people before used to tell me, "Don't tell stories; if you attack the church you make hard times for everybody." Now I'm old, and I keep my mouth shut, and still we have hard times. It's gettin' harder and harder, Sousette, it's gettin' harder and harder for everybody. I don't know why the Lord guided me back to this place, or even why I should still be livin' and all these other women are dead. I keep askin' the Lord every day, what is it that I need to do, and I hear nothin', just those dreams that won't allow me a decent night's sleep. I know there are those of you who believe I don't belong here. For most of my life, I've wanted to believe that too. It's always been so easy for me to leave here, and to turn away from the side of me that's Indian, except it's like turnin' my back on the only human being who ever truly loved me. My grandmother, who was Indian, told me once that it was not going to be easy livin' on the edge of two worlds, and I see that now, when my eyes are opened, that this has been true. When I walk in the Indian world, I hear them tauntin' me: "Teacher's pet, teacher's pet, hey little white girl, whatta you doin' 'round here. Are you a 'Wannabe'? One of those Bill C——31 Indians?" And when I walk in the white world, I hear them tauntin' me: "Little Indian Squaw, why don't you go back to the reservation where you belong? Hey, Pocahontas, you wanna come home with me and be my little Indian princess? You're not really like one of them, you're almost white. Well, almost is not good enough." I've come home to find out who I really am. I knew who I was when I was a little girl livin' in my titti's house before they took me away to that school. I knew who I was when she would light the juniper and guide my tiny hands over the smoke, pulling it up over my hair, across my heart, and down the rest of my body. She would turn me in a circle, always to my right, and she would tell me that the Creator gave me as a special gift to her, to watch over for a time. That, at that time, I was the most perfect and precious being, there was no doubt. I believed that with all my heart. What I seen in that school shocked me into silence, and disbelief in everything that was good. But it was NOT THE LORD that did that. I know that now. It was people just like you and me. I saw that girl, Theresa, refuse to stop speakin' Indian, refuse to quit prayin' to Napika. I saw her always encouragin' others not to forget they were Indian, and I admired her strength, and the depth of her determination. While no one else spoke to me, I had no friends you see, she would always stop to give me a kind word, and I grew to love her like the older sister I never had. I'd sneak her extra food. She'd break it into bits and share it. I saw her challenge them repeatedly, daring them to do what they finally did to silence her. I saw Sister Luke, hate and venom spewing out of her mouth, "You dirty, savage Indian!" and threw that girl Theresa down, down two flights and cement steps, and I said nothin'. My screams were silent and my agony all consumin'. I saw murder done in that school, and when they wrapped that broken body and sent it home to the mother tellin' her it was pneumonia that killed her little girl, she unwrapped her and runnin' her grievin', lovin' mother's hands across the bruised face, shoulders, legs and back, discovered the neck was broken, screamed out in agony, "Why? What happened to my baby?" and I said nothin'.

I saw little girls taken in the night from their beds. I heard the moans and groans, and sobbin'. Shut up, shut up, I said, glazed eyes, ravaged and torn bodies returned in a frightened, huddled mass beneath the sheets, and I said nothin'. "You're a good girl," they often told me. "These girls are bad. They need to be taught a lesson." I saw a baby born one night to a mother who was little more than a child herself. I saw her frightened, dark eyes pleading with me to save her child, and later on, when the grave was dug, and the baby lowered into the ground, I said nothin'. When my grandma died, I was only nine, and I had no one. At Christmas, and summer holidays, no one came to claim me, so "they" became my family. They stroked my light skin, and brushed my brown curls, and told me I was almost white. They pampered and spoiled me, and there was not a place in that school that I was not welcome. I had special privileges, and because I was so good at saying nothin' I became one of them. I was very loyal. When I left that school, Father put this cross around my neck, and he cried and wished me well, made me promise to come back and visit.

(MARIAH walks toward the door, then stops.)

I walked away. Never looked back. Not once. For a long time after that, I couldn't pray, and for years I believed in nothin'.

(SOUSETTE does not want MARIAH to leave. Gently she calls after her.)

SOUSETTE: Mariah, what do you believe in now?

(MARIAH turns back, her face is radiant.)

MARIAH: I believe what my grandmother told me, that I am the most perfect and precious being in all of Creation.
AGNES: And you are, Mariah, you're magnificent.
LUCY: Ah, you're still crazy.
SOUSETTE: I understand what she means, Lucy.
AGNES: So do I. Mariah, won't you come back and sit with us?
LUCY: Well, then you're all crazy.

(MARIAH comes back at AGNES's coaxing and sits. EVA brings her some tea.)

SOUSETTE: Maybe we are, Lucy. That school made us all a little crazy, even you. *(Everybody laughs, except LUCY.)* It was all so long ago, it hardly seemed worth talking about. I figured I could just forgive, and go on, but Eva and Suzie, they opened my eyes. *(SOUSETTE looks affectionately at EVA.)* Eva, my little girl, she lost a lot too. When they started to talk about residential schools, and even started an investigation, I didn't want to be involved. I thought we'd be better off to just keep the past behind us. When young people came to ask me about residential school, I wouldn't tell them nothing. I said it was a good place for me. Then one day, Eva, she opened my eyes.

(The light dims. EVA moves into the spotlight. SOUSETTE pulls a chair just to the edge of the spotlight. All other action freezes.)

EVA: How can you say it was a good place for you? How can you lie like that? I'm so sick of hearing about residential school. I'm sick of reading about it. I'm sick of hearing about how you all suffered from everybody else but you. What about us? What about me and how I've suffered? Does anybody care about that? Do you remember how you used to beat me, Mom? Do you even remember the bruises? Do you remember the ugly things you used to call me, and all those times you left me alone. I wouldn't have cared, if only you would have loved me. Do you even know what that means, love? Every time I go to hug you, you stiffen up. Do you know that you do that, Mom? Do you know how that makes me feel? And now I'm doing the same thing to Suzie. I push her away, Mom. I call her stupid, and I hit her, and I don't want to. Tell me again that residential school was good for you. Talk to me some more about forgiveness, so I can get angry. At least when I'm angry, I know that I'm alive. I know that I'm feeling something. The rest of the time, it's like I'm frozen.

(SOUSETTE is bent over in pain. She barely whispers.)

SOUSETTE: But Eva, I do love you.
EVA: No, you don't.

(SOUSETTE speaks more strongly this time.)

SOUSETTE: Yes, Eva, I do love you. I never meant to hurt you.

(SOUSETTE gets up and slowly walks over to EVA.)

Eva, if you hug me now, I won't stiffen up, I promise. Please forgive me. I'll make it up to you, if only you'll forgive me. I'll start talking about it. I'll tell you everything that happened to me, so you'll understand. We'll help one another to understand.
EVA: Oh, Mom, I'm so sorry.

(SOUSETTE and EVA sit on the floor. SOUSETTE rocks EVA like she is a little girl.)

SOUSETTE: It's okay, hush, hush, it's okay.

(Blackout)

SCENE 2

*Evening of the same day, very close to the time when SUZIE will return.
SOUSETTE and LUCY are sitting on the armchair and couch. AGNES is helping EVA peel carrots and potatoes. They are filling up a big soup pot. All the
ladies are dressed in their best traditional dress.*

AGNES: There. That should about do it. Do you need any more help?

EVA: No, everything is done now. By the time this finishes cooking, Suzie will
be here. *(Agnes moves to the couch.)* Here, Auntie, here's another pot of
tea. If you don't mind bringing it over, I'll bring the sugar and milk.

(AGNES gives EVA a warm, affectionate, one-arm hug.)

AGNES: I don't mind at all. You're a good little worker, you know. I'm proud of
you.

(EVA beams, and so does SOUSETTE.)

LUCY: I'm getting, hungry. *(EVA brings her a plate of cookies.)* Here, Auntie, I
don't want you to spoil your appetite.

*(AGNES reaches over to grab a cookie, and LUCY moves the plate, allowing
her only one.)*

AGNES: Yes sir, that school never taught me a thing about being a mother. My
babies, I had two of them, got swooped up by Social Services a long time
ago, and I never saw them again. When I sobered up I tried to get them
back, but it was tough. I remember them though. I'll always remember
their sweetness.

SOUSETTE: Maybe they'll come looking for you, Agnes. That's happening
more and more nowadays; kids come looking for their parents. I wouldn't
be surprised if they just showed up here one day.

LUCY: How would they even know where to find you, when you're always runnin' around all over the place?

AGNES: Well, if they came, Lucy, I would expect you could tell them where I
am.

SOUSETTE: Do you remember getting sick in that school?

AGNES: I remember getting sick and my neck swole up.

SOUSETTE: I don't know what that sickness was, but our necks used to get
really big; must have been hundreds of kids died of that sickness.

AGNES: One time, mine swole up so big I could hardly get my dress zipped up.
I thought for sure I was gonna die. In fact, that's what Sister Rose told me,
that I was gonna die. I was terrified to go to sleep, just in case I didn't wake
up.

LUCY: Is that why you didn't die, because you wouldn't go to sleep?

AGNES: No, Lucy, I think it must have been your prayers that kept me alive. We spent so much time praying, some of those prayers must have been for me.

SOUSETTE: Did I ever tell you about that man I met in Creston, when I was in my twenties? He asked me right out if I went to St. Eugene's. When I said yes, he asked if us kids used to get sick a lot out there. I told him about that sickness with our throats, and you know what he said? *(AGNES and LUCY are listening attentively.)* He said he worked in a factory back then that supplied flour to that school. He was the one who sewed up the sacks after they were filled. He was told to keep them St. Eugene sacks separate. Before he sewed them up he was to add a scoop of some white, powdery material to each one of those sacks. You know in those days, you just did what you were told, and you didn't ask questions. One day his curiosity got the best of him, and he asked what that powder was. The next day he was out of a job.

AGNES: Did he think there was a connection?

SOUSETTE: He seemed pretty sure that something wasn't right. No medicine could cure that sickness once it took hold, at least no medicine that they would give us Indians. They were always sending kids home in those bags. One time, one of the girls from here died, and they put her in a bag and slung her over the back of a horse; they had to tie her down so she wouldn't slide off. They made me and this other girl bring her back to the reserve. It took us all day to get home. We were just little girls then and I remember we were riding through the bushes and we got into a fit of giggles because that other girl, she was watching Molly, that was the name of the girl who died, and she said, "Lookit Molly's head bouncing up and down. I wonder what she's thinking?" Gee, we musta been crazy just laughing at her like that. These old men came along from our village and they really bawled.

(The women can't help but laugh at this memory. Suddenly the mood changes, becomes somber. The lights dim. SOUSETTE gets up and moves to the center spotlight.)

When my neck swole up, Sister sent me to the infirmary right away. When I got to the room I noticed there was another girl there. Her name was Sarah. I tried to talk to her, but she told me to pretend I was asleep, or someone else would come and bother.

(Sound of two girls)

SOUSETTE, AS A GIRL: *(giggling)* What're you doing here, Sarah? Are you sick too?

SARAH: Be quiet. When he comes in keep pretending you're asleep. Sometimes he just goes away.

SOUSETTE: I didn't know who she was talking about, but I pretended to be asleep until I got so tired, I almost did fall asleep. Then I heard someone talking, a man's voice. I peeked out and I could see Father LeBlanc.

MAN'S VOICE: I come to visit you again, Sarah. Huh? Who's that in the other bed? What a nice surprise, it's Sousette. I think I'll visit her first. You don't mind, do you Sarah?

SARAH: She's asleep, maybe you shouldn't bother her. She's real sick.

SOUSETTE: He just ignored Sarah. I kept my eyes tightly closed, hoping he'd go away. I felt the weight of him lean against the bed as he knelt down. At first I thought he was going to pray over me, so I just lay still. Then I felt his hand under the cover, touching me, down there. I tried to push his hand away, really I did.

MAN'S VOICE: No, Sousette, you just lie still.

SOUSETTE: He kept feeling around, and I kept pushing his hand away. I started to cry because I didn't want him doing that and he told me to be quiet, but I couldn't stop crying. Finally he got mad, and he left.

MAN'S VOICE: I'll go over to Sarah, she's not scared. She's not a crybaby like you.

SOUSETTE: I shut my eyes and covered my ears. I tried not to listen. It made me sick to hear that, and Sarah, she didn't say a word. Didn't make a sound. Didn't even cry. He must have done that to her a lot. Do you remember how she was always sick, always in the infirmary?

She finally died, too. That was probably a relief for her. She suffered so much.

(The lights slowly fade. EVA goes to her mother and gently leads her back to her chair. She tucks a shawl around her shoulders. She is full of tenderness, and SOUSETTE is grateful. EVA stays close to her mom.)

After that time, I wouldn't lie in the infirmary when I got sick. I'd get a whole bunch of coats, and I'd pile them in the toilet, and I'd sleep there. It sure was cold, but I didn't care. It was better than going through that with Father. I couldn't stop him forever though. One day he just did what he wanted with me, and oh, how I've hated him. He did awful things to us. I sure used to hate getting sick. I still do. Whenever I get sick now, I gotta be half dead before I go to bed. Isn't that right, Eva? *(EVA smiles and nods.)* I used to think I was the only one that happened to, so I took my anger out on everybody. Then other women began to speak up. Even my mother, before she died, said that same thing happened to her. And my Eva, I couldn't protect her. I was too busy running away.

(SOUSETTE is very sad. EVA reaches over to take her hand.)

EVA: But you taught me how to keep Suzie safe and how to celebrate her becoming a woman.

AGNES: That's right. Suzie will turn the whole world right side up again, the way it was meant to be, and we will celebrate.

EVA: When I hear your stories, I feel so lucky that you are one of the handful of girls who did survive. I can't imagine what my life would have been like without you. Even when you were not there, you taught me something. You taught me how to get through tough times, and how to survive. All of you went through so much. Someone should write about it. They should make a movie about how you survived. I feel real proud sitting here among you. You're just like old warriors.

AGNES: Maybe you'll write that story, Eva. You sure must get an earful sitting around with us old ladies.

LUCY: I don't mind being called a warrior, Eva, but I'm really not that old.

AGNES: Oh, Lucy, you're falling apart just like the rest of us.

EVA: Suzie's here. I'll go help her with her things. She'll be so pleased that you're all here.

(*SOUSETTE gets the dress and holds it tenderly. AGNES gets the cape and hands LUCY the moccasins and MARIAH the hair ties. They all stand, waiting expectantly. SUZIE bursts through the door wrapped in a beautiful Pendleton blanket. Her hair is wet; she has just come from a swim. EVA carries her bundle. She hugs each of her grannies long and tenderly, starting with SOUSETTE.*)

SUZIE: (*To AGNES*) I dreamed about you in the lodge. I saw you dancing on the mountain. I'm so happy you're here. (*To LUCY*) Granny Lucy, you're always here for me, always. (*To MARIAH*) Granny Mariah, I prayed for you to be here, and Napika brought you. (*To EVA*) Mom, I need to get dressed right away, the people are waiting.

EVA: Let's hurry, we've got lots of celebrating to do. Agnes, help me with the blanket. Mom, you can bring the dress.

(*EVA and AGNES hold up the blanket around SUZIE, while SOUSETTE helps her into the dress.*)

SUZIE: Next I'll need my moccasins.

LUCY: Come here, my girl, put your feet up, I'll put them on you.

(*LUCY puts on the moccasins while SUZIE visits with the others.*)

SUZIE: Aunt Agnes, there was an eagle flying around the lodge every time I came out to take a swim.

AGNES: Now that's a good sign. Did you see anything else?

SUZIE: I saw the two little deer that came to great-grandpa when he was hunting for the hides for this dress. They came right inside the lodge, and they talked to me.

SOUSETTE: What did they say?

SUZIE: That I was going to have a long life, and that my daughter will someday wear this dress.

AGNES: Another good sign. Lucy, hurry up, can't you see? Let me help you.

LUCY: Get away. The moccasins are mine. I'm just about done.

(LUCY finishes. SUZIE stands up so AGNES can put the cape on.)

AGNES: Now you gotta bend over cuz you're too tall for me.

SUZIE: Oh, Granny, what a beautiful cape.

AGNES: Its just perfect for you. Mariah will do your hair. It's still wet so it will be easier.

(EVA moves a chair for SUZIE to sit, and MARIAH begins to braid her hair.)

EVA: It's so short, Mariah, she just got it cut. You might have to struggle with it.

MARIAH: It'll be fine. Bring me some more water in case I need to wet it.

SOUSETTE: Suzie, while Mariah is doing your hair, I'm going to explain to you what will happen at your feast. Everyone is waiting for you. Nothing will begin until you get there. Your mom and your Granny Agnes will cover you with the blanket again. The blanket is a gift from your great-granny Marceline. We will surround you when you come into the hall, and the aunties who helped you will lead the way, and some will fall behind. There is an arbor built of spruce and cedar inside the middle of the hall. All the medicine people will sit inside this arbor.

We will lead you to the very center and we will remove the blanket and place it in a spot set aside for you to sit. There will be an honor song, and a special prayer, which we will all stand for. When this is done, all the women will make the victory call. Do you remember how that is done? Agnes will show us. *(AGNES makes the victory call. All the women join in, laughing.)* When you sit down, the Chief will come with all the dignitaries to congratulate you. You will invite them to sit with you to eat, and you will gift them for being there to witness this great day.

SUZIE: How will I know what to give them?

SOUSETTE: We will stay around you all the time. We will help you to know who gets what and how things will happen. We are there, just like old buffaloes surrounding the young, to protect you.

LUCY: Oh, now I'm an old buffalo.

AGNES: Well, there are worse things, Lucy. *(The women laugh.)*
SOUSETTE: We'd better get going.

(EVA and AGNES wrap SUZIE in the blanket. LUCY carries her bundle. MARIAH brings the medicine, and EVA trails behind with the pot of soup. As they leave, an honor song begins. The room darkens behind them. Exit to blackout.)

Te Ata

A PLAY WITH MUSIC BY JUDYLEE OLIVA

ORIGINAL COMPOSITIONS AND MUSICAL ARRANGEMENTS BY JAY VOSK

LYRICS AND ADDITIONAL COMPOSITIONS BY JUDYLEE OLIVA

MUSICAL REVISIONS BY RHENADA FISHER

Premiered in 2006.

Characters

Elder Te Ata—90-year-old Chickasaw Indian woman; a spirit, so age can vary

Te Ata—Chickasaw Indian woman; younger version of the above; 15ish–40ish;° English name is Mary Thompson; tall, attractive, long dark hair and eyes

Miss Davis—30-year-old white woman; Te Ata's teacher; attractive, charismatic

Dr. Clyde Fisher—50-year-old white man with shocking white hair; Te Ata's husband; formal in manner, twinkling eyes

Kuruks—Young Indian man; tall, mischievous, catching smile; plays flute/sings

Margaret°—20ish–30ish white woman; friend of Te Ata's; adventurous, blond with beautiful blue eyes; plays violin

Ataloa°—15ish–40ish Indian woman; Te Ata's cousin; sings opera

Chorus—Comprised of 3 men and 3 women, all of different ethnic groups, including Indian; various ages; play a variety of characters

Setting

The play travels back in time from the 1990s to 1907, the year Oklahoma became a state. We see the play as Elder Te Ata remembers it so that the chronology of events is not as important as the events themselves. The characters' ages are approximate and are given only to help establish relationships to Te Ata. Some characters do not age as we move forward through time; others age only slightly. The play begins and ends in spring. Each scene melts into the other. There should be no stop in the action except between the two acts.

Most of the action takes place on a bare stage. An Oklahoma sky is seen

---

°These characters' ages are suggestive only. They must give the essence of the age but not necessarily look much different as the time changes.

throughout. We see a variety of levels suggestive of the geography of Te Ata's life. Always present is a tall tree and a large tree stump. The tree is symbolic of Te Ata's father, and she often talks directly to it. The stump is symbolic of Te Ata's mother. Miss Davis's classroom and the New York apartment and other locations are just slightly suggested with minimal props and furniture.

Notes on Corn Ceremony

According to the real Te Ata's records, this is the basic ceremony: First, offer the basket of corn to six directions; with basket in left hand and rattle in right, make movements as if digging a hole and go around in small circle; place rattle in basket and take out with right hand four kernels of corn and make a movement of dropping four into each hole dug and stamp around each; place basket on floor down center . . . keep rattle and through song make movements of singing and bringing up the corn, occasionally shaking as if getting rid of evil spirits lurking in the fields; toward end of song make movements of sun coming down and rain coming down; dance in straight line but first dance standing in almost same place, making movement of corn knee high, then waist high, then tasseling . . . tear off an ear and place in basket; offer the corn back to east, south, west, north, down below and up above; ending dance with arms over head holding basket to the Great Spirit back toward audience.

Overture—Native flute

ACT ONE
Scene 1—Elder Te Ata
Scene 2—Oklahoma, 1907
    Dance/Narration: "Ribbons of Corn"—Elder Te Ata, Kuruks and Chorus
    Orchestra: "Pied Piper of Hamelin"
Scene 3—Oklahoma College for Women, Chickasha
Scene 4—Chautauqua
    Orchestra—"Stars and Stripes Forever"
    Song and Dance: "Ode of the Peg-Leg Pirates"—Male Chorus
    Song: "Miss Chamberlaine's Bird Renditions"—Miss Davis
    Song: "Shoosh, I'm Indian, Don't Tell"—Female Chorus
    Song: "Rocks in Your Head"—Ataloa and Te Ata
Scene 5—Carnegie Tech
    Orchestra Instrumental: "Rocks in Your Head"
    Orchestra Instrumental: "Ithanna—Seekers of Knowledge"
    Song: "Ithanna—Seekers of Knowledge"—Company
    Orchestra—Violin Solo—"Seekers of Knowledge"
Scene 6—New York

False Face Society—Te Ata and Chorus

"Drum Song"—Drum Group (prerecorded)[1]

Scene 7—Wedding

"Drum Song"—Drum Group (prerecorded, continued from above)

Violin Solo—"The Wedding March"—Margaret

Song with Violin Accompaniment: "Beloved, It Is Morn"—Margaret and Ataloa

"Drum Song"—Drum Group (prerecorded, continued from above)

Flute Solo[2]

Intermission

ACT TWO

Flute Solo[3]

Scene 8—Hyde Park

Orchestra Instrumental—"The Land of the Sky Blue Water"

Native Flute Composed—"Red Throated Spring"—Kuruks and Te Ata

"Red Throated Spring" Reprise—Kuruks

Scene 9—Loon Island

Violin Solo—"Eerily"—Margaret

Dance: "The Dance of the Loons"—Te Ata and Company

Song: "Feather Gone in Wind"—Miss Davis and Chorus

Scene 10—Under the Stars

Orchestra: Violin and Native Flute Duet—"Coming Together"

Song and Dance: "Clyde's Love Song"—Dr. Fisher, Te Ata and Chorus

Scene 11—The Circle of Life

Orchestra: Violin Solo—"Margaret's Song" (prerecorded)

Scene 12—The Other Side

Dance—"The Dance of Youth and Age"—Elder Te Ata, Young Te Ata, Company

Song: "Gone Away People"—Company

Epilogue—Final Pose—Young Te Ata

Note about Music: The drum sounds called for in the text should be played on a powwow drum from the orchestra. There are a few instances in which a hand drum is played by a character onstage. Drum sound effects are not numbered as part of the musical score. Margaret and Kuruks play their instruments onstage, live, but there are instances in which the violin and native flute are played in the orchestra, as in "Margaret's Song" and "Coming Together." Whenever the "Drum Song" is called for, the music is prerecorded, as it reflects a memory, and it is not necessary to see the drum group. Nor is it appropriate or feasible for the orchestra to attempt to play powwow music, which is performed strictly by Native drum groups.

Production Notes: There should be no breaks between scenes as one scene should flow into the next with the help of sound, music, and light shifts as transitions.

ACT ONE

SCENE 1

Music: Native flute

At Rise: As the house lights fade to black, KURUKS enters and stands in place. Lights fade up to soft light and highlights KURUKS who plays flute solo. An Indian shawl is preset, draped over the stump, where there is also a music box and a ribbon stick.

The Native flute concludes, followed immediately by the beating of the drum.

Music: Drums

ELDER TE ATA enters as if through the sky. She is dressed in a Dakota skirt, multicolored with long-sleeved blouse and a squash blossom necklace and an assortment of silver and turquoise bracelets. Her long gray braids are pulled up in a bun and covered with a cotton turbanlike cap. There is still something quite elegant about her. When she gestures, it is lovely to watch, and it becomes obvious that the years of theatrical presentations were greatly enhanced by her expressive hands.

ELDER TE ATA: *(Extending her arms, in performance mode)* "The drum is full of dreams"
"The drum is full of memories"
"The drum sings for me, the song of olden things"
"I am very small, as I dance upon the drumhead: I am very small . . ."
"I dance upward with the day; I dance downward with the night . . ."
"Someday I shall dance afar into space like a particle of dust. . . ."

(The drums fade out.)

(To audience)

These bones . . . don't work like they used to. They take too much time. Don't they know I am not a patient woman and I have things to do . . . I have letters to write . . .

ELDER TE ATA: Mother always said, "Mary Thompson, you must learn to be patient, like the corn. It takes its time to grow, just so that it can be sweet and yellow and crunchy. It is patient and waits on the sun and waits on the rain and it does not grow ill tempered and sulk into the ground."Mother taught me the names of all the flowers and the birds and . . .

(With a twinkle in her eye)

And Dr. Fisher, my husband. He knew them too. We went on walks . . . And we wrote letters. Such wonderful letters . . .

(Chanting)

Hey, yah, hey, yah, hey, hey, ha . . .

(Dances in place as she chants, stops, picks up ribbon stick and practices writing in air)

(To the audience)

I was practicing you know. Writing my name.

(Gestures, writing her name in air)

(Three Chorus Members dressed as children, carrying ribbon sticks, enter from three areas and stand in place, writing in air.)

I must write. People expect me to. I have many friends . . . And the children . . . I must sign my name. "Te Ata Ohoyo" that is actually more correct. "Ohoyo" means woman. That is how it should be.

(Stops writing, thinking)

Sometimes I forget what I am going to say and I have to try so hard to remember it. I don't know why. I am getting old, that's it. Did you know, I can remember what happened during Indian Territory but I can't remember what happened yesterday. Indian Territory . . . I remember it . . .

(She writes in air, as do the children, who follow her lead and scratch it out.)

"Indian Territory" written on stationery. I remember. And I remember Father *(scratching out with ribbon stick)* scratching out those words, "Indian Territory," and writing the words "Oklahoma." Okla—homa. Oklahoma.

(Children dance out as we hear faint sound of Swiss music box. ELDER TE ATA crosses to stump, wraps shawl around her and opens music box.)

SCENE 2

*Faint sound of Swiss music box grows louder. YOUNG TE ATA enters, near
ELDER TE ATA, who magically gives TE ATA her Indian shawl as she exits.
TE ATA, a young girl of about 15 or so, pretends to do a rain dance. SNAKE,
played by a Chorus Member, and ATALOA enter running and playing. They
carry schoolbooks, which they discard. They become aware of TE ATA's dance
to the music box and stop, watching.*

SNAKE: What ya doin', girl?

ATALOA: She's doin' a rain dance to the grandmother's music box.

SNAKE: Nah, she don't know how. She's only dancin' in her head. Father says
she imagines things. Goofy Injun girl. Sits in the cornfield and tries to hear
the corn grow . . .

TE ATA: *(Stops dancing, shyly indignant, closes music box)* So, so what. Just
because you cannot hear it.

(Places shawl on ground, listens for the corn)

SNAKE: *(Half kidding, half curious)* What does it sound like, the corn growing?

*(TE ATA sits Indian style on shawl, invites SNAKE to join her. SNAKE hesi-
tantly sits. ATALOA scoffs at them, but sneaks closer to listen. As TE ATA tells
the story she becomes quite animated and gestures with her hands, eloquently.
Her voice fluctuates for effect; but at times she seems to be uncertain as if she
may be making the whole thing up as she goes.)*

TE ATA: *(Assuming the role of a storyteller)* I will tell you, about the sound of
the growing corn, and you too may hear it, if you know the ways to listen.
The sound is not like any other that Mother Earth sings. It sounds like . . .
leaves of ribbons dancing in the wind as each stalk floats toward the sky. It
sounds like . . . hair growing as it twists and twines and covers each treasure
with hundreds of stringy braids. And you can hear the kernels waking from
sleep as they stand together in rows of yellow. Listen! Shshsh . . .

*(ATALOA has lost interest in the story. She sneaks behind them, pretends to be
a giant stalk of corn, and "shoots up" to scare them.)*

ATALOA: Yahhhheeee! Listen to me, I am Giant Corn; bet you didn't hear me
"pop" out, now did ya!

*(TE ATA and SNAKE scream. SNAKE is embarrassed. ATALOA collapses on
the shawl laughing. SNAKE rises in disgust.)*

SNAKE: Ah, girls are no fun. I'm headin' home to take the horses out for a ride. Beat ya.

(*He retrieves books. As he exits, kicks shawl, lets out a "whoop." The girls both screech.*)

ATALOA: There is a reason why they call him "Snake" instead of Gene! (*Looks around for schoolbooks*) That was an interesting story, Mary. Did your father tell it to you, or was it one you heard from the old ones or maybe you just made it up?

TE ATA: I didn't finish.

ATALOA: Well, don't whine like a white girl. Get your books and you can finish on our way.

TE ATA: I don't have books. They get in the way. You can't run with books.

ATALOA: How can you learn if you don't read your books?

TE ATA: (*Places shawl over her head, sits on stump, puts music box on ground*) I'm going to be a forest ranger. I don't need numbers and spelling words. Mother taught me the name of every flower and every tree and . . .

ATALOA: (*Balancing book on head*) I know, Mary. I know. And you alone can hear the corn grow. And you were the first in the family to taste celery. And Uncle Doug let you use that new telephone machine first, before any of us other kids. Girls cannot be forest rangers, Mary Thompson, especially Indian girls. You better learn to type and to spell. No one will pay you to tell them how the corn grows.

(*TE ATA sits defiantly and looks straight ahead, then remembers. She digs into her pocket, pulls out a handful of dirt, smells it and keeps it tightly in her fist.*)

ATALOA: What is that?

TE ATA: Dirt.

(*TE ATA crumbles the dirt out of her hands, slowly, as she turns around on the stump peddling with her feet. She makes a circle of dirt around the stump, and then faces ATALOA and smells the remaining dirt in her hand.*)

And I CAN hear the corn growing. And I can smell tomorrow in the earth. And I can run and jump way higher than any boy, and especially any white girl, and only Indian girls who are afraid of their fathers need books, Ataloa. (*She pauses briefly.*) Ho! I have said it.

(*TE ATA slightly pushes ATALOA who angrily runs offstage. TE ATA opens the music box, listens a moment, walks toward tree, stops, looks up, as if for wisdom, exits. As the sound of the music box fades away, we hear the sound of a single Indian flute, played by KURUKS who appears US.*)

(1. Dance with Indian Flute Solo: "Ribbons of Corn" Instrumental)

(CHORUS of three Indian Women enter and do a stylized version of the Corn Ceremony. They are dressed in a stylized version of the Chickasaw native dress, calico and apron, and ribbons. Lights reflect the colors of the ribbons. They each carry a small basket with kernels of corn, and a rattle. ELDER TE ATA enters and narrates. For a description of the Corn Dance, see "Notes on Corn Ceremony.")

ELDER TE ATA: *(As the dance is enacted)*
>When the Moon of the Rains comes
>Planting can begin
>The kernels of colored corn
>Are offered to the six directions of the earth
>To the North
>
>To the East
>To the South
>To the West
>To the Up Above
>To the Down Below
>
>Then the corn is given to Mother Earth
>Where it will grow strong and beautiful
>First . . . with a digging stick
>The hole is made
>Four kernels are dropped into each hole
>For four is a sacred number
>And the woman covers it over
>With her bare feet
>
>Soon the corn will appear
>Like a beautiful feather headdress
>But not without help
>Night after night
>The Indian planter walks about the field
>Singing up the corn
>There is a song for the corn when it is
>
>As high as the knee
>When it is waist high
>And when it begins to tassel.
>When the corn ripens
>they shall eat . . . our children

And all our friends too
Who come from afar.

(*The Indian flute music is overtaken by a European flute and we hear, barely discernible, "The Pied Piper of Hamelin" as dance ends and KURUKS exits.*)

(*2. Music: "The Pied Piper of Hamelin"*)

ELDER TE ATA: (*To audience*) Always listen to your Earth Mother.

(*ELDER TE ATA exits as TE ATA enters.*)

(*During the Corn Ceremony, TE ATA changes costume or makes adjustments to her clothing to signify that we have moved to another time.*)

SCENE 3

"Pied Piper of Hamelin" music gets louder. TE ATA practices jumping over stump as MISS DAVIS enters with chair and CHORUS member brings in small blackboard with ruler on edge. MISS DAVIS is a young professor at the Oklahoma College for Women, the OCW. We have moved in time to around 1917. MISS DAVIS is a "take charge" woman full of passion. Like TE ATA she has a charisma about her. She wears the dress of the day, stylish and with a flair and has dark hair and eyes. The music of "The Pied Piper" fades out as MISS DAVIS speaks. TE ATA is older, but still seems innocent and naive. MISS DAVIS brings chair toward center and lays it down.

MISS DAVIS: Come now, Mary, let's make OCW proud. Let me see you jump over this chair. Show me how you can leap without losing your posture.

(*MISS DAVIS beckons TE ATA over, and stands waiting for the exhibition. TE ATA walks hesitantly to the chair. Awkwardly, with her head down, she steps back a few feet in preparation to jump over chair.*)

MISS DAVIS: Head up, Mary. None of my girls at Oklahoma College for Women walks with her chin on her chest, my dear. Be proud of who you are!

(*TE ATA runs and jumps over the chair. MISS DAVIS then gives TE ATA a ruler.*)

Excellent, Mary! Now, here is your "flute." Pretend that you are dancing your way, leading all the children out of Hamelin to a place where no one ever finds them. And don't forget your gestures.

(*TE ATA jumps over both stump and chair, holding her "flute" and awkwardly gesturing.*)

Yes! Head up. Enjoy yourself, Mary!

(TE ATA finishes and shyly but proudly comes up to MISS DAVIS.)

I am pleased with your progress. In a few short weeks, I believe you will astound the audiences with your special rendition of "The Pied Piper of Hamelin." Then it is on to Shakespeare, dear one. *(Touches TE ATA's shoulder and sits her down in a chair)* Now sit down, Mary. Let us talk about your future. What is it that you wish to do?

(TE ATA sits with her head down, catches herself, correcting both posture and head. MISS DAVIS notices, smiles, but says nothing.)

TE ATA: My father believes that I should learn important skills like typing.
MISS DAVIS: And your mother?
TE ATA: My mother . . . agrees with my father.
MISS DAVIS: I see. And what about you? What do *you* want?
TE ATA: *(Too embarrassed to say)* I . . . don't know.

(MISS DAVIS realizes questions are making TE ATA uneasy. She changes the subject as she stands.)

MISS DAVIS: I believe you are going to be an actress, Mary Thompson. I feel sure of it! So, we must continue working on rounding your vowels and improving your confidence.

(She gathers her things to leave.)

I'll see you at rehearsal tonight my dear.
TE ATA: Yes. All right.
MISS DAVIS: *(As she puts on sweater)* You can stay and practice your lines here on the classroom stage if you like.
TE ATA: I know all my lines.
MISS DAVIS: *(As she exits)* Good! But tonight I'll want to be able to hear them from the BACK of the auditorium. Farewell!

(She exits with a flourish.)

(TE ATA crosses to an area to practice. She is reciting her lines when a young white girl enters the room. MARGARET plays the piano and the violin and lives in the same dormitory as TE ATA. MARGARET carries violin case and books.)

TE ATA: Follow, follow. *(Remembers what MISS DAVIS said about volume)* FOLLOW, FOLLOW, children, everywhere. Listen to my magic flute . . .

(Practices different gestures but stops when she sees MARGARET)

MARGARET: Oops, I didn't know you were rehearsing. I was looking for Miss Davis, is she here?

TE ATA: She's gone already.

MARGARET: Phooey, I wanted to ask her if she needed me at tonight's rehearsal. I have a violin lesson.

TE ATA: You play violin, too?

MARGARET: I'm learning. I really like the lessons; much better than piano.

TE ATA: You already know how to play the piano. Why are you still taking lessons?

MARGARET: Well, I'll tell you what my teacher, Miss Waldorf, says.

(She mimics the voice of her teacher, not unkindly.)

"Music is never *learned;* nor mastered. You will take lessons all your life."

TE ATA: All your life?

MARGARET: All my life!

(She laughs.)

MARGARET: Would you like an audience? You were practicing when I came in; would you like me to prompt you on your lines?

TE ATA: Oh! No.

MARGARET: Everyone says that you are like a little Miss Davis in the making.

TE ATA: *(Surprised by this comment, slowly sits down by MARGARET)* They do?

(Shaking her head adamantly)

I'm not though. Miss Davis is . . .

MARGARET: She's a wonder. We all love her. *(Rises)* It's almost time for the dinner line to open, are you eating?

TE ATA: *(Shy once again, but longing to make a friend)* No, I . . . I saved my sandwich.

(There is an uneasy silence.)

MARGARET: Well, we could have a picnic here.

(Crosses, retrieves an apple from her violin case)

TE ATA: A picnic? Here?

MARGARET: Sure! Or, we could just talk. If you wanted. I've seen you at the dorm, but, well, your door is usually shut.

(MARGARET makes herself comfortable, sitting on the floor. She offers the apple to TE ATA.)

MARGARET: Wanna bite?

TE ATA: *(Shakes her head, then answers)* No. Thank you.

(TE ATA slowly crosses, sits near MARGARET, and the two eat in silence for a few moments.)

TE ATA: I don't know anyone in the dorm.

MARGARET: Well, silly, it's hard to get to know people when you are hiding behind a door all the time. Is it hard being the only Indian girl in school?

TE ATA: *(Taken by MARGARET's frankness)* I don't think about it.

MARGARET: It makes you unique. You stand out. In a good way, I mean. *(She smiles brightly.)* So, do you live in a tepee?

TE ATA: *(Shocked and immediately upset)* Oh, No! We live in a house. We have a store. We . . .

MARGARET: Mary, I'm teasing you! You're very serious, aren't you?

TE ATA: Yes. I get that from my father.

MARGARET: Does he live in a tepee?

TE ATA: *(Falling for the joke again)* No, he . . . Oh . . . you're teasing again.

MARGARET: Yep! That's me. Best in the dorm, at teasing, I mean. Margaret, the tease.

TE ATA: My cousin, Ataloa, used to say that she wanted to live in a tepee, until my Uncle made her sleep all night in one.

MARGARET: Is she in school?

TE ATA: Yes, she goes to an Indian school. My father says that, sometimes . . . the education at an Indian school isn't as good as . . .

MARGARET: *(Nonchalantly)* As a white school?

TE ATA: As . . . this school.

MARGARET: Is your cousin, Atoolola, coming to the play?

TE ATA: Ataloa. No . . . she wouldn't . . . no.

MARGARET: Are your parents coming?

TE ATA: If they can, May is busy for them.

(It begins to turn dark outside. We see stars. Lights create magical shadows as the young women ponder their future.)

MARGARET: *(Becoming aware of the dark and the lateness of the hour)* Goodness me, it is getting dark outside. Can't believe it's May already! This term is almost over. So what'cha going to do for the summer?

(TE ATA is caught up in her own dreaminess.)

MARGARET: Mary?

TE ATA: Oh. I'm going to perform in the Chautauqua. Tour with the Redpath Circuit. Miss Davis helped me get an audition.

MARGARET: That's wonderful! What will you do?

TE ATA: Stories and Indian things.

MARGARET: What kind of stories? What kind of Indian things?

TE ATA: Ones that we pass down. Ones that my father told me.

MARGARET: I'd love to hear one.

(TE ATA holds her head down, not knowing how to get out of the request.)

Oh, go ahead. It's just us. You can practice your "rounded vowels" while you're at it.

TE ATA: You know about rounded vowels?

MARGARET: Haven't you heard all of us in the dorm practicing our "rounded vowels"? Really, Mary, I honestly would like to see it. I admire your talent.

(TE ATA feels a bit more encouraged having heard this last comment. She crosses to a performance area. As in the first scene she begins shyly and softly, but by the time she finishes she has become quite engaging. We can hear the improvement in her speech and see it in her presentation. She uses her hands eloquently and once she gains her full confidence, her voice is powerful, and lovely.)

TE ATA: "Omishke! Tillifashi is haklo"—That means "Listen I will tell you a story." *(She uses some broken English throughout.)* Why Rabbit and Owl don't get along. Now long 'tam ago Old Man in the Sky made everybody just the way he wanted to be. He came along like a cloud in the sky one day, Old Man Earthmaker did. He looked down and he saw Rabbit shivering in the cold. Well, Old Man knew that was not what Rabbit really wanted. Rabbit was making a song and dance, trying to tell Old Man how he really wanted to be. Old Man looked down and he watched very careful. He liked that song and dance, Old Man did, so he said to himself, "Rabbit say he want to have long hair, keep him warm on cold days. He want long ears too. And he think he might as well have long legs like deer, to carry him fast and light over cold ground. Well, I like that song and dance. I make a magic for Rabbit." So Old Man in the Sky say to all animals. "While I make magic for Rabbit, you all keep eyes shut." The Old Man start in. He pull Rabbit's hair, make it long like Rabbit wanted. Then he pull Rabbit's ears way-y up, make them long too. He start to pull legs and make them long when he look up and see Owl have his eyes open, peeking to watch the magic. Old Man got so mad, he grab Owl and push his head down into shoulders and say, "You stay that way. And you stay up in tree all day long, not even come out to see Sun shine," and Owl have to stay that way. Then Old Man go back to finish

Rabbit's legs, but Rabbit done hop away, his legs just half down. So he have to hop 'bout like this. Rabbit never come back to have legs fixed right, so he have to stay that way. So Rabbit don't like Owl. Owl don't like Rabbit. That's the way it is.

(There is a moment of quiet, which makes TE ATA uncomfortable, so she adds the last line for finality. It is to become her trademark.)

TE ATA: Ho! I have said it!

MARGARET: *(Rushing to Te Ata, bubbling)* Mary! Mary! I loved it. Your hands . . . and your expressions! Ho . . . I have . . .

(Looks at her watch)

Ho, I've got to go!

(She runs and gathers her things, while TE ATA remains. MARGARET will need to be ready to play violin once off.)

See you after rehearsal. No more hiding behind the door.

(Exits)

(Stars are glistening. TE ATA stands briefly in the fuzzy light. The tree seems to be lit by a star.)

TE ATA: *(To herself, smiling)* "So Rabbit don't like Owl. Owl don't like Rabbit. That's the way it is. Ho! I have said it!"

(TE ATA smiles, liking what she has discovered about herself, exits. As she exits, we hear bursts of fireworks for the 4th of July followed immediately by music.)

(3. Music: "Stars and Stripes Forever")

(During "Stars and Stripes Forever" a crowd enters from all areas of the stage, some removing previous scene props and furniture while others carry balloons on sticks, small flags, etc., to set new scene. They are dressed in attire of the day, some carrying banners that read "The Original Chautauqua Tent Show—Educational, Entertaining, a Must for the Entire Family," etc. Some can carry posters, noting time, etc. TE ATA enters amid the crowd after quick costume change. Crowd mills around as music plays. At one point DR. FISHER and ELDER TE ATA pass each other and there is a brief moment between them. He nods to her, and perhaps gives her a balloon. He does NOT wear a hat so that we will always notice him when he is onstage. Standing out among the crowd are the THREE MALE CHORUS MEMBERS dressed exactly alike. They wear some sorts of man-made elevations [paint cans, etc.] suggesting a peg leg. They wear a patch over one eye, tall cowboy hats, bandanas, etc.)

SCENE 4

"Stars and Stripes" music fades as we hear "Ode of the Peg-Leg Pirates."
THREE MALE CHORUS MEMBERS take stage on one level. Accompanying
dance is ludicrous and comical.

(4. Song and Dance: "Ode of the Peg-Leg Pirates")

THREE MALE CHORUS MEMBERS:
 We're the Peg-Leg Pirates
 Of North Platte Nebraska

 Pretty near half the state
 Away from Omaha

 Not the kind of Pirates
 On ships in Alaska

 But like Captain Hook—we
 Scratch our foot with a saw
REFRAIN:
 We step with the good
 Swing t'other round
 Prairie Dancin' Pirates
 From a one-horse town
THREE MALE CHORUS MEMBERS:
 Cherrywood Joe lost his right
 Fighting for our land

 Wilford talks about a Bull
 Steppin' on his toe

 Frank took an arrow
 From the Kiowa clan
 And now we three Peg Legs
 Star in our own tent show
REFRAIN:
 We step with the good
 Swing t'other round
 Prairie Dancin' Pirates
 From a one-horse town

(Song and dance conclude. Onstage crowd applauds and ad-libs as two of the
MALE CHORUS MEMBERS move to the side. THIRD MALE CHORUS
MEMBER introduces next act.)

MALE CHORUS MEMBER: And now, ladies and gentlemen, children in attendance, we will now be treated to the trills, and thrills of Miss Charlotte Chamberlaine, noted Bird Warbler and Chirping Champion of the Red Path Circuit.

(Audience greets her with jeers and cheers and bird imitations. MISS CHAMBERLAINE is played by MISS DAVIS. She is dressed outlandishly with a large hat and wig. TE ATA quietly appears and awaits her turn.)

MISS CHAMBERLAINE: Thank-you. Thank-you.

(5. Song: "Miss Chamberlaine's Bird Renditions")

(As she makes the sounds of the various birds, she also enacts them physically.)

(Music lead-in for bobwhite)

(She echoes sound of piano.)

Thank-you and as most of you know, that was the recognizable call of the bobwhite. See if you can guess this next delicious sound.

(Music lead-in for tufted titmouse)

(She echoes sound of piano.)

Ah, now how many of you knew that that silly serenade was none other than our friend the tufted titmouse! This next rendition is one that has taken me a good while to perfect. Listen carefully, as some of you out in the pastures of Nebraska have most surely heard this next fair fowl.

(Music lead-in for the purple-crested cowbird)

(She echoes sound of piano.)

Well I gather from your laughter that you not only have heard, but have seen the purple-crested cowbird! You are a very astute audience. I shall now conclude my bird aria with the grand finale—a call that no other warbler, male or female, has ever been able to imitate.

(Music lead-in for the hollow-headed higgety hen)

(She echoes sound of piano.)

Thank-you, your applause is most touching. That imitation, my friends, has astounded even the masters of musicality—That was none other than the glorious hollow-headed higgety hen!

(Act concludes to huge applause. She exits.)

(Without introduction TE ATA approaches stage dressed in a buckskin dress and a one-feather headdress, carrying a small bow and arrow, which she places at her feet. Onstage audience applauds, jeers. Comments overlap. ATALOA enters with hand drum.)

FEMALE CHORUS MEMBER: Quiet! The Indian is going to speak!

MALE CHORUS MEMBER: Is that yore war bonnet, missy? Missin' some feathers, ain't ya?

SECOND MALE CHORUS MEMBER: Hey, quiet you all or she'll come out here and scalp us!

SECOND FEMALE CHORUS MEMBER: Go on honey, we white folks get along with Injuns now a'days!

THIRD MALE CHORUS MEMBER: You shore are pretty for a redskin!

ALL: Shshshs!

(Crowd quiets. TE ATA is nervous but determined. She uses her hands eloquently as she tells the story. Hand drum is heard sporadically, to reinforce parts of story, played by Ataloa.)

(Music: Drum)

TE ATA: Now, long time ago, Old Man sit up on top of sky, all by himself, and he began to think. After all the work making all the animals, he guess he make somebody for to talk with and to walk with on the earth. So Old Man in Sky, he come down to earth and picked out everything he needed to make him a man. He pushed this 'away, and out that way; and under this way. Then he make all things that go on face and then he think . . . Weeelllll . . . Maybe better fix a place to bake him, so he stay that way.

So Old Man in Sky put Man in to bake. Only Old Man got excited, and pulled Man out too quick, so he just 'bout half baked! So Old Man took him by the leg and threw him across big body of water, out'a sight. And that's how White Man came to be. And ever since, poor White Man has been pale and sickly looking.

But Old Man in Sky, think, . . . Weellll . . . mebbe try again. This time, he leave Man in too long. Turned out all black. And that's how he happened to make Black Man. So he took him by the leg and threw him across another big body of water. Out'a sight.

Old Man think, if he keep on tryin' he oughta make pretty good man after a long time. So he try again, put Man in oven, and this time he was verrry careful, and he pulled him out and this time Man, he just 'bout right. He nice and brown and red. A perfect man. And that's how our people came to be. That's how Indian man was made. Ho! I have said it!

(Drum beats louder and faster. She picks up her bow and arrow and dances,

enacting a hunter in search of prey. She enters audience and uses audience members to theatricalize the act. They ad-lib responses.)

Hey ya! Hey ya! Hey Ya!

(Drumbeats grow faster and louder. TE ATA spots her prey offstage, let's out a piercing "Whoop," shoots the arrow offstage and runs off.)

Haaaaaa!

(TE ATA reenters holding a stuffed, green rabbit. She throws the rabbit to crowd, bows shyly and exits. Crowd laughs, applauds, jeers, etc. Onstage audience exits ad-libbing. Lights have slowly shifted to the end of the day. THREE FEMALE CHORUS MEMBERS remain, speaking to one another.)

CHORUS WOMAN: I thought the Indian girl was best.

SECOND CHORUS WOMAN: Yes, the Indian girl.

THIRD CHORUS WOMAN: We live next door to an Indian family. No trouble with them.

FIRST CHORUS WOMAN: Really?

THIRD CHORUS WOMAN: Yes.

SECOND CHORUS WOMAN: Hmm . . .

THIRD CHORUS WOMAN:: Well . . .

FIRST CHORUS WOMAN: Did you know . . . that I'm. . . .

SECOND CHORUS WOMAN: What?

THIRD CHORUS WOMAN: Well . . . I'm . . .

(6. Song: "Shoosh, I'm Indian, Don't Tell")

CHORUS WOMEN: *(Each one takes one line.)*
> I am Cherokee
> I am Seminole
> I have Potawatamie blood in me

TOGETHER:
> Shoosh, I am Indian, don't tell
> Half breed
> Mixed blood
> Full blood
> Blue blood

TOGETHER:
> Who are we?
> Ohoyama siah hoke

CHORUS WOMEN: *(Each one takes one line.)*
> I am the Indian Woman
> I am the Planter of Seeds

I am the Gatherer of grain
I am the maker of trails
In my footsteps civilization follows
The traffic of a nation hollows
I am the pioneer of every frontier
I am the Indian Woman
Ohoyama siah hoke

I am Cherokee
I am Seminole
I have Potawatamie blood in me

TOGETHER:

Shshsh, I am Indian, don't tell
Shshsh, I am Indian, don't tell

(WOMEN exit, humming the song. TE ATA enters, carrying her bow and arrow. She is dressed in street clothes, wears a stylish hat and carries a purse. She sees tree and is aware of its presence. KURUKS enters carrying larger bow and arrow.)

KURUKS: Excuse me, Miss. Excuse me. Grandfather say that his hunting days are over. You will make better use of this. Grandfather say, the one you use is not a real hunting bow.

(He hands TE ATA the bow and arrow.)

This one made for shooting fish.

TE ATA: Thank you. Please tell your Grandfather thank you. I am honored to have it.

KURUKS: My Grandfather is Chief White Eagle. We live in Pawnee. Oh, yes, uh, my name is Ralph. Ralph Allen. Kuruks Pahitu, Lone Bear.

TE ATA: My name is Mary Thompson. I am called "Te Ata"—"Bearer of the Morning."

KURUKS: I very much enjoyed your act, Te Ata. I am also an actor. Someday, I want to go to New York City and study. I . . . I thought maybe you could get me an audition for Chautauqua.

TE ATA: I don't know. I could try. It is not up to me.

KURUKS: Well, you know, seeing as how we're both . . .

(He steps back apologetically.)

I'm talking too much. I hope to see you again, Bearer of the Morning. Our people are honored by you.

(Hands her a piece of folded paper)

Just in case, I put my name on this paper.

(*ATALOA enters and the two almost collide. She drops a handful of sheet music. She is older than when we saw her last.*)

KURUKS: Uh, excuse me. Sorry.

(*He exits.*)

ATALOA: (*On the ground gathering up the sheet music*) Te Ata, wait. The bird lady's sheet music. That man has been a nuisance all evening.

TE ATA: (*Helping pick up the sheet music and sorting it*) Thank you for playing for Miss Chamberlaine on such short notice. I don't know what happened to . . .

ATALOA: I've told you before, you can't count on that one-legged man.

TE ATA: His name is, Thurlow Lieurance. Mr. Lieurance gave me this job, Ataloa. And don't call him a one-legged man.

ATALOA: That's what you called him, the first time you saw him, remember?

TE ATA: Yes, well . . . I had never seen . . . Oh, it doesn't matter.

ATALOA: He isn't classically trained. I play circles around him, but he didn't cast me, so what does that tell you?

TE ATA: He didn't cast you because you refused to play an Indian.

ATALOA: I don't have to play an Indian, Te Ata. I am Indian. I don't know how you can do what you are doing.

TE ATA: (*Trying not to lose her temper*) I am entertaining. It's a job. I'm making a salary. Miss Davis . . .

ATALOA: It's not real theatre. I'm learning opera. The real thing. Can you imagine me in a buckskin singing an aria, it's laughable. Didn't you hear them jeering at you?

TE ATA: (*Almost in tears, takes the sheet music out of ATALOA's hand*) They jeer at everyone. They appreciate . . . That Indian man gave me his grandfather's bow . . .

ATALOA: That Indian man's full of craziness, too. He talked my leg off backstage. "Wants to go to New York. Wants to be an actor. Can I help him? Indians have to stick together."

TE ATA: But the legends . . . the Indian legends that . . .

ATALOA: They don't care about the legends. They like to see you run around and shoot your bow and arrow. And with all your training, you use broken English in some of your stories . . .

TE ATA: That's how the old people . . . don't you remember . . . Old Aunt Mary . . .

ATALOA: They don't hear your words. That's why you have to do that last part. They want to see you act like *they* think an Indian acts like. And a green rabbit!!!!

(She shakes her head in disgust.)

TE ATA: It's just for show . . . they appreciate . . .

ATALOA: How can they appreciate what they don't even understand?

TE ATA: But Miss Davis said . . .

ATALOA: Miss Davis has put rocks in your head.

(ATALOA crosses to stump. We hear first few chords of "Rocks in Your Head." TE ATA crosses opposite direction. They each ponder the past. Lights reflect muted colors, like memory. ELDER TE ATA appears along with Elder Woman from CHORUS. Both watch.)

TE ATA: But don't you remember . . .

ATALOA: No, don't YOU remember . . .

(7. Song: "Rocks in Your Head")

ATALOA AND TE ATA:
> Don't you remember, the Grandmother saying
> While we were playing
> Long years ago?

(The next part of song is sung like an echo with ATALOA singing first and TE ATA following. They come together on the last line.)

ATALOA: To listen not talk

TE ATA: To give more than take

ATALOA: To keep our ways

TE ATA: To share our dolls

ATALOA	TE ATA
To walk the path our grandfathers made.	To bury bad thoughts under a tree

(THEY become young girls, dancing in circles slowly and stylized, NOT realistically, as OLD CHORUS WOMAN joins them. Lights suggest ribbons/girls dancing.)

OLD CHORUS WOMAN:
> Come little children dancing
> Come little children do
> Come little children dancing
> Come little children do
> Come little children dancing
> Braids in the wind
> Sunburn Faces smiling
> Holding hands 'til the end

ATALOA AND TE ATA:
> I remember, the Grandmother saying
> While we were playing
> Long years ago

OLD CHORUS WOMAN	ATALOA	TE ATA
Come little children dancing	To listen not talk	To give more than take
Come little children do	To keep our ways	To share our dolls
Come little children dancing	To walk the path	To bury bad thoughts
Come little children do	Our Grandfathers made	Under a tree

OLD CHORUS WOMAN:
> Come little children dancing
> Have no rocks in your head
> Float away to heaven,
> Little children, instead.

(TE ATA and ATALOA end up facing away from each other as music goes into another version of the song—darker and more intense. CHORUS WOMAN exits, followed by ATALOA. Lights shift.)

(8. Music: Orchestra Instrumental—"Rocks in Your Head")

TE ATA: *(Standing center, as if lost)* Miss Davis, Miss Davis!

(MISS DAVIS appears. ELDER TE ATA stands in another area of light. Both face audience.)

> Miss Davis, Miss Davis! I did Chautauqua Miss Davis. The Red Path Circuit, as you said. I did my best Miss Davis . . . I . . .

ELDER TE ATA: *(Takes over the line)* I did my best for you, Teacher. I was good Injun. Mr. Lieurance say I can come back, but I . . .

TE ATA: I want to go to graduate school. I want to learn more about real theatre. Do you think I can? Do you . . .

ELDER TE ATA: Do you think I can? Do they take Indians at Carnegie Tech?

TE ATA: Carnegie Tech?

MISS DAVIS: Carnegie Tech. In Pittsburgh. You'll have to audition. And yes, my dear pupil, they take Injuns. But they will take you because you are an actress. You have experience now; you have a degree. What do your parents say?

ELDER TE ATA AND TE ATA: How much will it cost?

MISS DAVIS: Oh, how exciting all this is for you! Are you at all afraid?

(Both speak at the same time.)

ELDER TE ATA: Yes!

TE ATA: No!

MISS DAVIS: Carry on then. Go, stir! I suggest "Hiawatha," which you do so well, and then perhaps the piece from "River of Stars."

SCENE 5

MISS DAVIS fades out of sight. Lights focus on ELDER TE ATA and TE ATA. Both practice. We begin to see suggestions of a bustling city—Pittsburgh, in the 1920s. The scene has a surreal look, a frightening memory. Music fades. We hear the beat of a drum.

Music: Drum

ELDER TE ATA: "Should you ask me, whence these stories,

ELDER TE ATA AND TE ATA: Whence these legends and traditions . . .
    I should answer, I should tell you,

ELDER TE ATA: From the forests and the prairies

TE ATA: From the great lakes of the North-land

ELDER TE ATA: From the land of the Ojibways

TE ATA: From the land of the Dakotahs,

ELDER TE ATA AND TE ATA: From the mountains, moors, and fen-lands,
    Where the heron, the Shah-sha-gah
    Feeds among the reeds and rushes

TE ATA: I repeat them as I heard them

ELDER TE ATA: From the lips of Nawadaha,
The musician, the sweet singer.
Listen to these Indian legends."

(Both stand as if waiting to be dismissed. Enter one male and two females from the CHORUS, who portray faculty members at Carnegie. They march in one behind the other. One carries a gigantic clipboard, one wears oversized glasses, one carries a giant watch. The drumbeat changes to enhance their marching. The THREE speak, staccato, finishing each others' sentences. The exchange is quick, quirky, and comical. Lights are surreal.)

TEACHER ONE: You were late with your application, Miss Thompson.

TEACHER TWO: Late with your application!

TEACHER THREE: Late!

TEACHER ONE: Have you another selection?

TEACHER TWO: Another selection?

TEACHER THREE: Selection?

ALL THREE TEACHERS: *(Peer at her)* Well?

(Drumbeat stops abruptly. YOUNG TE ATA is frightened. The THREE freeze. We hear soft sound of a drum beating, like the beating of a heart.)

(Music: Drum)

TE ATA: *(She turns in a panic to look for MISS DAVIS who is not there.)* Miss Davis! . . . Miss Davis—I'm afraid. These people don't like me. These people aren't like you. They don't look like teachers, Miss Davis. I don't think I belong here . . .

ELDER TE ATA: *(Prompting)* "The lights from a hundred cities . . ."

TE ATA: *(Listening, but not knowing to whom or why)* "The lights from . . ."

ELDER TE ATA: You cannot learn if you do not believe in yourself first. How badly do you want to learn? And are you brave enough to be different?

(She prompts her one last time.)

"The lights from a hundred cities are fed by its midnight power . . ."

(Once TE ATA has picked up cue, ELDER TE ATA disappears as if through the sky. As TE ATA performs the piece, TEACHERS change and become normal. Spot narrows on TE ATA. This is her best performance yet.)

TE ATA:
"The lights from a hundred cities are fed by its midnight power.
Their wheels are moved by its thunder. But they, too, have their hour.
The tale of the Indian lovers, a cry from the years that are flown

(She assumes a pose enacting the Indian lover.)

She watched from the Huron tents
till the first star shook in the air.
The sweet pine scented her fawn-skins,
and breathed from her braided hair.
Her crown was of milk-white blood-root,
because of the tryst she would keep,
Beyond the river of beauty
That drifted away in the darkness
Drawing the sunset thro'lillies,
with eyes like stars, to the deep.
He watched, like a tall young wood-god,
from the red pine that she named;
But not for the peril behind him,
where the eyes of the Mohawks flamed
Eagle-plumed he stood. But his heart

was hunting afar, where the river of longing whispered . . .
And one swift shaft from the darkness
Felled him, her name in his death-cry,
his eyes on the sunset star.

(Drumbeats are louder. Lights wash the stage with red, except for light on TE ATA.)

She stole from the river and listened. The moon on her wet skin shone.
As a silver birch in a pine-wood, her beauty flashed and was gone.
There was no wave in the forest. The dark arms closed her round.
But the river of life went flowing,
Flowing away to the darkness,
For her breast grew red with his heart's blood, in a night where the stars
   are drowned.

Teach me, O my lover, as you taught me of love in a day,
Teach me of death, and forever, and set my feet on the way, . . .
She rose to her feet like a shadow. She sent a cry thro' the night,
Sa-sa-kuon . . . Sa-sa-kuon!

(Arms outstretched)

Teach me, O my lover, as you taught me of love in a day,

(Defiantly)

Teach me of death, and for ever, and set my feet on the way."

(Lights slowly dissolve into normal. All that we hear is the drum beating, which fades as teachers speak. They applaud.)

TEACHER ONE: Young lady, that was excellent. I believe we have a place for you.
TEACHER TWO: Now what was your name, dear?
TE ATA: *(She crosses to them.)* Te Ata Thompson.
TEACHER THREE: Lovely. Lovely. An Indian name, I presume?
TE ATA: *(Instinctively drops her head at hearing the word "Indian")* Yes . . .
TEACHER TWO: *(Putting her arm around TE ATA's shoulder)* I know your town. I played Oklahoma City with a Shakespearean company some years ago, and we spent a night in Sheeeek a shay.

(The word "Chickasha" is mispronounced.)

How well I remember the—the Geronimo hotel, was it?
TE ATA: *(Brightening at the sound of familiar places)* Yes, Oklahoma College

for Women, where I went to school, is in Chickasha. And so is the Geronimo hotel, but I have never stayed there.

TEACHER ONE: Well, here you'll stay in the annex.

TEACHER THREE: Yes, the annex.

TE ATA: *(Not knowing what the word "annex" means)* Oh, uh,

(mustering up her courage)

my father would not want me to stay in an annex.

TEACHER TWO: Nonsense. The annex is fine. Good luck, my dear. We will see you in class, tomorrow.

(All three teachers disperse to various areas of stage, slowly, ad-libbing lines, chuckling about the "annex." TE ATA stands alone for a moment, then crosses, sits on floor. We hear the faint sound of the music box for a few seconds. This sound gives way to the tinkle of a bell, signaling the start of a class. CHORUS Members enter, one rolling a blackboard, with various writings and scribbles from an assortment of classes, including words and their definitions and especially the word "annex." This scene is a "collage" enacted. Fragments of dialogue overlap and reflect a year's worth of events remembered by TE ATA. All six CHORUS Members, as well as ATALOA, MARGARET and KURUKS, are in this scene. Sound of bell grows louder as final characters enter. DR. FISHER enters and takes a place near teachers. MISS DAVIS enters and sits, apart from the others. The melody of a song, "Ithanna—Seekers of Knowledge," underscores the dialogue.)

(9. Music: Orchestra Instrumental—"Ithanna—Seekers of Knowledge")

TE ATA: "Dear Teacher, It is the 25th Sun of the Hunting Moon, 1920, and I am finally settled in . . ."

CHORUS MEMBER OF TEACHERS: I don't believe she knew what the word "annex" meant!

(Laughter among them)

CHORUS MEMBER OF TEACHERS: I was worried that she didn't have any training in the classics, the real classics I mean.

CHORUS MEMBER OF STUDENTS: I have to room with the Indian girl! I hope she speaks English.

CHORUS MEMBER OF STUDENTS: You know she doesn't look Indian; well, she's not as dark as some.

TE ATA: *(Continuing her letter)* "Miss Davis, I thought annex was a place where they put Indian students."

MISS DAVIS: *(Writing at her desk)* "Dearest Pupil, you mustn't be troubled by things you don't understand—especially words! Remember, you have mastered Shakespeare."

CHORUS MEMBER OF TEACHERS: I told her that we were all going out for libations and she looked at me as if I had said a dirty word!

TE ATA: "Miss Davis, will I ever know all the words I need to know? I love words when I say them onstage or when I read them in a play. But I hate them when they fool me. Did you know that "libations" are drinks, I think some kind of alcohol?"

MISS DAVIS: "Te Ata, dear, I am sending you a dictionary. Keep it with you . . ."

(All cast members hum "Ithanna.")

TE ATA: "Even Indian words. Did you know that OCW's annual, *The Ithanna*, means "Seekers of Knowledge"?

CHORUS MEMBER OF STUDENTS: She doesn't seem like an Indian to me, except when she tells her stories.

TE ATA: Indian words, teacher words, words white people know, words in books. I'm ready to leave here Miss Davis. And maybe, one day, I will have all the words I need to understand . . . Do white people worry about what red people say? Shouldn't we all seek to . . ."

(One member of the CHORUS OF TEACHERS begins a song and others join in. They are memories in TE ATA's mind. One by one they finish their day, their classes, closing books, erasing the blackboard, putting their sweaters on, etc.)

(10. Song: "Ithanna—Seekers of Knowledge")

MALE MEMBER OF CHORUS OF TEACHERS:
  We are the seekers of knowledge.
ONSTAGE CAST:
  We seek to know what words can mean
  And a place where all words
  Mean the same thing

  Words that know no colors
  Where sound and silence are heard the same
  We seek the understanding that lies
  Past the knowledge of the flame

  We are the seekers of knowledge
  Chanting our heartbeats
  Singing from the souls of here and gone
  Finding the word path where all the world meets

One word—our hand in hand
One mind—our truth unhid
One place—our circle made
One heart—our journey's end

(*We continue to hear the piano accompaniment to the song. CHORUS exits, like a fading memory. MISS DAVIS and DR. FISHER remain, lit with hazy light. The Pittsburgh of the 1920s becomes New York City of the 1930s. We also see some twinkling stars. ELDER TE ATA appears. There is a moment of stillness among all of them, as they all seem to connect in some mystical way. They stare straight out.*)

TE ATA: "Miss Davis, will you reserve a room for me, at the Three Arts Club? That sounds much better than an annex!

ELDER TE ATA: "New York will find you quite a rarity. Good luck."

TE ATA: "Ataloa says she is tired of being on display as the Resident New York Indian, so I must hurry. And Kuruks, you remember me telling you of him. He told me . . .

ELDER TE ATA: "Remember, we have to stick together. Our color doesn't always fit in."

TE ATA: "Miss Radcliffe advised me to say . . .

ELDER TE ATA: "That I have been trained at Carnegie Tech; that might be better than saying I was from Oklahoma."

TE ATA: "And dear Margaret, she's in New York, studying at Columbia. She said,

ELDER TE ATA AND TE ATA: "Don't forget your Indian stories . . . the simple words and the lovely way your hands . . . she said don't forget your Indian stories . . ."

(*We segue from the piano of "Seekers of Knowledge" to a version on the violin, which plays under dialogue. ELDER TE ATA, DR. FISHER and MISS DAVIS exit.*)

(*11. Music: Violin—"Seekers of Knowledge"*)

TE ATA: (*Near the tree*) "Father thinks I am crazy but he has long since given up trying to change me. But I think secretly he is proud; at least he is pleased that I have schooling and can manage my money affairs—most of the time. Mother sees that this is my dream. Must get this letter to you. I am in desperate need of a long walk. The azaleas are still blooming here. I'll pick one for you. My very best love to you, your pupil."

(*Music: Segues from violin to music box*)

(TE ATA touches the tree, circles it as we hear music box. Stars disappear and the New York buildings appear a bit brighter.)

SCENE 6

Music box slowly fades out as sounds of city fade in. Various CHORUS Members enter from all parts of stage, hawking newspapers, telegrams, etc. They walk fast and chaotically to set up for the False Face Society scene. Lines overlap. During this TE ATA crosses US.[4]

CHORUS MEMBER: "Explorer's Club to hear *Silent Enemy* film star Long Lance speak on Indian Culture."

CHORUS MEMBER: "Get your tickets for *Trojan Women* with Estelle Winwood and Bela Lugosi."

CHORUS MEMBER: "See farewell appearance of the famous Miss Duse playing her last engagement."

CHORUS MEMBER: "Mrs. Samuel Tucker to host the Three Arts Club Tea."

CHORUS MEMBER: "I have tickets here for Red and Adele Astaire playing in Gershwin's *Smarty*."

CHORUS MEMBER: "Mrs. Franklin Delano Roosevelt entertains at New York home."

CHORUS MEMBER: "Te Ata—Indian Princess Performs."

CHORUS MEMBER: "Telegram for Te Ata—Long Lance, star of *Silent Enemy*, commits suicide."

CHORUS MEMBER: "Indian actor said to be part Negro—Get your *New York Post*, read all about it."

(Music: Drums)

(Drums begin to beat in odd rhythm. City sounds are more surreal, as if in a dream. ELDER TE ATA enters as if through the sky. TE ATA enters with purse and hat. The lights shift to glaring shafts of color and shadow, as if all the lights of New York City were suddenly possessed. Throughout the following speeches by ELDER TE ATA, we see members of the False Face Society emerge and block TE ATA's path. She mimes what ELDER TE ATA says. False Face Society is composed of the CHORUS Members. They don masks that are oversized heads with misshapen faces, but only on one side. On the other side they are perfectly normal—working-class citizens of New York. Their movements are frightening if they are facing one way, and then change to a stylized version of walking and going to work on the other side. Drumbeat varies from ominous to frightening. Additionally, during this scene, CHORUS members bring on what

is necessary to suggest TE ATA's New York apartment, including a Navajo blan-
ket, an Indian rug and a bouquet of flowers, glasses and champagne, etc., while
portraying False Face Society.)

ELDER TE ATA: *(To audience)* It seemed as if I walked right out of the azaleas
and into another world.

(TE ATA walks, only to be blocked by light and a member of the society.)

I thought I saw a totem pole, but it was only a light post with graffiti on it—
words and a sign language I did not know.

(TE ATA mimes this, and her path is blocked again.)

I thought I saw a row of blackjack trees in the fields, but it was only the
shadows of buildings, side by side on 5th avenue.

(TE ATA mimes this, her path is blocked again. Drum and city sounds grow
more frightening and intense, as does the movement, which is creative,
unworldly, with intermittent images of normal people walking to work.)

I thought I saw Mother and Father and Snake, but it was another family
with no color to their skin and no faces that I remember.

(TE ATA mimes this, and again her path is blocked. She is clearly lost.)

And soon there were faces all around, like in a dream. And for a moment I
thought I heard the elders chanting . . . Hey yah, hey yah . . .

(Her voice trails off.)

But it was not them. I was lost.

(ELDER TE ATA exits. Movement reaches a climax as it engulfs TE ATA.
Slowly the light shafts disappear and drum and city sounds soften. Members of
the False Face Society exit, showing normal side of face, as the music fades
away. TE ATA is left standing alone. We hear MARGARET calling.)

MARGARET: Te Ata! Te Ata! Aren't you coming?
TE ATA: *(In a daze)* Margaret? Margaret? I . . .
MARGARET: *(Crosses to TE ATA)* Didn't you have a long enough walk? Everyone is waiting for your return, my dear Indian Princess. I think Dr. Fisher
was worried about you. He kept looking out the window. He wants to make
a toast.
TE ATA: *(Realizing now where she is)* Oh, yes. I'm sorry. I just had to take a
walk. All this talk of Long Lance. Sometimes I just want to pretend that . . .
Never mind.

(Shakes off somber mood, grabs Margaret's arm and they walk to apartment.)

Margaret, what do you think of Dr. Fisher?

MARGARET: Must you ask? We all think he is charming. Even your cousin, Ataloa, likes him. Te Ata, what are you asking me?

TE ATA: Well, you know I've been dating a few others. Many people thought I was seeing Long Lance. But we were just good friends.

(Again a somber mood engulfs her, and again she shakes it off.)

Anyway . . . I just wanted to know what you thought . . .

MARGARET: I think Clyde Fisher is head over heels in love with you and I believe you already know that.

TE ATA: What about, the . . . the differences . . .

MARGARET: What about the glint in his eye when he looks at you? I'm waiting for you to "tiss him." Remember that song you sang when we lived at the Three Arts Club? "T'ome on and tiss me, tiss me, I wouldn't resist . . .

(They both sing the rest of the song, finishing just as they arrive at the apartment, where they simply "step into" the action.)

MARGARET AND TE ATA: "I dot scolded today. My mama told me not to. But when I feel this way, I dot to, dot to, dot to. There is no harm in a tiss. I don't care if there tis. Cuz I'm a tiss me doll."

(They laugh and then as they enter the apartment MARGARET squeezes TE ATA's hand. TE ATA sits far apart from others, takes off her shoes. MARGARET and TE ATA join KURUKS, ATALOA and DR. FISHER. DR. FISHER has shocking white hair and is at least 15 years older than the rest of the group. He feels comfortable in this setting, sitting on floor. They have glasses in their hands and KURUKS holds a bottle of champagne.)

KURUKS: Well, now that the princess has rejoined us, its time for a toast, to our friend.

(They rise solemnly and hold their glasses up.)

DR. FISHER: To Long Lance. May he be remembered by those of us who knew him well, as a man of many talents.

KURUKS: An actor

MARGARET: A pilot

DR. FISHER: And above all, a gentleman.

ALL: To Long Lance.

(There is a brief moment of reflection until KURUKS breaks the mood. ATALOA and TE ATA exchange glances and then bow heads.)

KURUKS: You know, he wanted me to be in that film of his, *Silent Enemy*, but as it turned out . . . well, I couldn't do it. So, do you think he did himself in cuz of all the rumors?

ATALOA: Let's not start another one, okay, Kuruks? He was in over his head. I'll just say this—he didn't bring much honor to his people.

DR. FISHER: I'll have to disagree with you there, dear lady. He often entertained at the Explorers Club, told stories of his ancestors, and he had everyone quite engaged.

MARGARET: *(Overly positive)* My friends, we promised ourselves that this dinner and toast would be in honor of Long Lance, and that we would try our very best to keep the occasion a happy one, remember.

TE ATA: *(Who has been quiet and distant until now)* Margaret is right. I hope now that he is at peace. I didn't know how troubled he was, by the talk. We understand each other based on our own needs. We touch each other's skin to feel our own.

(SHE stops and there is a strange eerie feeling that engulfs the room, until KURUKS breaks it.)

KURUKS: It doesn't matter to me whether it was true or not. He was some kind of actor. Took chances. Man I wish I had the breaks he had. If he could have just slid some more of his work my way . . .

ATALOA: Indians don't get "breaks" Kuruks, they get exploited. He was a token Indian actor, just like most . . .

TE ATA: *(She looks very sternly at ATALOA, who turns away.)* I wonder if all that talk was just his way of trying not to feel lost.

(There is an uncomfortable silence and the tension among all of them is obvious. DR. FISHER keeps his eye on TE ATA.)

MARGARET: *(With a determined energy)* And *I* wonder how much more we can go on wondering. So, everybody up, its time for a walk to Fanny Farmer's for fifteen cents of goodies and goo. And Kuruks, YOU are buying. Ataloa cooked, Dr. Fisher brought the champagne and Te Ata stayed out of the kitchen.

(They all move, except TE ATA, putting glasses away, fetching purses, etc.)

KURUKS: Ah, shoot. You want me to spend my last few cents . . .

ATAOLA AND MARGARET: Yes!

DR. FISHER: Now, I can certainly pitch in a few pennies. . . .

MARGARET AND ATALOA: No!

DR. FISHER: Sorry, Kuruks, I'm outnumbered.

(Crossing to TE ATA, still a bit concerned about her)

Coming?

TE ATA: Please go ahead without me. I've already had a walk today.

DR. FISHER: Why don't the three of you go? I'll stay to keep Te Ata out of trouble.

MARGARET: *(Before anyone can raise any objections)* Even better. Just enjoy the evening and don't bother with the dishes, that's my contribution.

ATALOA: Te Ata, did you thank Dr. Fisher for the flowers, now that you know they're from him?

(ATALOA and TE ATA exchange looks and then ATALOA, MARGARET, and KURUKS exit, taking away props. There is an immediate change in the emotional atmosphere. Both DR. FISHER and TE ATA let out a sigh. They smile at each other. DR. FISHER crosses over to her, takes her hand and escorts her to where the flowers are sitting. He spreads the Navaho blanket and they sit on it, as if they have done this many times. They are formal, but comfortable with each other.)

TE ATA: I have to get my own apartment. I'm not sure I can wait for Ataloa to move back to Oklahoma.

DR. FISHER: Yes, I was thinking something along those lines as well. You two are very different.

(He touches a petal on the flower and frowns a bit.)

Did you honestly think they were from someone else? I just assumed you would know . . . perhaps I should have signed my name . . . I . . .

TE ATA: No, no. I knew. I knew they were from you. And thank-you. It did cheer me up.

DR. FISHER: It was a dangerous thing for a sober, serious, scientist to do . . .

TE ATA: Why?

DR. FISHER: Well, I . . . It took me a long time to find just the right ones. These specimens, *Hustonia coerules,* are called Quaker Ladies or Inno-cence . . . I felt it the perfect choice for you, especially at this time. I know how Long Lance's death has troubled you.

TE ATA: C.F., you always know just the right thing to do. You are so like my father. You listen to what people don't say.

(She looks at him, peering into his eyes deeply.)

I feel I've known you all my life.

DR. FISHER: And of all people to introduce us to one another—

DR. FISHER AND TE ATA: Ataloa!

(They smile. He takes her hand and holds it in his.)

DR. FISHER: I've enjoyed our walks. I enjoy having you at my lectures.

(Leans toward her, very close)

TE ATA: *(Wants to fall into his arms but is too nervous, so changes subject)* Yes, I've been meaning to speak to you about that. All those scientific names for the constellations—the Indian names are much more fitting. Maybe the Planetarium would let me tell my version.

DR. FISHER: Do you really think our versions are that dissimilar?

TE ATA: Hmmm, just the words. And the, uh, "perspective."

DR. FISHER: Ah! So you remember our lesson on that word do you?

TE ATA: Yes, Teacher, I do. And I remember the other lessons on other words—like astrology and astronomy. And do you remember the lessons I have taught you?

DR. FISHER: I believe I learn from you every day.

(Again he leans toward her and touches her face.)

TE ATA: Well, it's good to know that *my* wisdom is appreciated too. And if you are real good, Meester Feesher, I just might keep it a secret about your nickname.

DR. FISHER: My nickname?

TE ATA: One of the last stories that Long Lance told me was about you and your Indian name, "Mata Koki Papi."

DR. FISHER: Mata Koki Papi—Afraid of Bear. So, he told you about my adventures with the Blood Indians. Well, Indian Lady, I am not ashamed to say that I am indeed afraid of bears! Isn't everyone?

(She smiles, looks into his eyes, feels like kissing him, but doesn't.)

TE ATA: I can't imagine that you would be afraid of anything. You are so wise and strong and . . . practical.

(She crosses away and stares out.)

DR. FISHER: Practical. What might you be looking at, or maybe I should ask what are you trying not to look at?

TE ATA: *(Not looking at him)* You.

DR. FISHER: May I ask why?

TE ATA: No, you may not.

DR. FISHER: *(Picks up the Navaho blanket and stands near her)* You know, Te Ata, I'm more afraid of you than afraid of bears.

TE ATA: *(Turning to face him)* Why, 'fraid I'll sneak up on you one day and scalp all that beautiful white hair?

(She makes a meager attempt to laugh and then gasps at what she has said, wishing the words had never come out. DR. FISHER is also stunned by the comment and waits a moment before speaking.)

DR. FISHER: *(Wrapping the blanket around her and gently forcing her to face him)* I'm afraid that one day you won't be there to sneak up on me at all.

TE ATA: It was an awful, awful thing to say. I'm sorry. I don't know why I said it.

DR. FISHER: Sshh. I know that you are afraid of what we are feeling for each other. I am too. Please know that. I am desperately afraid and delighted at the same time. And I realize that now may not be the best time to talk about this, but well . . . I love you. I am in love with you.

(She lets out a moan, which is half in fright and half in delight.)

TE ATA: Ohhh . . .

(Her knees are wobbly.)

Ohhh dear!

DR. FISHER: *(Holds her up, almost chuckling at her reaction, but afraid of it as well)* Steady there, my knees are none too strong at the moment either.

(She looks at him, trembling, wanting to fall into his arms, but instead remains stiff and afraid to move.)

TE ATA: Dr. Fisher . . . Clyde . . . after all the things people said about Long Lance, I . . . And yes,

(She takes a breath. Then the words and emotions come, fast and furious.)

I love you, too. But I'm afraid of what people will . . . You are so much . . . And I have said nothing to my father . . . What would happen if we . . . I don't know . . . I'm afraid . . . C.F., don't make me choose . . .

(She sinks to the ground, wrapped in the blanket, like a rag doll. He kneels down by her, but keeps his distance.)

DR. FISHER: Te Ata, look at me.

(TE ATA doesn't look at him. She looks trapped. He backs away farther, trying desperately to think of a way to explain the situation.)

Do you remember the very first meal that you made for me? How you had planned this extravagant 5-course dinner. And you spent the whole day just working on the dessert, the lemon meringue pie. And when I arrived that was the only course ready. But we were determined that that was enough. And you pulled it out of the icebox, only to find that it had never quite congealed just right. So that night, you and I had lemon meringue soup—from straws, no less. And we laughed and you cried. And it didn't matter whether it was pie in a pan, or pie in a cup, it had all the same ingredients. People, pie, we all have the same ingredients, dear special one, even though we may look different.

TE ATA: *(She looks up at him and smiles through tears.)* That's not a very scientific way of explaining . . .

DR. FISHER: Say that you will marry me . . .

TE ATA: I . . . Mata Koki Papi . . .

(He kisses her softly on the lips. Immediately we hear thunderous crash, as if two universes had collided, followed by the shrill shout of an INDIAN WARRIOR and Drum Song. We see one lone WARRIOR in shadows, holding a spear. TE ATA is both alarmed and allured by the kiss. She panics and runs away, out of DR. FISHER's arms and out of the scene. DR. FISHER exits with blanket and flowers.)[5]

(Music: Drum Song—prerecorded)

(Lights segue from the light of the apartment to hazy, surreal areas of light. We hear Drum Song throughout.)

TE ATA: *(Runs toward one hazy area of light)* Miss Davis! Miss Davis . . . I met a man. He's a white man. He kissed me. Miss Davis, I don't like mouth kissing. It's too personal . . . But, Miss Davis. This man . . . He is wise, like my father . . . He says I should perform my Indian legends and not worry about acting on Broadway . . .

(ELDER TE ATA appears. INDIAN WARRIOR appears and disappears throughout scene.)

ELDER TE ATA: White men like mouth kissing. And their wisdom is different. And no one ever explained to me, exactly, what love is between a man and a woman.

(She disappears out of the light.)

(TE ATA hears ELDER TE ATA as if listening to her own thoughts. She looks for MISS DAVIS, but she does not come. TE ATA runs toward the hazy area near the stump. WARRIOR lurks.)

TE ATA: Mother, what would Father say if I told him I was seeing a white man? He told me not to trust them. But this man, he is wise like father.

Only he is a very white, white man. He has white hair. He has studied the Indians and he knows all the names of the plants and the stars and he is writing a book about the moon . . . Will people think it strange, if we became married?

ELDER TE ATA: Will it hurt my career to marry? And will a white man's circle around my finger be too confining? People will talk and say things. They will not see his wisdom; they will see his age and they will wonder.

(*TE ATA runs to hazy area near tree, which has cast an overbearing shadow. WARRIOR lurks.*)

TE ATA: Father. He is like you. He is quiet and gentle. He has taught me about the white culture. I will not forget . . .

ELDER TE ATA: Father will say nothing. He will stand alone and look into the blue skies of his land and question, again, the choices his daughter has made. And we are to honor our father and mother. And we are to preserve the ways of our people. I am trying. I am trying to do both. But I am lonely.

TE ATA: I am lonely.

(*ELDER TE ATA disappears. TE ATA looks lost and uncertain as she disappears in the haze.*)

SCENE 7

The Drum Song fades away. Lights dramatically shift. Immediately, we hear Mendelssohn's "The Wedding March" played on a violin by MARGARET. MALE CHORUS member appears dressed as a minister.

(*12. Violin Solo: "The Wedding March"—MARGARET*)

The wedding party enters—entire cast except for cast members who play INDIAN BRAVE and INDIAN MAIDEN . MARGARET leads them in, playing violin. ATALOA leads others in. They make a semicircle around the stage. Two of them place Navaho rug on floor for ceremony.

TE ATA appears from one side. DR. FISHER appears from opposite side. TE ATA wears a stylish suit of dark brown crepe with fur and holds a small bouquet of pink tea roses. She wears a stylish hat. DR. FISHER wears a dark suit, with a small boutonniere, also of tea roses. They walk to center stage and meet, face-to-face. They step up to another level onto Navaho rug and face US. Lights should strangely suggest designs of the Navaho rug.

MALE CHORUS MEMBER: Mr. and Mrs. Thomas B. Thompson welcome you to their daughter's wedding on this 28th day of September, 1933, here at Bacone College Lodge. It is another beautiful Indian summer day in Muskogee.

(Once TE ATA and DR. FISHER step on the rug, they kneel. MARGARET plays "Beloved, It Is Morn" on the violin and ATALOA sings the song. Both women face audience.)

(13. Song: "Beloved, It Is Morn")

ATALOA:

> Beloved it is morn, a redder berry on the thorn
> A deeper yellow on the corn
> For this good day newborn, Pray sweet for me
> That I may be, faithful to God, to God and thee.

(As the first words of the song are sung an INDIAN BRAVE [same person who played warrior] and an INDIAN MAIDEN enter. They are both dressed in traditional Indian wedding regalia. The INDIAN BRAVE carries a beautiful Indian shawl. The INDIAN MAIDEN sits, as if waiting.)

ATALOA:

> Beloved it is day, and lovers work, children play,
> With heart and brain untired all way.
> Dear love, look up, look up and pray, look up and pray.
> Pray sweet, for me, that I may be faithful to God
> And thee, faithful to God and thee.

(INDIAN BRAVE approaches the MAIDEN slowly and lays the shawl at her feet. They do not look at each other. They are enacting a simple version of the Indian Wooing Legend, while TE ATA and DR. FISHER "get married." INDIAN BRAVE, after leaving the shawl, walks away, waiting. The MAIDEN picks up the shawl ritualistically and stands, wrapping it around herself, and then turns US. The BRAVE sees this and joins her. We now have two sets of couples, juxtaposed. The second verse of the song may be omitted depending on time needed for action.)

ATALOA:

> Beloved it is night, it is night! Thy heart and mind are full of light,
> Thy spirit shineth clear and white, clear and white.
> God keep thee in his sight, God keep thee in his sight.
> Pray sweet for me, that I may be faithful, faithful to God and thee.

FULL CAST: Amen.

(TE ATA and DR. FISHER rise and face each other, holding hands.)

TE ATA: Until death do us part.

DR. FISHER: Until death do us part.

(DR. FISHER kisses her first on the forehead and then very briefly on the lips. They hug each other. They step down from the level off the rug, as we hear a Drum Song.

(Music: "Drum Song"—prerecorded—continues where it left off.)

Cast members onstage form a circle, which becomes the wedding party's receiving line. There are ad-lib responses and gestures as each greets and congratulates the couple. The Indian couple is immersed among the others. The crowd completes one rotation of the circle during the following exchange.)

(MISS DAVIS and ELDER TE ATA come through the circle.)

ELDER TE ATA: Chisno pisa yukpah siah it tika na sa.
MISS DAVIS: *(Has on a corsage and is dressed in a becoming suit, with flair)*
    And I am glad to see you.

(She takes ELDER TE ATA's hand and keeps it clasped in hers.)

    I will always remember your wedding. I don't know what I was expecting. I guess I half thought you would walk down the aisle in your buckskin. At least it was in Oklahoma. I know that pleased your father and mother.
ELDER TE ATA: I sometimes still marvel that C.F. and I took the time to get married. We called it "our joint venture." I got to know him through letters; years of writing and trips together to places I had never expected to see. It was an adventure we took, sometimes together, sometimes alone. But it was an adventure—my hand in his . . .

(MISS DAVIS melts into the wedding circle, which has now come full circle, and all cast members exit. Lights on the stage slowly narrow. The Navaho rug used at the wedding has been left behind and is spread out on the stage floor. ELDER TE ATA looks lost for a moment as she realizes that MISS DAVIS has slipped away.)

ELDER TE ATA: As I have gotten older, I think . . . that we never married at all. That it was all a rehearsal . . .

(ELDER TE ATA walks toward the Navaho rug, passing TE ATA and DR. FISHER as they begin to cross DS. TE ATA is aware of a "presence"; DR. FISHER is not. ELDER TE ATA stands on the rug briefly, then disappears. TE ATA and DR. FISHER hold hands and walk DS. They are more comfortable with each other, though there is still a kind of formality between them that is always present. Drum Song fades.)

TE ATA: Now take my "pome" and put it in your little red book and write "Write Te Ata" and then mind what book say!

DR. FISHER: Yes, orders from the Chief. I took your dress and coat to the cleaners and I tucked away a box of Kleenex for you. I gave the Seminole doll to Susie and I won't forget to forward any communications from your bank.

TE ATA: *(Removes hat, doing a little dance/ritual around him as she speaks)* I will write every day and you better be on your best behavior while I'm gone and you better write me every day or I may forget that I am married and you will have to woo me all over again.

DR. FISHER: *(He stops her movement, takes her in his arms, and looks into her eyes.)* I miss you very much when you are gone, my slender Indian. Hurry back to me . . . The stars and the moon don't look the same when you are not sharing them with me . . .

TE ATA: I'll be back in our tipi soon . . . and then you will be the one gone. Between my performances and your lectures I expect we should take out stock in hotels . . .

(During this final exchange she begins to walk toward the Navaho rug as he walks farther away from her. Their lines overlap.)

DR. FISHER: Don't forget—amateurs try photographing at too great distances . . . Don't be an amateur . . .

TE ATA: *(As she slowly walks away)* I pinned a note to your pajamas . . .

DR. FISHER: *(As he walks away)* I mailed you some toothpicks, I hope the stamp canceling machine won't . . .

TE ATA: I have much to tell you, my "lily of de Ohio Valley." You best 'sprise me with a talking leaf . . .

DR. FISHER: I ate alone tonight, and thought of you, dearest Injun . . .

(He looks toward rug, then slowly fades away offstage. TE ATA is by this time standing on the Navaho rug.)

TE ATA: Are you feeling well . . . Have you bought new shoes . . . Have you been writing in the book . . . You have the whole table you know . . . And someone is wondering how many ham sandwiches on rye have been eaten and . . . which stars you find yourself most interested in . . . Goodnight Meester Fisher . . .

(She sits on her knees, writing the following letter. VERY slowly, as she completes the letter, the light narrows and narrows until just her face is lit by the final line of the letter. She suggests writing initially but then looks up and remembers each memory. Her delivery is intimate, not performed.)

"28th Sun of the Hunting Moon. On the High Seas. 1936. Dear Clyde. Three years of togetherness on the trail—and we have known the tang of

the desert sagebrush and seen the gnarled strength of piñon
and cedar.

*(Native flute music underscores remaining monologue. Kuruks should not be
seen.)*

(Music: Native Flute Solo)[6]

TE ATA: We have walked together under green hemlock boughs and marveled
at the dignity of the northern pine. We have sailed "big waters" and have
felt drawn and fascinated by the knowledge of the Ancient one. We have
loved the smoke and the beauty of the campfire and have felt the warmth
that comes from companionship and real friends. We have felt our alone-
ness and the sadness of parting—but always knowing we would feel as
much the keen joy and the sweetness and strangeness of coming together
again—and—we have caught a photographic cloud or two and had an occa-
sional dance among the stars! The 28th Sun of the Hunting Moon and an
Indian on the Atlantic sailing back to you!"

*(The one light fades to blackout. Music fades. TE ATA exits in blackout, with
rug.)*

End of Act One

ACT TWO

(Music: Native Flute[7])

SCENE 8

*Lights fade up on Kuruks playing flute. At end of flute solo lights fade up on
entire stage. We see nothing but the blue sky. From offstage we hear ELDER
TE ATA chanting and shaking a rattle. She enters as if through the sky.*

ELDER TE ATA: Hey ya, hey ya, hey ya, hey ya . . .

(She keeps beat with rattle, stops, stands in performance mode, recites.)

"You see, I am alive.
You see, I stand in good relation to the earth
You see, I stand in good relation to the gods.
You see, I stand in good relation to all that is beautiful

You see, I stand in good relation to you.
You see, I am alive. I am alive."

(To audience)

These moccasins have traveled many paths during my many moons. They took me to the White House where I performed for the Roosevelts. It was in the East Room and I slept in the Lincoln Room. These moccasins most surely got their share of excitement and not nearly enough rest. These moccasins took me to great places and small places. I accepted most any invitation, if they paid me. I was a professional, you know, and that is how I made my living, for ever so long. Performing my stories and telling all people, not just white people, but all people, about the Indian ways. And Dr. Fisher helped me and together we learned a good deal about life and how it was to live in this world where we think we are all so different, when really we are all the same.

(She slowly crosses.)

On the 11th Sun of the Wild Rose Moon in 1939, I performed for the Queen and King of England at the Roosevelts' family home in Hyde Park. Kuruks insisted on being a part of the presentation. So I let him. And Margaret, my dear friend, came with me. C.F. had me up with the sun. Bearer of the Morning was a correct title for me on that day, at least . . .

(KURUKS enters slowly beating a hand drum, almost ominous, as ELDER TE ATA slowly disappears, and a golden sun, just rising, fades into view. TE ATA appears dressed in her buckskins and carrying a rattle. She places the rattle at her feet and stands facing audience as if waiting for her cue. She is on a higher level than others to suggest a makeshift stage. Drum segues into music.)

(14. Music: Orchestra Instrumental—"The Land of the Sky Blue Water")

(As music plays, all CHORUS Members and DR. FISHER, ATALOA, and MARGARET enter, each dressed in the attire of the day. They all carry white lawn chairs and place them sporadically in groups around TE ATA's performance area. They chat and ad-lib among themselves. They look quite elegant, but not completely formal. Once they all sit, music fades. We see suggestive shadows of trees and foliage in varying shades of green. The onstage audience applauds as the music ends.)

TE ATA: *(In performance mode)* Many suns have crossed the sky since we last sat together. My friends, I give you my hand. I am happy to see you. My people say, "Chisno pisah yukpah siah it tika na sa."

(Uses Indian sign talk for "I," "happy" and "you" as she says the words)

I have come a long way . . . The berries have grown and ripened and the time has come for stories. Indians believe that all things have a story of their own. So draw close and I will tell you the story of romance from the Senecan tribe.

(Takes her rattle and shakes it as she begins, dances a few steps in place)

"Hey ya, hey ya, hey ya. . . ."

(During the telling of the story, the onstage audience should laugh and respond throughout.)

"Long time ago, there was a young maiden, live all alone beside a stream. She was old enough to get married. She oiled her hair and she painted her face and went down to the stream and looked in. She say to herself, 'I'm good looking enough for any man.' And she walked down the banks of the river.

After a little bit she came to a place where there was a camp and she sat down upon a log and she began to sing . . . 'Anybody round here want a wife? Anybody round here want a wife . . . anybody here want a wife?'

Someone answered 'I want a wife, I want a wife, I want a wife.'

'What shall we live on if we live together?' He answered, 'We will live on Hawthorn berries and roots.'

'I couldn't live on Hawthorn berries and roots . . . They are not good enough for a nice girl like me.'

And she walked on down the banks of the river. The Sun had been traveling across the sky trail and had reached about the middle of the sky. It was very hot. She found nice shady place and again sang her song . . . 'Anybody round here want a wife? Anybody round here want a wife . . . anybody round here want a wife?'

Somebody answered, 'I want a wife. I want a wife. I want a wife.'

'What shall we live on? What shall we live on if we live together,' she said.

'We will live on grass.'

'Oh, I couldn't live on grass. Grass is much too coarse for nice girl like me,' and she walked on down the banks of the river.

The Sun was riding low in the sky. She think if she is going to get husband that day she better hurry up. So once more she sang her song, 'Anybody round here want a wife? Anybody round here want a wife? Anybody round here want a wife?'

Somebody answered, 'I want a wife. I want a wife. I want a wife.'

'What shall we live on if we live together?' she asked.

'We will live on seeds.'

'Oh, I like seeds. Seeds are nice and soft and tender.'

'Did you understand what I said we would live on if we lived together?'

'Yes, seeds. I like seeds.' He came over and sat down beside her. He was so pleased with her answer and she was so pleased with him . . . that they flew off down the river together . . . for they were the first birds of spring." Ho! I have said it!

(Shakes rattle to conclude as audience applauds. She nods reverently, puts down rattle and begins her next piece, which is accompanied by flute, played by KURUKS.)

(15. Indian Flute Solo: "Red-Throated Spring"—KURUKS)

(For this poem, she uses the beauty of her voice and little gesturing, which helps make the distinction between Native pieces and this piece of poetry from the time period. She is almost motionless, save for slight hand gestures.)

TE ATA:

"Red-Throated Spring is calling me,
O Old Man Winter—man that I have loved
In the dark pine thatch beneath the falling snows;
Red-Throated Spring is calling me by the brookside.

I hear his pipe of scarlet willows
Ruddy-shrilling through the wind,
With its thousand notes of flame
Piping to the young wild Dawn by the brookside.
O Man that I have loved,
In the dark pine thatch beneath the falling snow,
I must go!
For my silent songs have wakened
And my lips are thirsting for his kiss,
For the kiss
Of Red-Throated Spring by the brookside;

And my heart is leaping from your hands,
O Old Man Winter,
With the sound of the blue ice cracking to his thousand notes of flame
I must go
Where his scarlet pipes are calling me,
To the dance of the young Wild Dawn by the brookside!"

(The flute finishes, audience applauds. KURUKS plays rattle to introduce next part of performance. Lights shift, suggesting the passing of the midday sun. There is more light focused on TE ATA. ELDER TE ATA enters as if through the sky and stands directly behind TE ATA, but on a higher area of the stage. Their delivery of the next piece is exactly the same with the same gestures. KURUKS stops playing rattle as the two begin speech.)

ELDER TE ATA AND TE ATA: *(They stand reverently for a moment.)*
> "Let it be beautiful
> when I sing the last song—
> Let it be day!
> I would stand upon my two feet,
> singing!
> I would look upward with open eyes,
> singing!
> I would have the winds to envelope my body;
> I would have the sun to shine upon my body;
> The whole world I would have to make music with me!
> Let it be beautiful
> When thou wouldst slay me, O Shining One!
> Let it be beautiful
> When I sing the last song!"

(The onlookers are quiet for a moment, then applaud for a length of time. TE ATA is pleased but wishes to exit the stage. She bows slightly, exits. Lights reflect late afternoon, with more shadows.)

(16. Indian Flute Solo: "Red-Throated Spring" Reprise—KURUKS)

(As the "guests" rise from their chairs and begin to exit, KURUKS plays flute; characters' movement takes on a different look and feel—somewhat suggesting the Pied Piper of Hamelin leading a group into a forest. The guests, carrying chairs, follow KURUKS snakelike, exiting. ELDER TE ATA remains onstage as if watching a memory.

Flute music fades, sun is almost down, and for a moment the stage is empty. Then from different areas MARGARET and DR. FISHER rush on, followed by KURUKS.)

MARGARET: Te Ata? Has everyone gone?

DR. FISHER: Hello? Ah, you are here. Where is Te Ata?

KURUKS: *(Carries rattle and flute)* Did you see? I talked with the Queen. I met her. She liked my music. Boy, oh boy, I just talked to a Queen. And the King. He liked me . . . Where's Te Ata? Hey . . .

MARGARET: We have to call Miss Davis. Right now. She will want to know the details.

KURUKS: We should celebrate. We should . . .

DR. FISHER: I agree with Kuruks, for once. We should definitely toast the evening. It isn't every day . . .

KURUKS: It isn't every day a Pawnee Indian from Oklahoma meets the Queen.

MARGARET: Well, it isn't every day that a Queen meets a Chickasaw Princess.

(TE ATA rushes in, looking lost.)

TE ATA: *(Calling names as she enters, carrying her buckskin dress)* Margaret? C.F.—Oh good, I thought I had been forgotten!

(Looks around at the surroundings)

The sun is going down. I didn't realize it was so late. I need to take a breath.

(They all meet together in the center, speaking at once. All are joyous except for TE ATA.)

DR. FISHER: *(Kissing TE ATA's cheek)* You were captivating . . . the audience was simply enthralled . . .

MARGARET: You could hear a pin drop during that last piece. It's always been my favorite. Did the Queen like the doll you presented her?

TE ATA: I guess. I was too nervous to really look at her for very long. I wish Father could have. . . .

DR. FISHER: He would have been proud. So, let's see, we need to find a telephone. And I'll bring the car around. Where might we go to mark this occasion? I'm afraid I'm slipping. I should have brought champagne and we could have celebrated under this beautiful sunset. We can't deny this setting that nature has given us, can we Te Ata?

TE ATA: No, I . . . just want to go home . . . or go . . . somewhere . . . to . . .

MARGARET: There is a pay telephone at that cabin place, that we passed, remember Te Ata? I promised Miss Davis we would call.

KURUKS: Hey, I got beer in my car. It isn't champagne, but its cold. Let's just stay here. Sit on the grass and get a little happy. We could pretend we're sitting on the plains of Oklahoma! Let's bring back the Indians across the Mississippi, hey, Te Ata?

TE ATA: No . . . we can't do that . . . We can't drink here. What would people say?

DR. FISHER: No, Margaret's right, Francis Davis must be called. I'm sure that's Te Ata's preference.

MARGARET: It might be fun, though, to sit out here and have a cold drink, a little adventure? I'm game. Miss Davis will forgive us.

(They talk at the same time. TE ATA moves away looking confused and distant. Lines overlap.)

MARGARET: Let's find a spot. Do we have a blanket or something to sit on?

KURUKS: Should I get the beer?

MARGARET: Hope we don't get arrested.

DR. FISHER: We're guests of the Roosevelts, aren't we?

KURUKS: I've certainly worked up a thirst.

DR. FISHER: Maybe we should drive to that cabin, get something to go with our champagne/beer. What do you think?

MARGARET: Who's going to drive?

KURUKS: We'll have our own little powwow right here. We'll dance the sun down.

Hey, ya, hey ha . . . *(He takes off piece of clothing, throws it down.)*

(KURUKS dances around DR. FISHER and MARGARET. They laugh and join in—in their own fashion.)

KURUKS: Hey, I shoulda ask the Queen if she ever had it with an Indian! Hey, ya hey yah whoo . . .

(DR. FISHER and MARGARET groan at last remark. They stop slowly, one at a time, as they notice TE ATA.)

DR. FISHER: Te Ata? Are you all right, my love?

(There is silence. They wait for her answer, which doesn't come for a long time. When she does speak, there is an anger and a loneliness coming from her voice that defies all that we know about her. She speaks with silent power facing directly toward the audience, and beyond.)

TE ATA: The Queen asked me if my people were proud of me. I could not answer. Did she mean my tribe? My family? The nation? Proud of me, for what? Knowing the Roosevelts, being an actress, marrying a New York doctor? "Let it be beautiful when I sing the last song." I suddenly realized that I don't know what that means. Father died three weeks ago. Ataloa was with him, since she decided to go back to teach in Oklahoma. Ataloa . . . not me! The last song . . . is everything that you add up to be . . . it's all the words in your life . . .

(She turns to them and looks directly at them.)

Don't ask me to play Indian with you Kuruks. Don't assume you know what I prefer, Margaret. And C.F., my darling, don't be kind to me, I don't deserve it. I have to go. I need some time to think. To . . . I don't know . . . to find . . . I need to have these clothes . . . this buckskin cleaned.

(She exits. There is a moment of silence and, one by one, they exit too.)

(We hear sounds of a loon bird, haunting and beautiful. The sun is setting. ELDER TE ATA steps out of the shadows and crosses closer to the audience.)

ELDER TE ATA: It was the 16th Sun of the Hunting Moon, 1943. We went to Loon Island. Loon Island, Lake Winnepesaukee, Lakeport, New Hampshire. Solitude. Me and Miss Davis and Margaret. Sometimes Dr. Fisher would come, too. But most times, we wrote letters. "Dear Fraid of Bear . . ." I wrote . . . many, many times.

SCENE 9

We periodically hear the sound of the loon bird.

We see suggestion of foliage and trees. There should be a lake. ELDER TE ATA listens to the loon, then disappears. MARGARET and MISS DAVIS enter, carrying a canoe with items for a picnic. In the canoe is MARGARET's violin. MISS DAVIS wears stylish slacks, and a hat, all in shades of green. MARGARET wears shorts and a blue shirt. Their colors look bright and lovely against the wooded backdrop, like two different birds. The sun is beginning to set. As the scene progresses, it grows darker and darker. TE ATA is offstage. She is dressed in a white halter top, with her hair in one braid and covered with a red scarf. She has on black shorts and a shell necklace and carries a white, lacy shawl.

MISS DAVIS: *(Laughing as she drops her end of canoe)* Come now, Te Ata, Margaret and I were just teasing you, weren't we dear?

MARGARET: *(Drops her end, spreads a blanket and unpacks)* Teasing, just teasing. We know you aren't afraid of most things, but a cockroach is hardly worth nearly capsizing the canoe. Don't be so selfish; he just wanted to take a ride on the water and get a wittle sun.

(Laughing)

No different than you, Te Ata!

MISS DAVIS: I thought she had seen a snake the way she was carrying on!

MARGARET: It's the same in their apartment, one little cockroach and she flies around the room like it was on fire. Dr. Fisher has to have it fumigated periodically just to keep the little varmints out of Te Ata's sight.

(MARGARET and MISS DAVIS unpack canoe, spread a large blanket and place their things on it, food, a book, the violin, small pillows, etc. TE ATA enters, her clothes splashed with water, carrying canoe paddles.)

TE ATA: (*Crossing to them, threatening with the paddles*) You two better behave or I'll put an Injun curse on the both of you!

MARGARET: Te Ata, how can a grown woman, who has stayed in Lord knows how many less-than-nice hotels, be so afraid of a harmless hungry cockroach?

TE ATA: (*She crosses to blanket, puts paddles down, sits, takes out notepad and pen.*) Indian woman no talk, must write her chief about bad treatment.

MISS DAVIS: Send my love to C.F., Indian woman, and thank him again for the book. I've been reading reviews about *The Yearling* but never got around to purchasing it. I love what we have read so far! The characters really come to life when one reads them out loud!

(*She crosses to TE ATA and lightly touches her hair.*)

Goodness, you did get yourself a shower from all that. You won't get chilled will you, when the sun goes completely down?

TE ATA: (*Pats MISS DAVIS's hand*) No, Frances, I'm fine. I have my shawl, and Margaret, the pioneer, is going to build us a fire, aren't you?

MARGARET: Yep, but let's wait just a bit, I dearly love to see the sun going down. It almost takes your breath away. Wish my Johnny were here to see it.

TE ATA: Just us ladies this time. Clyde is speaking in Staten Island for the Zoological Society. "Wild Animals Near Home" was the working title when I left.

MARGARET: Would wild animals near home include the cockroach?

TE ATA: Good thing it isn't your birthday! Now come on, I'm dying for Frances to open her gifts. Aren't you dying to, Frances?

MISS DAVIS: Dying to!

(*MARGARET and TE ATA each pull out wrapped presents from canoe. MARGARET plays "Happy Birthday" on violin. No one sings, so the song has a lovely sophistication to it. At the end MARGARET does one final "zip." They laugh.*)

MISS DAVIS: (*Smiling, taking in the atmosphere and the friendship*) How kind of you Margaret!

MARGARET: (*Handing a small wrapped gift to MISS DAVIS*) Happy birthday, Frances, and may we always be able to celebrate it together. Open it!

MISS DAVIS: I can't imagine what it might be, it is so tiny and light!

TE ATA AND MARGARET: 'Taint a bird. 'Taint a bee. So don't ask me!

MISS DAVIS: (*Opens the package, which is a lovely white embroidered lace handkerchief*) Oh, this is exquisite!

MARGARET: It's from my grandmother's collection. Real Dublin embroidered lace.

MISS DAVIS: Thank you, thank you. I believe I'll pin this on my white linen dress, won't that make an interesting look?

TE ATA: *(Giving gift)* Happy birthday, Miss Davis. Uh, Frances. Uh, it's Dean Davis now, isn't it! Funny, after all these years I still think of you as "Miss Davis."

MISS DAVIS: Quite all right. I still think of you as my students, even though you are both old married women! Now, what has my Injun given me?

MISS DAVIS: *(Opens gift, revealing a small Indian doll)* Oh, Te Ata, how sweet! I'll add this precious doll to my collection. Is it from New Mexico?

TE ATA: Yes! It reminded me a little of my mother; how she looked before . . . when she was young. I especially like the . . .

(She unexpectedly is overcome with emotion, then immediately apologizes.)

the calico apron. I . . . I'm sorry. I've been so weepy lately. I . . .

MISS DAVIS: *(Trying to lighten up the situation)* Well, I can't believe you kept it a secret. Usually she tells me what it is before I have a chance to open it. *(Beat)* Thank you. For everything! The invitation to come here, the gifts. I can't think of anything better in this world than being here, just now, watching the sun go down, and sharing my birthday with the two of you.

(SHE takes each of their hands and they in turn grasp the other, making a circle. It has grown darker; we hear the sound of the loon. Hearing the loon, TE ATA shivers, disturbed and distracted. She crosses to edge of "water" and stares in the distance. We see stars appear throughout this next scene, until all we see are stars, and the reflections on the water. We hear periodically the loons wailing. TE ATA sits by the water with shawl wrapped around her. She takes the red scarf from hair, ties it around her neck, and unbraids her hair.

MARGARET and MISS DAVIS have been setting up the campfire. They notice TE ATA's absence.)

MARGARET: She misses him.

MISS DAVIS: Dr. Fisher?

MARGARET: Oh, no, I meant her father. His passing was very hard on her. She won't even speak of it at all. And, yes, I am sure she misses Dr. Fisher too, but they have really gotten accustomed to being away from one another. Actually, I think it is the only way Te Ata could ever really live with anyone. They write constantly.

MISS DAVIS: I thought she seemed a bit preoccupied, but I decided that she just must be tired. So much traveling and performing. I'll go fetch Te Ata.

We should read a few pages of *The Yearling* before we go in, don't you think?

(MISS DAVIS crosses slowly to TE ATA. With unbraided hair TE ATA looks strangely wild and beautiful. MISS DAVIS sits beside her silently. They look out over the water. The loud wail of the loon pierces the moment. TE ATA is shaken.)

TE ATA: Some Indian tribes believe that the loon is an omen for death.
MISS DAVIS: Do you believe that?
TE ATA: I don't think my father ever saw or heard a loon. It would remind him of a wolf howling. I . . .

(Fights back tears, as she looks out over the water)

The loons have been around for millions of years. They mate for life. They come back every year to the same place. Since I have been coming here, this one pair of loons has come and gone and had children. And at night, especially during the Hunting Moon, they sing their song. They're beautiful birds. Their feathers are sacred because their markings are so rare. I'm haunted by the sound. My heart feels like it cannot beat.
MISS DAVIS: I never knew my father. But when my mother died, I remember at the graveside, I heard a mourning dove and I saw it perched high on the rooftop of the church. It seemed to me that at that moment my mother's soul had taken flight and there she was sitting on the rooftop of our church. And to this day, when I hear a mourning dove calling, I search the skies until I find her. It makes me smile and cry at the same time.
TE ATA: Are you sure you're not part Indian?
MISS DAVIS: Actually, I am not sure at all. Mother always said that I had an old soul, and a young heart, but nothing about Indians!

(She puts her arm around TE ATA's shoulder.)

No matter how old one gets or how many loved ones pass away, we never really get used to our mothers and fathers leaving us. But we mustn't let the memories make us forget the living and why we are here and what glorious things we can do and see and be!
TE ATA: *(She smiles and for just a brief moment she relaxes into MISS DAVIS's embrace, but only for a moment.)* You always have just the right words to give me, Frances.

(She rises, crossing away from the water.)

It isn't just father's death. Mother is so frail these days. And sometimes when I look into C.F.'s eyes I see . . . well, he hasn't been well, either.

Maybe his is just homesickness; away from his tepee and his Indian far too much, he says. And . . .

(17. Violin solo: "Eerily"—MARGARET)

(MARGARET plays her violin, very softly. We don't recognize the tune. It is both lovely and eerie.)

TE ATA: Margaret's serenading us.

(There is a moment of silence as both listen to the violin.)

When I come here, to Loon Island, I always leave feeling so torn. I can find solitude here, and pinecones, and rocks, and wild asters and . . . here I don't have to perform for my supper. Here I don't have to justify my choices. I lose all obligation . . . My mind can just slumber. No Ataloa reminding me of what I should do; no Kuruks reminding me of what I haven't done . . . mainly for him. No C.F., who just by his presence reminds me that . . . I wish I were more like Margaret. She never looks back. And you, you are always so sure. Sure footed, like a deer. I live in the hard brick buildings of New York, with a white man, and I only wear my buckskins for performance . . . And . . . on the phone . . . when Ataloa called me to tell me that Father . . . She said . . . his last words . . . he spoke in broken English like the old people . . . like, she said . . . the way I do when I . . . He thought Ataloa was me . . . He tried to tell her the story of the owl and the rabbit . . . Then he . . . She laughed at his confusion . . . I think of myself like a paper doll, with paper clothes, and depending on what clothes are put on me, that's the way I must behave and that's who I must be for a day, or an hour . . .

(MARGARET's violin music crescendos here, and ends. MARGARET picks up the blanket and stirs the campfire, which has grown very dim. The moon is out full and provides the major source of light. She stands for a moment holding the blanket and the violin, uncertain about interrupting.)

I don't know who I am, except when I am here, or when I'm home, in Tishomingo, picking up handfuls of red dirt and putting them in my pocket to remind me of where I come from. Spirits are calling me, calling me, all the time . . . in the loon's cry, in the moon's light, in the wind's path . . .

MISS DAVIS: *(Crosses to her)* Would it really make any difference if you wore your buckskins all the time and lived in a tepee surrounded by buffalo?

(MARGARET crosses carrying blanket and violin.)

MARGARET: So what are you two talkin' 'bout out here under the moon? I'm cold and I'm hungry and the fire's gone out and this pioneer woman is headed for more civilized sanctuary. So is everyone okay?

MISS DAVIS: I tell you what Margaret, if you'll start the coffee, Te Ata and I will secure the canoe. I can't wait much longer to find out if Jody finds the fawn.

MARGARET: *(Crossing)* He'll find it. I'm readin' Jody this time. Coffee in a few tick tocks. And shake a leg, I'm not going to come lookin' in the dark for you two. Last one in is a rotten one.

(MARGARET exits.)

TE ATA: Frances, go on ahead, with Margaret. I've been rude to keep you all to myself. I'll see to the canoe.

MISS DAVIS: Be careful out here, by yourself. *(Crosses, then turns back)* Te Ata, there is really only one voice who calls.

(MISS DAVIS exits. TE ATA crosses to canoe and starts to push it toward the water, but is interrupted by haunting sound of the loon. The yodel of the loon sounds like a woman laughing. It is followed by another loon answering in the distance. TE ATA stands erect, as if in answer to the loon.)

TE ATA: They shoot Flag, Frances, the beautiful yearling dies, and Jody is never the same, even though he becomes a man. Jody's Pa said he was uneasy all his life.

TE ATA: *(Pushes canoe in " water" and steps in, clearly in another world as she recites, in performance mode)*
"From the red deer's flesh Nokomis
Made a banquet to his honor
All the village came and feasted

All the guests praised Hiawatha
Called him Strong-Heart-Soon-ge-taha
Called him Loon-Heart, Mahn-go-taysee"
Mahn-go-taysee!!

(As she says the following a second time, it sounds less like words and more like a loon cry. It is the most bewildering moment in the play.)

Mahn—go—tayyyseeeeee!!

(She pushes canoe into the water and gets in, as the entire stage becomes water. All is blue and shadowy, sparkly and surreal. The loons answer her call. We hear the various wails, tremolos and yodels of the loons and the night sounds of the island. It is not peaceful. TE ATA stands in canoe. She looks wild and beautiful. Slowly the LOON PEOPLE emerge from all over the stage.)

The LOON PEOPLE are ATALOA and the six CHORUS Members. They wear the colors of the loon—black, white and red. They have feathers, and their faces look like a loon's with the red eyes oversized. Yet, there is something human about them.)

(18. Dance: "Dance of the Loon People")

(We hear faint sound of a drum, over the sounds of the night, like a heart beating. All the LOON PEOPLE come together in a circle around TE ATA who remains standing in the canoe. They beckon her with various loon sounds. Music evolves from the sounds and they dance the "Dance of the Loon People," which TE ATA is a part of, at first, as one who runs from them, but then as one who becomes one of them. The LOON PEOPLE eventually become one entity, one beautiful bird on the water, with TE ATA finally at the "helm."

When the dance is complete, the music fades, but drumming remains. We hear only distant sounds of the loons. Lights move from night to day. LOON PEOPLE remain in various areas of stage and watch, leaving TE ATA in the canoe. Stars fade away and we see a blue-gray sky, the first light of morning. TE ATA gets out of the canoe, pulls canoe to "land" and turns it over. She traces some of the steps from the dance and finds a feather, sits on canoe and braids her hair. She has changed. She looks older and more at peace. We hear morning sounds of birds. ELDER TE ATA appears as if through the sky, carrying TE ATA's new buckskin and moccasins. ELDER TE ATA lays the buckskin on the canoe and helps braid TE ATA's hair. TE ATA is aware of a "presence" but is not afraid. MISS DAVIS appears as if to check on TE ATA. Drum fades as we hear the opening bar of "Feather Gone in Wind.")

(19. Song: "Feather Gone in Wind")

MISS DAVIS:

 Feathers do not last forever
 Eventually, they fall away
 Gone in the wind
 And time blows forward
 A different life, a different day

(TE ATA works on braiding her hair alone, deep in thought, as LOON PEOPLE help TE ATA into her buckskin and sing chorus parts. New buckskin is completely beaded on the bodice with turquoise. TE ATA lets her old clothes fall away as in a ritual.)

 Some like you are chosen
 To tell the story of the song
 It's no burden,

Regret not your choice
Though your heart may long

For feathers do not last forever
Eventually, they fall away
Gone in the wind
And time blows forward
A different life, a different day

Hindsight will keep you singing
Melodies for tomorrow's child
Wisdom whistles
In the words and rhymes

And a feather's made
Feathers do not last forever
Eventually they fall away
Gone in the wind
Time blows forward
A different life, a different day.

(*Music fades away, replaced with drum, faintly. TE ATA emerges as the LOON PEOPLE disappear, taking away TE ATA'S old clothes. MISS DAVIS exits through the sky.*)

ELDER TE ATA: They will be here soon.

(*TE ATA nods her head yes but says nothing, smiles, and exits. ELDER TE ATA remains. We hear drum for a few more seconds, then it fades away.*)

SCENE 10

We immediately hear a collage of children's voices (prerecorded). DR. FISHER enters, carrying a large telescope and a notebook, in which he is writing. He stands opposite of ELDER TE ATA. He wears a suit.

DR. FISHER: Dearest Indian Poet. It is the 18th Sun of the Leaf Falling Moon, 1946. I'm here at the . . .

ELDER TE ATA: (*Picking up the line*) American Museum of Natural History. Central Park West at 79th Street. Department of Astronomy, Hayden Planetarium. Curator and CHIEF!

(*TE ATA enters opposite side of DR. FISHER, carrying writing notebook. She pulls canoe over to her side. She sits on canoe and writes.*)

TE ATA: 21st Sun of the Leaf Falling Moon, 1946, Clyde Dear, I'm here at . . .

ELDER TE ATA: *(Picking up the line)* Commissioners of the Palisades Interstate Park, Bear Mountain Inn, Iona Island, New York.

TE ATA AND DR. FISHER: I'm awaiting the children.

*(The collage sound segues into the live sound of children as they enter. The chil-
dren enter from both sides. On TE ATA's side, enter MARGARET, three
FEMALE CHORUS MEMBERS, MISS DAVIS and ATALOA. On DR.
FISHER'S side, enter KURUKS and the THREE MALE CHORUS MEMBERS.
ELDER TE ATA crosses to DR. FISHER's side. The female side carries TE
ATA's necessary props, including: hand drum, rattle, cradle board, and Indian
blanket. The male side carries an easel, a pointer, and a small stool. They enter
"paradelike" as if on a field trip, ad-libbing lines. The girls are from a campfire
group in the Bronx; the boys are from a Catholic Church school in Manhattan.
ELDER TE ATA plays the boys' teacher.*

*TE ATA and DR. FISHER take a breath, and for a brief moment their eyes
look in the direction of each other's performance area. They smile, take another
breath, turn away from each other, and cross to their respective lecture areas.*

TE ATA is outside at dusk, at a camp retreat.

DR. FISHER is inside the planetarium.

*Children on both sides sit on floor in anticipation. We should see a few stars
just beginning to show on TE ATA's side. As TE ATA and DR. FISHER begin
their presentations the lights should dim onstage a bit and a subtle spotlight
should appear on both of them.)*

*(20. Music: "Coming Together" Indian flute and violin duet by MARGARET
and KURUKS)*

*(We hear the instrumental music "Coming Together" on flute and violin played
by MARGARET and KURUKS. Music underscores the whole scene. Entire
scene is done in mime. It should look like a duet dance, as TE ATA and DR.
FISHER tell the children about the moon, and Indians, and explain their various props. At times their gestures are exactly the same, other times in complete
opposition. Both are animated and reverent at same time. Action is listed where
dialogue would normally be.)*

DR. FISHER: *Introduces himself as the curator of the planetarium, gestures to
the area.*

TE ATA: *Introduces herself as a Chickasaw Indian princess and signs a greet-
ing of welcome.*

DR. FISHER: *With a gesture the lights turn off as the planetarium stars appear
on the Sky Cyc, he points to a particular constellation.*

TE ATA: *She points to the heavens, as if to say that "Indians have believed in
many legends as the universe has developed." She then points to the setting*

sun, and the Sky Cyc on her side begins to merge with the planetarium stars until everyone is under one big sky. She then points to the moon and mimes how it is round and how so many things are round, the tepee, the drum, etc.

DR. FISHER: *At the same time he points to the moon, and their gestures and facial expressions should be very similar. He then demonstrates the telescope and shows how it is used and what one can see with it.*

TE ATA: *She then instructs all the girls to lie down and stare up at the sky to see what they might imagine, as did the Indians. They do so and then she picks up cradle board and explains how it is used, etc.*

DR. FISHER: *He then shows how a meteorite can fall to the sky and he passes around several small chunks of a meteorite. He then demonstrates how a meteor shower might look to Indians of long ago, like falling stars.*

TE ATA: *She explains that when we look at the stars twinkling, that it could be babies' eyes twinkling back from faraway planets; or maybe the twinkling stars are campfires up in the heavens like we have here now. She then gets the drum and teaches how important it is to Indian people, the sound it makes, the unending circle, etc., and then she teaches one child to play it.*

(Music: Drums)

(Once the child has started to play the drum, we hear all over the stage the sound of beating drums.)

DR. FISHER: *The various constellations appear, as he points to them, and we begin to see the stars take on physical shapes, The Gemini Twins, the tail of the Scorpion, the head of Leo, the sword of Orion, etc.*

(The physical shapes of the star patterns appear all over the stage and engulf the stage with "star characters." Both sets of children are now seeing the same thing. TE ATA begins to dance, by herself, making a huge circle. As she does so, we see overlaid onto the star characters, suggestive images of powwow dancers dancing under the stars, so that we have three layers—the star patterns, the powwow dancers, and TE ATA. It is the dance of the universe, "Coming Together."

TE ATA makes a complete circle, and when she reaches the starting spot the drums stop and music is complete. The lights remain as if all were sitting outside in late evening. All star patterns are gone and we see, simply, the light of the moon and the twinkling stars as both TE ATA and DR. FISHER finish aloud. We hear sounds of the night—crickets, frogs, etc., which grow louder as the children leave.)

TE ATA: Ho! I have said it.

DR. FISHER: I believe . . . I believe our time is up. Thank you. You have been a most attentive audience.

(Both TE ATA and DR. FISHER take small bows and the children applaud. Groups on both sides rise and form a line to shake hands with their host as they exit. The next exchanges are simultaneous.)

CHILD (ATALOA): I liked the part about the cradle board, uh, "Ullosi Afohka."

TE ATA: Thank-you, dear, teach your friends those new words.

CHILD (MALE CHORUS MEMBER): Can you see heaven through that telescope?

DR. FISHER: No, son, not quite that far.

CHILD (MISS DAVIS): At school we have a bulletin board with Indians on it.

TE ATA: Do you now?

CHILD (MALE CHORUS MEMBER 2): Do you open the ceiling so that we can see the stars?

DR. FISHER: It seemed that way didn't it, Neil?

CHILD (FEMALE CHORUS MEMBER): Are there really oil wells in Oklahoma?

TE ATA: Oh, yes, you will have to come there and visit one day.

CHILD (MALE CHORUS MEMBER 3): I guess this was worth fifteen cents.

DR. FISHER: I'm delighted you feel your money was well spent, Christopher.

FEMALE CHORUS MEMBER 2: Thank-you very much. It was an honor to meet a real Indian princess.

TE ATA: It was an honor to meet a real campfire girl.

CHILD (KURUKS): Thank-you, sir, I'm going to do my report on eclipses.

DR. FISHER: Excellent choice. There are postcards of some in the lobby; be sure to take a few.

CHILD (FEMALE CHORUS MEMBER): *(She uses Indian sign language to say)* "I Love You"

TE ATA: *(uses Indian sign language to say)* "I love you."

ELDER TE ATA: Thank-you, Dr. Fisher. I am sure we will have a lively discussion in the classroom tomorrow, especially about a man on the moon. Goodness, I had to laugh at that one.

DR. FISHER: Please come again! And you'll have to forgive me for that man on the moon speculation; just a scientist's idealistic view of the possibilities of the future.

(Two girls carry off the canoe while others carry the other props. The boys carry DR. FISHER's things except for a stool.

ALL exit except for TE ATA and DR. FISHER. She crosses, sits, takes off moccasins, rubs her feet, takes off headband, looks out at the stars. It has grown dark, but the moon and the stars provide special light. Night sounds grow louder. DR. FISHER carries the stool opposite of TE ATA. He sits as if looking at his stars in the planetarium. TE ATA pulls a folded letter from her moccasin, while DR. FISHER, takes a small red book out of his jacket pocket and also unfolds a letter. We hear their letters almost echo each other's, so that the words in bold are almost said at same time. At times they talk at the same time, as noted by the two columns. It should have the feel of a spoken aria.)

TE ATA: "Clyde, dear—Just completed my program for the evening. I do so love these outdoor presentations, but this **Injun** is way past tired.

DR. FISHER: "Dearest **Indian** Poet, once again I find myself alone under my stars. I trust your presentation went well for the girls. I had a few very bright fellows from the Catholic school this evening. Since I seemed to be able to control the universe, **One** boy asked if I was God.

TE ATA: **One** young thing asked if I owned my own tepee.

DR. FISHER: **An older** boy, Neil, I believe he said,

TE ATA: **An older** girl, Sandra, I believe she said,

DR. FISHER: Told me that he wanted to be the first man to walk on the moon.

TE ATA: Told me that she wanted to be the first woman supreme court judge.

DR. FISHER	TE ATA
I chuckled, but secretly wished him well.	I smiled encouragingly, but wondered what her chances of attaining that dream would be.

DR. FISHER: Are you behaving yourself, Mrs. Mato-Koki-Papi?

DR. FISHER	TE ATA
Haven't had a talking leaf in several days and this paleface is wondering if his dawn girl has forgotten him.	**Haven't** had a talking leaf in several days and this Injun is wondering if white man has forgotten her.

TE ATA: How is the **moon** book coming?

DR. FISHER: **The moon book** is very near completion. Doubleday-Doran seem pleased.

TE ATA: And did you receive and **place** in the bank my check for $600.00?

DR. FISHER: I **placed** in the bank your check of $600.00.

TE ATA: I've been sending checks to pay debts and I had visions of being sued or jailed or something—I'd hate to have you come to prison to **see** me.

DR. FISHER: And when shall I **see** you, gorgeous one? I wonder if we should try harder to engage our programs closer together in the same cities. Do you imagine that could be **possible?**

TE ATA: Are you being a good boy or at least as good as **possible?** Do you button up your overcoat and leave it buttoned till you get there and put on your rubbers when it rains, and brush your collar and wear your house slippers and your robe? I worry about you, a little more lately. Are the **elevators** and buses still on strike?

DR. FISHER: **The elevators** and buses are still on strike so I am getting quite a physical workout.

TE ATA: I must seal this talking leaf and give it to the wind to send to you. You must know, dearest, that I realize what a generous man I walk the trail with; at least we walk it together occasionally. I'll be back in our tepee soon. And no more smokin' a pipe, unless it is a peace pipe. I am dear Mato, your most mischief Indian, counting the suns until my hand is in yours. **And at this moment,** counting the stars, on the clear fall night . . .

DR. FISHER: **And at this moment,** counting the stars . . . and wishing for one tall, slender Indian . . .

(There is a gust of wind. We hear for a few seconds the music box of years ago. TE ATA rises, mystified. DR. FISHER, as if he had been called by someone, walks directly to TE ATA and waits for her to turn around. The wind sounds create a surreal world. She turns and faces him.)

TE ATA: I was thinking of you, so I must be dreaming? How did you get here?

DR. FISHER: The wind. Because time, well, listen . . .

(Suddenly all the sounds have halted and there is complete and utter silence.)

I had to stop time, just for a moment, so I could simply say, I love you, most tenderly, and wish to kiss my Indian under these stars and to dance with her while time stands still and the wind holds its breath.

(He takes her in his arms, kisses her passionately.)

Dance with me?

TE ATA: There is no music.

DR. FISHER: *(Still holding her)* Shut your eyes and think of all the sounds that we have shared in our years together. Think of the sounds of our life, that made it so interesting, so curious, and yes, at times lonely.

(21. Song and Dance: "Clyde's Love Song")

DR. FISHER: *(Begins the dance slowly as he speaks this monologue)* Remember the curious language of the Incan people; the foghorn of the ship as we went hunting for eclipses of the sun; the Canadian Blood tribe's song at the Sun Dance; the purr of Frances Davis's voice reading *Wind in the Willows;* the street sounds of New York; the radio announcer's deep-throated reporting of the war; the funny voice of Fanny Brice; even the sound of the apartment door opening and the chain lock lightly tapping the frame, as one of us hurried home to the other. Think of these and you will hear our music.

(As they begin to dance, the six CHORUS Members enter, men dressed in glorious white tuxedos, women in sparkling, silvery gowns. The CHORUS dances around DR. FISHER and TE ATA.)[8]

DR. FISHER:

>Come dance with me for all eternity
>The stars have invited us
>They shine for you and me.

>I've missed you so
>The empty chair, the unread book
>The fond look, from those brown eyes.

>Come dance with me for all eternity
>Star-stepping across the sky
>Our love for all to see.

DR. FISHER AND CHORUS:

>Come dance with me for all eternity
>The stars have invited us
>They shine for you and me

DR. FISHER:

>My hand in yours
>The words unsaid, the warmth of you
>I never knew, more love than this.

ELDER TE ATA enters through sky and replaces TE ATA. TE ATA exits. DR. FISHER dances last part of dance with ELDER TE ATA.

DR. FISHER AND CHORUS:

Come dance with me for all eternity
Dark haired lady of my dreams
This night sky, you and me.

(CHORUS Members exit. As the song ends DR. FISHER steps away from ELDER TE ATA, holding her hands with their arms extended. She touches his face. At that moment he disappears through the sky and is replaced by TE ATA. Stars have faded away, and we see blue sky and clouds. TE ATA's hand is now touching ELDER TE ATA's face.)

SCENE 11

TE ATA: *(Touching ELDER TE ATA's face and then her own)* I've grown old . . .
     I've grown old, haven't I?
ELDER TE ATA: Do you feel old?
TE ATA: No.
ELDER TE ATA: Then you have not grown old, not just yet. Do you know what old is?

TE ATA: I . . . uh . . . no.

ELDER TE ATA: Then you must learn that first. Age is not found in one's face; it is found in one's heart and in one's footprints.

(*Music: Drums*)

(*A drum begins to beat. Areas where MISS DAVIS's classroom was, the New York apartment, the stump, and the tree are dimly lit, but should look like a memory.*)

ELDER TE ATA: Can you hear the drum?

(*TE ATA nods her head yes.*)

Then you must now follow the beat of your heart and walk the memories of your life. I'll be near, but you should also take a friend. Margaret is waiting for you just beyond that tallest of trees. Winter is coming. Find some warmth to sustain you until spring.

(*TE ATA exits upright. ELDER TE ATA crosses slowly DSC. There is a feeling of cold and doom in the air.*)

ELDER TE ATA: (*To the audience*) Dr. Fisher passed on in January of 1949. I do not speak of it much. It is private. I had my work to do. And Mother and Miss Davis are now gone away. Still, I have my work to do. To tell the children about the Indians. To explain to them what legends are and what a heritage is and how to preserve their cultures. I did not preach to them. I told them stories. I acted many, many parts and over the years I learned many words; words that seemed like music when I spoke them from my heart.

(*She looks around her.*)

But now the weather warrior—Tush ka ko cha—is coming. And the time of me is very near.

(*ELDER TE ATA turns and walks directly UC and watches next scene. MAR-GARET and TE ATA enter arm in arm. TE ATA now has on the same clothing as ELDER TE ATA, the Dakota skirt, etc., but TE ATA is still "young." MAR-GARET has aged, but she, too, is still "young." As they enter we hear a violin, playing "Margaret's Song" (prerecorded). With each change in the music, TE ATA grows older.*)

(*22. Music: Violin Solo, prerecorded—"Margaret's Song"*)

(*MARGARET and TE ATA walk toward the tree. The area around tree takes on a different light. They eventually walk a complete circle, clockwise. As TE ATA walks the circle with MARGARET, she slowly transforms into ELDER TE ATA. ELDER TE ATA remains, watching her life pass before her. When TE ATA speaks the Chickasaw words ELDER TE ATA says them with her. When TE ATA begins to drift in and out of reality, those lines are also said by ELDER TE ATA.)*[9]

TE ATA: I am not pigeon-toed. How can you say that after all these years? You've never said anything to me about being pigeon-toed.

MARGARET: *(Laughing)* What was there to tell you? You are blessed with all kinds of beauty, Te Ata, but it stops at about your ankles.

TE ATA: *(Laughing)* Well, then it is a good thing I wore my moccasins during performance then, isn't it?

MARGARET: Yep!

TE ATA: *(Turning her nose in the air and posing)* Well, Margaret Malowney Ball, I won't soon forget you pointing out my faults, especially now, when I am too old to do anything about them.

MARGARET: You will never be old Te Ata, you're too naive!

TE ATA: There you go again!

MARGARET: You never did take teasing well, my friend, and that makes it twice as much fun. *(Pause)* I'm glad that you chose me, to take this walk with you; lifelong friends is quite special.

TE ATA—ELDER TE ATA: *(only bold and italics) (Looking at the tree)* Yes . . . Father told me when I was very, very young that I must choose my friends wisely. **Aki** . . . Father was simple in his ways, but he had complex thoughts *. . . I dreamed of flying long before I knew of airplanes . . . flying hoe . . .* From my father I got my pride and my strong awareness of the oneness of things.

(Violin music changes to another level. TE ATA's walk, speech change, reflecting her aging.)

MARGARET: Come, let's walk on. I remember how you used to hide out alone at Loon Island. Lived on blueberries the whole day. My Johnny laughed so, at your blue mouth.

(As they cross to the stump, light changes in that area. TE ATA sits.)

TE ATA—ELDER TE ATA *(only bold and italics)*: When I think of simple things I think of my mother . . . I remember . . . *I dreamed I came home to mother . . . to an underground room where I lay on the ground . . .* My mother had among her treasures a small card showing a picture of a little angel with long yellow curls. They made me impatient with my long, straight, black braids. Mother couldn't manage yellow curls for me, but she saw a little white girl wearing a sunbonnet and she said, "If you wear that sunbonnet, you may get yellow curls." I wore that sunbonnet day in and day out. It was a mother's gift, **ishki . . . tombi** . . . She was the grand nurturer; like soft rain.

MARGARET: *(Crossing behind TE ATA and picking up her braids)* Your mother was right. You can now have yellow curls, just like you keep these braids black.

TE ATA: *(A bit uncomfortable but also a bit amused)* Margaret, please don't tell anyone I dye my hair. It's just that old man winter keeps sneaking in and throwing snow on it.

MARGARET: Te Ata Fisher, you are vain, that's all there is to it!

TE ATA: *(Wishing to change the subject)* We should walk on.

(The music changes. They walk from the stump to the area where the New York apartment was. The sky slowly clears. We see glimpses of the sun. TE ATA continues to age with each change in music.)

TE ATA: C.F. and I took so many walks . . .

MARGARET: *(As they walk)* How long were you and C.F. married?

TE ATA: Sixteen years. Why do you ask?

MARGARET: Seems like yesterday. Remember how taken Clyde was of the technicolor films? Remember, *The Three Little Pigs* at . . .

MARGARET AND TE ATA: at the Roxy!

TE ATA—ELDER TE ATA *(only bold and italics)*: Yes, and he insisted that we purchase tickets for the Irish Sweepstakes! I teased him . . . a superstitious scientist. We teased . . . , especially in letters. Talking leafs we called them . . . **Hatak hilitopah** . . . *It was hard to be intimate . . . I crossed the great abyss . . .* He taught me that the world was much larger than . . . I could . . . ever . . . imagine. C.F. would say a person understands himself only when he understands others first.

(The music shifts to another level. More sun is seen. TE ATA is caught between youth and age.)

MARGARET: I miss them. The older I get the more I miss those we have lost.

(They cross to area where MISS DAVIS's classroom was. Lights change in this area.)

TE ATA: *(They are now facing the area that was MISS DAVIS's classroom.)* Yes, my memories . . . I don't remember in order, do you?

MARGARET: *(Laughing in recognition)* Kinda like my music these days, sometimes I can play Debussy but other times all I can recall is the harmony to "Happy Birthday."

TE ATA—ELDER TE ATA (*only bold and italics*): Oh, Margaret, you can't forget . . . those "Happy Birthday" serenades . . . the canoe . . . Loon Island . . . Those . . . best times . . . **A yuk pa** . . . Miss Davis . . .

MARGARET: There will never be another one like Frances Davis.

TE ATA—ELDER TE ATA (*only italics*): I would have never been successful without her . . . I loved her . . . *feathers do not last forever* . . .

MARGARET: I loved her too. My favorite memory of her was when we sat around a fire reading a book out loud. I could see the actress in her and I could see how proud she was of you.

(*The music shifts one last time. They cross from the classroom area back to the tree and then to USC. There should be no difference now between TE ATA and ELDER TE ATA in terms of voice and physicality. ELDER TE ATA exits.*)

TE ATA: My . . . goodness, we're back to where we started . . . It feels warmer . . . It will be spring soon . . . I can feel it in my bones.

MARGARET: I'll say good-bye then, Mary Te Ata Thompson Fisher, my friend in life. I'll see you in the spring.

(*MARGARET embraces TE ATA, steps back from her and smiles. The violin music fades away. We hear drums then music. Lights shift.*)

SCENE 12

Music: Drums

MARGARET exits as if through the sky. ELDER TE ATA remains, watching. Two FEMALE CHORUS MEMBERS enter from one side, each wearing a fringed shawl. ATALOA and the other FEMALE CHORUS MEMBER enter from other side, each wearing a fringed shawl. The MALE CHORUS MEMBERS and KURUKS enter and stand in place. They all wear blankets.

(*22. Music: "The Dance of Youth and Age"*)

They watch the dance. The two female couples dance the "Dance of Youth and Age," which is to suggest one has grown old. It is a stylized version of a shawl dance. When dance is finished we hear beat of a lone drum, which sounds like a heartbeat. Dancers remain.

Music: Drumbeat

ELDER TE ATA: (*She breaths heavily and pauses often, clearly showing her age.*) I do not wish to have small thoughts behind big words . . . One day I was young and the next day I grew old . . . I am old now . . . All my people have left me . . . I am tired. My dreams are confusing. I wish to be on the last trail for I can no longer see with insight. I can no longer hear with understanding . . . The sounds I hear now are of long ago. I hear the weeping of the Choctaw women on the Trail of Tears; I hear the loon mother wailing for her mate; I hear the cry of the hunted doe. My maker is calling for me.

(ELDER TE ATA turns with her back to audience, facing upstage. MISS DAVIS and DR. FISHER enter from opposite sides, she wearing a shawl and he a blanket. They cross to USC as they lead in the song. MISS DAVIS carries a white shawl.)

(23. Song: "Gone Away People")

FULL CAST:
> Gone away people
> Lullaby sleep
> Gone away people
> Your soul to keep

> Grandmother, baby
> Reborn in this land
> Come take my hand,
> Come take my hand.

> Those of us before you
> Hear the song of life's silence
> For we are the hands across history
> Joining today and tomorrow

> And we will walk with you,
> Across the dawn
> Where we can wear colors
> And taste the morning sun

> Your soul has no shadow now
> Your heartbeat joins the drum
> And you breath in the rhythm
> Of those who've already come

> So walk forward Indian lady
> Reborn in this land

(MISS DAVIS and DR. FISHER walk together to ELDER TE ATA, place white shawl around her, and go back to their places. Entire cast extend their arms toward ELDER TE ATA, as she walks toward them and turns.)

Come take my hand,
Come take my hand.

Gone away people
Lullaby sleep
Gone away people
Your soul to keep

(Song begins to fade here and we hear refrain sung in Chickasaw.)

Gone away people
Hattak ahliha ayat tok

Lullaby sleep
Talowa cha nosi

Gone away people
Hattak ahliha ayat tok

Your soul to keep
Chi shilombish at ishisashki

Grandmother, baby
Aposhi, chipota iskannosi

Reborn in this land
Yakni yappa ala tok

Come take my hand,
Minti cha salbak ishi

Come take my hand.
Minti cha salbak ishi

(We see the sun just rising over the horizon. The cast should divide and stand on either side of the stage so that the sun can take precedence in the center. TE ATA enters through the sky, dressed in her buckskin, and assumes the pose that appears on her publicity brochure, arms extended to the heavens. Lights fade to black. We hear the Chickasaw refrain of "Gone Away People" during curtain call.)

THE END

Dedication

Helen Te Ata Cole and Linda Kay Harris

Helen and Linda, members of Te Ata's family, embody the same lovely spirit and goodness as did Te Ata. With their kindness and support they enabled me to examine Te Ata's private archives and to complete my research. Their joy in sharing their memories of Te Ata's life touches me deeply. They welcomed me into their family as one of their own, so it is with a profound sense of dedication and love that I pay tribute to my two spirit sisters. I know that Helen watches from above and Linda remains to celebrate the realization of seeing Te Ata's story come to life onstage, in hopes that one day many, many people will know the story of their Aunt Te Ata.

Acknowledgments

I wish to humbly thank the following for their financial support early in the development of the play: the University of Science and Arts of Oklahoma (Te Ata's alma mater), including Dr. Roy Troutt, Dr. John Feaver, Dr. Ann Frankland, and especially Professor Roger Drummond. Friends and family members also contributed financially, including: Hiawatha Estes, Helen Te Ata Cole, Ralph and Linda Harris, Keith Thomas, John R. McKee, Ann B. Rose, and Christy Stanlake.

For the realization of the 2006 world premier production, I wish to additionally thank the Chickasaw Nation, including Governor Bill Anoatubby, and Lona Barrick and her division, People in the Arts and Humanities; the Honorable Tom Cole, member of Congress; the many students who participated in the early workshop productions of the play, and the well-wishers who attended those early workshops as we continued to develop and refine the piece and make it ready for a full production worthy of Te Ata's story.

Notes

1. In the world premier of the play we used a selection from "Intonations," by Alex Smith and Cheevers Toppah, with the permission of Canyon Records and for a small fee.

2. Both flute solos can be original selections from the Native flute player's repertoire, chosen to set the mood in the beginning and to softly underscore the monologue at the end.

3. Flute solo chosen from the Native flute player's repertoire to set the mood for the opening of Act Two.

4. Chorus members are dressed as various workers from New York—waitress, telegram boy, butcher, and so. They do *not* need to carry any props, as these are the sights and sounds Te Ata remembers of the city.

5. We used the clash of two garbage can lids, which was quite effective. The most important thing is that it be immediate and loud and earth shattering.

6. Native flute solo chosen from Native flute player's repertoire—should be soft and haunting.

7. Native flute solo chosen from Native flute player's repertoire to set the mood for Act Two.

8. If there are strong dancers, all chorus members should dance and sing. If not, they can be placed around stage as if waiting their turn to dance and one couple can dance the entire stage while Dr. Fisher and Te Ata dance in center.

9. There are three levels of reality here, and actors and director should explore how best to portray the three.

Winnetou's Snake Oil Show from Wigwam City

SPIDERWOMAN THEATER

Produced by Spiderwoman Theater (Lisa Mayo, Gloria Miguel, and Muriel Miguel, with Hortensia Colorado).

Cast/Characters

HORTENSIA COLORADO / Wild-Eyed Sam, Witch #1, Mother Moon Face, Demon #2, Hordes #1, Hortensia

Wild-Eyed Sam is a true American. I was inspired by Gabby Hayes, cantankerous, know-it-all, a racist who appears to be a funny old man. He would burn the woods and not think twice about it. Spits over all creation, kills four-legged creatures, fish and winged animals for sport. Knows more than any foreigner that comes to these shores. Tolerates Indians and makes sure they keep their place.

Witch #1 evolves from Wild-Eyed Sam, the dark side becomes the flamboyant. With her power, she will put in motion history in its most ridiculous vein.

Mother Moon Face prances out of the Witch. She was given her name by Grandfather in a workshop. She was inspired to become a horsewoman when, as a child, she put a nickel in the gyrating horse in front of the Kmart. She wants to be loved by men and women. She's nearsighted. The Wild West Show is her life.

Hordes #1 evolves from Mother Moon Face as all the stereotypes there ever were of Indians. So steeped in stereotypes is she that she goes off into impersonations of various stereotypical Indians. Like worms in your skin.

Hortensia comes out of the hordes of Indians, out of being put down by her own family and other Indians. Reclaiming her ancestors, her blood, she stands in her circle—a woman of power celebrating her ancestors and looking to the future in an ongoing struggle.

LISA MAYO / Gunther, Witch #2, Princess Pissy Willow, Demon #3, Lisa Mayo

Princess Pissy Willow, a sharpshooter in the Wild West Show. In the Plastic Pow-Wow Workshop, I reveal myself as a plastic shaman, willing to sell shamanistic secrets to people for a fee.

Demon #3 is a dung beetle who is a facet of who Lisa Mayo is: a voracious eater, one who gorges himself.

Witch #2 is one of the three witches who create the Winnetou Snake Oil.

Gunther is a German tutor who becomes a brave man of the West.

At certain moments, during the serious times of the play, I am Lisa Mayo, Kuna/Rappahannock.

GLORIA MIGUEL / Bear, Klekepetra, Witch #3, Minnie Hall Runner,
   Demon #1, Hordes #2, Gloria

Bear is a happy bear. He represents the last vestiges of life that the greedy
   white person was killing, the killing of the last animal. It isn't enough just to
   kill him and be over with it; it is overkill that is used, as was used on this
   country.

Klekepetra is an elder and Winnetou's dumb sidekick.

Witch #3 is an evil character who mixes potions.

Minnie Hall Runner is a copy of an Indian princess who does nice sweet things,
   but she's all show business.

Demon #1 is not only the dark side that is a part of us all; it also represents the
   spirituality within Native tradition that our people believe in.

The Hordes are Indians in the forest.

As Gloria, I voice my political feelings toward plastic shamans and people who
   want to steal spirituality for their own gain. This is my reaction to spirituality being stolen, how we've grown from being Indian princesses to political
   awareness using our deep spiritual commitment.

MURIEL MIGUEL / Winnetou, Ethel Christian Christiansen, Muriel

Winnetou is a noble savage as seen from an outsider's viewpoint. He is a noble
   savage of the forest, plains, or anywhere in North America. He is smarter,
   faster, stronger than anyone. Winnetou is willing to befriend Gunther and
   teach him everything he knows. Winnetou is then surprised when Gunther
   thinks he knows more and is better than Winnetou and then leaves Winnetou to die.

Ethel Christian Christiansen is the golden darling. She is a mixture of Ethel
   Kennedy and Lynn Andrews. She thinks she can see the future but makes
   sure she leaves nothing to chance in the present. Underneath her shyness
   and gold lamé lies a heart of steel.

Muriel. I think at the age of nine I was politicized. Social studies in school
   insisted that we were a dying culture and that there were very few Indians
   alive. I could not comprehend how a teacher, who was supposed to know,
   could tell such lies. I would look around at the faces of my family and my
   family's friends and knew we were not dying.

Author's Note

Winnetou's Snake Oil Show is the result, the culmination, of all these feelings
over all these years, the feelings of our culture being taken away from us. Years

ago, "hobbyists" (non-Indian people who take up native cultures as a hobby) were content to don the outward manifestations of our culture (clothes, jewelry, dancing, etc.). They didn't give a damn about what was really happening inside of us. We had something to hold onto for the time being. As years went on, though, they started to become interested in the spiritual part of us. They suddenly knew more about Indians than the Indian people themselves. The question, as a result, becomes, for me, how do I approach this stealing of spirituality? Do I confront each incident of theft or do I ignore it, let it slide and then feel like I am a sellout?

Setting

There is no set of which to speak, except for Spiderwoman's signature backdrop made of many different pieces of cloth to form a hodgepodge patchwork quilt and a projection screen made of old sheets. The stage is bare. All props that are used are brought on by the cast.

The film footage used in the play was shot by the Miguel sisters' Uncle Joe and consists of "home movies" of old powwows dating from the early 1940s into the 1970s. The more recent footage was filmed in the 1980s by Bob Rosen in the same style as Uncle Joe. The idea is to juxtapose the real powwow imagery against the Snake Oil Show.

As the house lights go out, the theme to the Magnificent Seven *begins. The movie then comes on. Lights up on WILD-EYED SAM. As he begins to speak, the music goes out.*

WILD-EYED SAM: First time out West? Hey! I say, first time out West? Gunther, come on!

(The movie goes out, full stage light bumps up, Gunther *enters.)*

I'm going to show you how we hunt out West.

GUNTHER: *(In a German accent)* Yah, Wild-Eyed Sam, I am willing to learn. I will follow you.

(GUNTHER mimics WILD-EYED SAM as he walks around the stage.)

WILD-EYED SAM: Did you tether your horse? Horses have been known to run away on such an occasion.

GUNTHER: What occasion? . . . BEARS!!!!

WILD-EYED SAM: Are you scared? Hey, hey, sometimes the bears out here are nine feet tall, weigh as much as a thousand pounds or more.

GUNTHER: Yah?

WILD-EYED SAM: Makes the ground shake when they walk. Teeth are this long.

GUNTHER: Yah?

WILD-EYED SAM: There are rules to follow. Do you have a knife and a rifle?

GUNTHER: I have one knife, two revolvers and your hammer.

WILD-EYED SAM: Good. Don't use them 'til I tell you. Follow me.

(They walk another circuit of the stage.)

GUNTHER: Are there any Indians around here?

WILD-EYED SAM: If there was, you'd smell them.

(We hear a bear roar. The BEAR enters. It attacks WILD-EYED SAM. GUN-THER shoots the BEAR. It releases WILD-EYED SAM and stalks GUNTHER. GUNTHER shoots the BEAR, hits the BEAR with a hammer, then stabs it. The BEAR dies in an elaborate death scene.)

WILD-EYED SAM: The Bear is dead, thanks to my quick thinking and agility. You foolish greenhorn, you broke my hatchet!

GUNTHER: What! I saved your life! I killed that Bear with a hit on the head, a shot in the eye, a stab in the chest.

WILD-EYED SAM: That ain't true! Are you gonna stand there flat-footed with your bare face hanging out and tell me that you killed that there Bear?

GUNTHER: It is an indisputable fact that I killed that Bear with a hit on the head, a shot in the eye, a stab in the chest.

(WILD-EYED SAM and GUNTHER fight. As the fight is happening, the BEAR is quietly crawling off, leaving the costume in the center of the stage. The fight continues. KLEKEPETRA enters.)

KLEKEPETRA: Stop! Have you gone mad, gents? What reason could there be for white people breaking each others' necks?

WILD-EYED SAM: Klekepetra! Ugly. . . . UGLY! Did a horse walk on your face?

KLEKEPETRA: Well you can't judge a frog by its croak. *(Spots the BEAR)* Oh, oh, there's that fellow we've been after. He is dead. What a shame. *(He yells offstage)* EYAH! EYAH! EYAH!

WINNETOU: *(From offstage)* UFF! UFF!

KLEKEPETRA: EYAH! EYAH!

WINNETOU: UFF!

KLEKEPETRA: *(Screaming)* EEEEYAHHHHHHHHHH!

WINNETOU: UFF!

(WINNETOU *enters. The following sequence is sung in an operatic style.)*

KLEKEPETRA: Winnetou!

WINNETOU: I am Winnetou, a grizzly bear. Boom,boom,boom,boom. This

Bear has been hit on the head, shot in the eye, stabbed in the chest. Who did this deed?

GUNTHER: I did.

WINNETOU: He killed the grizzly bear with a hit on the head, shot in the eye, stab in the chest. I shall call him Old Shatterhand.

ALL: Shatterhand . . . Shatterhand . . . Shatterhand.

WINNETOU: He shall become my blood brother.

GUNTHER: Blood brother.

(We return to a normal manner of speaking.)

KLEKEPETRA: Let the ceremony begin. First we will smoke our peace pipe, then we will cut our wrists and become blood brothers.

(They do a choreographed, ceremonial dance, which quickly disintegrates into confusion.)

GUNTHER: Hough, hey, hey, hey. Hough, hey, hey, hey. Hough, hey, hey, hey.

KLEKEPETRA: Her?

WILD-EYED SAM: Who?

WINNETOU: Him.

GUNTHER: Me.

(Lights fade to center special, demon light. All exit except WILD-EYED SAM. He crosses to garbage can, which is offstage right, and drags it to center stage. He then does an interpretive dance in the style of Martha Graham while turning into the WITCH.)

WITCH #1: What shall this concoction be? Pure white cat, daughter of a pure white mother. Porcupine piss, boiled 'til the hair falls off. Velvet antlers of a well-hung moose. Find the left hind leg and suck the marrow out. Bull turd.

(WITCH #2 and WITCH #3 enter.)

WITCH #2: Bat shit.

WITCH #3: Yum, yum from a bum. Cockeyed sheep eyes.

WITCH #1: Toenails of a lounge lizard.

WITCH #3: Vomit sauce.

WITCH #2: Skunk come.

WITCH #3: Putrid liver from a dead cat.

WITCH #1: What shall this concoction cure?

WITCH #3: Running asshole.

WITCH #1: Constipation.

WITCH #2: Half-breeditus.

WITCH #3: And the name . . .
ALL: YATAHOLAY INDIAN SNAKE OIL.

(Lightening and thunder begin. The movie begins. The cast moves stage right to change HORTENSIA from the WITCH to MOTHER MOON FACE and to put on their jackets. They pick up coconut shells. MOTHER MOON FACE picks up her mop [horse] and rides into the film followed by the rest of the cast playing their coconuts and horses' hoofbeats.)

ALL: *(singing)* Rollin', rollin', rollin'.
Keep them doggies rollin', RAWHIDE!

(They make a spectacular configuration onstage and all gallop off except for PRINCESS PISSY WILLOW. As they leave, the lights bump up to full and the movie goes off and PRINCESS P.W., in a circus ringmaster's voice, announces)

PRINCESS P.W.: Ladies and gentlemen, welcome to the Winnetou Snake Oil Show from Wigwam City. Now, for our Grand Entry, I would like to introduce to you three genuine Indian princesses. Princess Mother Moon Face *(she gallops around in a circle and gallops off)*, Princess Ethel Christian Christiansen *(she does some odd choreography in a circular motion and then goes off)*, Princess Minnie Hall Runner *(she walks around in a circle and then goes off)*, and your mistress of ceremonies tonight, I am Princess Pissy Willow. As your first entertainment, I present a magnificent act, a woman all the way from New Mexico, whose mother was a full-blooded Apache and whose father was German, which is why she likes eating fry bread with her sauerkraut.
ALL: *(offstage)* HA! HA!
PRINCESS P.W.: Not only is she an expert bullwhipper, she is also a famous opera singer. Ladies and gentlemen, I present, Minnie Hall Runner!

(MINNIE H.R. enters with her imaginary whip, singing in an operatic voice.)

MINNIE H.R.: Snap! Crackle! Pop!

(From stage right trot her two assistants.)

PRINCESS P.W.: As her two assistants we have, Mother Moon Face and Ethel Christian Christiansen, ladies and gentlemen.

(ETHEL C.C. and MOTHER M.F. exit stage left and pull on a box with their props in it. For the first trick, they each pull out a tube of rolled-up newspaper about one foot in length, ETHEL C.C. holding it in her right hand, MOTHER M.F. in her left. They face MINNIE H.R.)

PRINCESS P.W.: Each of our Indian princesses is holding a rolled-up tube of newspaper in her hand. Watch, ladies and gentlemen as Princess Minnie Hall Runner snaps the end off each side until the newspaper tubes are both gone.

(MINNIE H.R., facing ETHEL C.C. and MOTHER M.F., snaps each side as they alternatively crunch the tubes into their hands until they disappear. There is applause. MINNIE H.R. bows.)

PRINCESS P.W.: Yes, ladies and gentlemen, wasn't that terrific?

(ETHEL C.C. and MOTHER M.F. next pick up a rolled-up newspaper about two feet in length and hold it between them in their mouths.)

PRINCESS P.W.: Princess Ethel Christian Christiansen and Princess Mother Moon Face are holding a larger tube of the *New York Times* in their mouths. Princess Minnie Hall Runner will cut the tube in half without touching their noses.

(MINNIE H.R., facing them, snaps the tube in half, ETHEL C.C. actually cutting it with a pair of scissors. Applause. MINNIE H.R. bows.)

PRINCESS P.W.: Let's hear it for her, ladies and gentlemen.

(ETHEL C.C. and MOTHER M.F. next hold an open sheet of newspaper between them, holding it at the top corners.)

PRINCESS P.W.: Princess Ethel Christian Christiansen and Princess Mother Moon Face are holding a sheet of the *New York Times* between them. Princess Minnie Hall Runner will snap the sheet in two from behind her back. Watch her now as she takes a bead on her object. Are you ready, Minnie?
MINNIE H.R.: *(singing)* Yes.

(She snaps the whip. ETHEL C.C. and MOTHER M.F. carefully tear the newspaper in half by each pulling at her corner. There is applause and MINNIE H.R. bows.)

PRINCESS P.W.: Isn't she wonderful?

(MOTHER M.F. next blindfolds MINNIE H.R., then goes back to stage left where ETHEL C.C. places a red cowboy hat on MOTHER M.F.'s head.)

PRINCESS P.W.: Now, ladies and gentlemen, a most dangerous trick. As you can see, Mother Moon Face has blindfolded Princess Minnie Hall Runner. Ethel has placed a hat on Mother Moon Face's head. Minnie Hall Runner will knock the hat from Mother Moon Face's head. One false move and she could be decapitated. Watch her now as she feels her space. Are you ready, Minnie?

MINNIE H.R.: Yes

(*MINNIE H.R. snaps the whip. ETHEL C.C. knocks the hat from MOTHER M.F.'s head.*)

PRINCESS P.W.: Ladies and gentlemen, Princess Minnie Hall Runner! Let's give her a big hand.

(*There is incredible applause. MINNIE H.R. removes the blindfold, bows, takes her props offstage and returns. ETHEL C.C. goes out into the audience to pick a contestant for later and PRINCESS P.W. introduces MOTHER M.F.*)

PRINCESS P.W.: We now present to you a magnificent act. All the way from the Ponderosas of Colorado, an equestrian par excellence. She has been around horses most of her life, in fact she was born on a horse. I now present to you, the one, the only, Mother Moon Face!

(*Applause. MOTHER M.F. comes onstage riding her horses [two string mops]. She canters, trying to control the animals. PRINCESS P.W. tries to get her to stop moving.*)

PRINCESS P.W.: I now present to you, two magnificent animals, Silver Turkey and Pinto Bean. These animals are highly educated in mathematics. Pinto Bean, give me the sum of two plus two.
MOTHER M.F.: Two plus two, two plus two.

(*She stamps her left foot, counting. When she reaches four, PRINCESS P.W. starts the applause.*)

PRINCESS P.W.: Yes ladies and gentlemen, what an intelligent animal. Now, Silver Turkey, not to be outdone, I give him the sum of nine divided by three.
MOTHER M.F.: Nine divided by three, nine divided by three.

(*She stamps her right foot, counting. When she reaches three, PRINCESS P.W. starts the applause. They all acknowledge it.*)

PRINCESS P.W.: Amazing, amazing. Now ladies and gentlemen, these animals will play dead.

(*MOTHER M.F. throws the two mops on the floor in front of her.*)

PRINCESS P.W.: Yes, ladies and gentlemen, let's give them a big hand. Now, ladies and gentlemen, for your edification and pleasure, Mother Moon Face will now ride around this ring with two horses, jumping from horse to horse.

(MOTHER M.F. rides around the stage, jumping from mop to mop, to great applause. At this point, ETHEL C.C. has found a contestant and has brought her onstage and is instructing her.)

PRINCESS P.W.: The next trick, the next trick is so difficult that it can only be executed with one horse. Minnie Hall Runner, will you lead one of the horses away?

(MINNIE H.R. leads one of the horses off with some difficulty.)

PRINCESS P.W.: Mother Moon Face will now ride backward on one foot, with her eyes closed with this fluffy in her mouth.

(MOTHER M.F. does this after having had difficulty in keeping the instructions straight. There is thunderous applause. She bows.)

PRINCESS P.W.: Ladies and gentlemen, Mother Moon Face!

(She bows again. Exits with her horse. PRINCESS P.W. then picks up her rifle and moves to stage right.)

ETHEL C.C.: Ladies and gentlemen, Princess Pissy Willow is not only a marvelous mistress of ceremonies, she is also a crack shot. She is known from Brooklyn to Tierra del Fuego.

(ETHEL C.C. asks the contestant her name. PRINCESS P.W. gets ready to shoot. MOTHER M.F. gives the contestant two balloons. She is put into position, holding a balloon in each hand above her head.)

ETHEL C.C.: Princess Pissy Willow will now attempt to shoot the balloons out of (name's) hands.
PRINCESS P.W.: Are you ready, (name)?
NAME: Yes.
PRINCESS P.W.: I am going to shoot the balloon out of your right hand.

(Everyone points to the correct hand.)

PRINCESS P.W.: One, two, three.

(PRINCESS P.W. shoots the balloon in the right hand, it pops. Applause.)

PRINCESS P.W.: Now I am going to shoot the balloon out of your left hand.

(Everyone points to the correct hand.)

PRINCESS P.W.: One, two, three.
PRINCESS P.W.: *(PRINCESS P.W. shoots the balloon in the left hand; it pops. Applause.)*

ETHEL C.C.: Minnie Hall Runner will now rotate Princess Pissy Willow around three times. One, two, three. Now bend her over.

(PRINCESS P.W. is turned around three times. She bends over, the rifle is pointing in the wrong direction. She is turned so that the rifle is pointed in the correct direction. The contestant holds one balloon over her head with both hands.)

ETHEL C.C.: Ladies and gentlemen, Princess Pissy Willow will now attempt to shoot the balloon out of (name's) hands.
PRINCESS P.W.: Are you ready, (name)?
NAME: Yes.
PRINCESS P.W.: One, two, three.

(PRINCESS P.W. shoots the balloon; it pops. Applause. PRINCESS P.W. bows. The contestant is thanked and escorted off the stage by MINNIE H.R.)

PRINCESS P.W.: Thank you, ladies and gentlemen. Last but not least, we have a trick roper. And now we present Princess Ethel Christian Christiansen. She uses a rope so fine it cannot be seen by the naked eye. Watch her, ladies and gentlemen.

(ETHEL C.C. takes the invisible rope and, using it as a lariat, makes a very large circle. She keeps twirling it until it becomes a very tiny circle.)

PRINCESS P.W.: Wonderful, ladies and gentlemen.

(There is applause. ETHEL C.C.'s second trick is to make another very big circle and to insert her very graceful foot into and out of the circle formed by the rope.)

PRINCESS P.W.: Ladies and gentlemen, Walking My Baby Back Home.

(There is applause. ETHEL C.C.'s third trick is to form a very large circle again, a vertical one this time. She jumps back and forth through the circle.)

PRINCESS P.W.: Ladies and gentlemen, isn't she terrific?

(Great applause. ETHEL C.C. goes to get two ropes.)

PRINCESS P.W.: Ladies and gentlemen, she now has two ropes of a finer denier than the first. Watch her now as she begins twirling one, and now the other.

(MOTHER M.F. and MINNIE H.R. are on either side of her. ETHEL C.C. snags each of them with a rope and pulls them toward her at center. Applause. She releases the two princesses.)

PRINCESS P.W.: Now, ladies and gentlemen, this next trick is known as the psychic rope trick. This particular trick has never before been performed in public.

(MINNIE H.R. gets a rope. MOTHER M.F. gets a stool. ETHEL C.C. sits on the stool. She goes into a trance.)

PRINCESS P.W.: Now, we take a rope and tie her up. *(MINNIE H.R. and MOTHER M.F. tie her up.)* Ethel, can you hear me?
ETHEL C.C.: Yes.
PRINCESS P.W.: Do you have a message from the other side?
ETHEL C.C.: Yes . . . I have hemorrhoids.
PRINCESS P.W.: This ties in with our sale of Yataholay Indian Snake Oil. Our snake oil comes in three different varieties. *(MINNIE H.R. demonstrates with her plastic hammer.)* We have a liquid, a salve and tonight, we have the aerosol can. Minnie Hall Runner will now administer this to Ethel Christian Christiansen. *(MINNIE H.R. taps the back of the stool with the hammer.)* Ethel, can you hear me?
ETHEL C.C.: Yes.
PRINCESS P.W.: Do you have a message from the other side?
ETHEL C.C.: Yes.
PRINCESS P.W.: What is it?
ETHEL C.C.: I HAD hemorrhoids. *(She is untied and stands up unsteadily.)* Where am I? Movie, please.

(The lights fade and the movie comes on. DEMON #1 appears stage right.)

DEMON #1: EEEEEEEEEE. *(Two other demons appear center stage with the first demon joining them.)* Sulubevia, Oloindalgina, Matchahapipi. My father believed in demons. Listened to Chief Nele and captured tortoise. At the age of thirteen, his body was covered with blue dye from the Ploi Wala tree. And he slept three nights and three days alone in the rain forest. EEEEEE. He left Naranga on the San Blas Islands and became an able-bodied seaman. EEEEEEEE.
DEMON #2: My father worked the fields, he washed dishes, he swept floors.
DEMON #1: He travelled to Marseilles.

(DEMON #3 exits)

DEMON #2: He paid his way.
DEMON #1: Cologne, Monte Carlo, Paris, New York City. He still believed in demons. To chase away the demons, he gulped down a bottle of whiskey.

DEMON #2: He followed the demon serpent, winding his way north. He followed the feathered serpent, Quetzalcoatl.

DEMON #1: He never returned to Naragana. He still believed in demons. He believed in demons until the day he died.

DEMON #2: He crossed to the other side.

(All the DEMONS exit. The movie goes out; the lights bump up to full. WINNETOU and GUNTHER enter. There are animal noises from offstage.)

WINNETOU: Hear that? That is Indians talking to each other. We must be very careful.

GUNTHER: Yes, but they are not ready to attack yet. Among Indians, the leader gives the signal with a shout, then the rest join in. *(WINNETOU is making faces because GUNTHER really is a know-it-all.)* The screaming is intended to scare the shit out of people.

WINNETOU: I can make that sound. *(WINNETOU woowoos.)* Like that.

GUNTHER: I hear no birds, I hear no animals.

(The theme from The Good, the Bad and the Ugly *plays. We hear the sounds of Indians offstage. The HORDES OF INDIANS enter.)*

GUNTHER: We are surrounded by hundreds of Indians!

WINNETOU: We are captured and I am wounded.

(GUNTHER and WINNETOU are herded to the center of the stage by the HORDES OF INDIANS and tied to each other.)

HORDES #1: You mangy cur, you cheeky bugger, toilet bowl, you diarrhea lips.

HORDES #2: *(operatically)* Yes, Mr. Winnetou. You are going to be speared, impaled, poisoned, stabbed, shot, put on the wheel, hanged, tortured in front of your wives and your children. Ha, ha, ha!

ALL: *(operatically)* Tortured in front of your/our wives and your/our children.

GUNTHER: Halt! You can't do that. He is my blood brother. I beg you not to kill him.

HORDES #1: You shall have your wish, if you fight a duel.

GUNTHER: With whom and with what?

HORDES #1: With a huge Indian with a real sharp knife.

GUNTHER: Bring him on!

(HORDES #2 has exited to remove her blanket. She returns to downstage left and begins to assume various bodybuilding positions. WINNETOU is crawling off stage right.)

HORDES #1: First we will make two loops or zeroes, like a figure eight. *(She outlines them on the floor.*) You will not be allowed to step outside of these zeroes. A fight to the finish.

(*HORDES #2 walks forward into the zeroes, egging GUNTHER on.*)

GUNTHER: Braggart!
HORDES #1: Braggart, braggart.
HORDES #2: You dare insult me! I shall have the vultures devour your entrails!

(*HORDES #1 exits. During the following speech, HORDES #2 continuously changes the position of the knife in her hand to conform to what GUNTHER is saying at any particular moment.*)

GUNTHER: Entrails! So he is not going to run his knife through my heart, he is going to slit my stomach. Aha! His right arm is hanging straight down. He is holding his knife so that its handle is resting against his small finger and the blade is sticking out between thumb and index finger, cutting edge turned up. If he was going to strike downward, he must hold the knife so that the edge of the handle rests against the thumb and the blade protrudes alongside the little finger.
HORDES #2: Attack, white coward! (*Thunder and lightning. They fight. HORDES #2 is wounded.*) Mangy cur!

(*GUNTHER and HORDES #2 exit as lights go down. HORTENSIA enters, blowing a conch.*)

HORTENSIA: Tlatzoteotl in her jardin. Sweat beads on her forehead. Mama smell. (*LISA enters.*)
LISA: You have a lovely mother. (*GLORIA enters.*)
GLORIA: Six times seven is forty-two. Don't sit on the stove. Scratch your head and blow your nose. (*MURIEL enters.*)
MURIEL: I would have liked, I would have liked her to have been taller. I would have liked her to be like every other mother in the neighborhood.
HORTENSIA: Hummingbird, Mama Metiza.
LISA: You have a lovely mother.
GLORIA: I thought she was so pretty.
MURIEL: I would have liked, I would have liked.
LISA: She came into the world with an extra piece of skin covering her head. It was a caul. C-A-U-L. And Grandma said that she saved the caul and that one day she was going to give it back to Mama. Grandma kept the caul all wrapped up in tissue paper in a special box. And one day she showed it to me. She let me hold it. It looked like a piece of wrinkled brown paper bag. And then she wrapped it up again and she put it away. Grandma said "Your

mother was born with a caul, so she has strong psychic powers. She can tell the future. She can see through anybody." And Mama could tell the meanings of the symbols left by coffee grounds and tea leaves in the bottom of cups. Mama would go into a trance and she said everybody changed in the world. All sound stopped and it became so quiet that you could hear sounds that had been there before. And people who had been there before. She could actually see them and then thoughts would come into her body and she would tell you what she had received. But no one paid Mama any money. They brought crackers, buns and tea and all her friends came to her. And those friends told other friends. And so it continued. And Mama became a wise woman.

HORTENSIA: And Grandma said . . .

GLORIA: Be a good girl.

MURIEL: And Grandmother said . . .

HORTENSIA: You should be thankful . . .

GLORIA: You have a gifted mother.

LISA: And Grandma had that gift, too. And all of my grandmother's children have that gift. And all their children's children have that gift, too.

(There is a continuous repetition of these lines as they all move together and upstage and then to exit. The lights bump up. ETHEL CHRISTIAN CHRISTIANSEN enters.)

ETHEL C.C.: I used to be a white woman. It's true. I was Irish . . . , German . . . Norwegian . . . ? Then one day, my skin turned bronze and I became a shamaness. I must share with you this vision I had. I was in the subway, waiting for the F train and there was this noise and I looked up and a white light was coming toward me. No, it wasn't the F train. It was a white buffalo. And seated on that white buffalo was a noble savage, naked . . . except for his loincloth. His skin was the color of bronze, with just a touch of gold. His hair was the color of Lady Clairol No. 154, midnight blue. He wore it in long braids, intertwined with rattlesnake skins. And growing out of his skull was an eagle feather, signifying he was a chief. He was a chief, I was a shamaness. His eyes were as black as coals and energy came at me like flick, flick, flick . . . and his eyes pierced my skin and seared my heart. His lips moved, what were they saying?

(She stares as he moves closer. She starts channeling, her body contorts, she begins to sing.)

ETHEL C.C.:
Your cheatin' heart will tell on you
You cry and cry, the whole day through . . .

(PRINCESS PISSY WILLOW enters carrying a large plastic water cooler bottle on her shoulder. MINNIE HALL RUNNER enters with a large placard. Both these items are emblazoned with the words Yataholay Indian Snake Oil.)

PRINCESS P.W.: Ladies and gentlemen, two weeks ago this woman was nothing but a plain old white woman but after taking one swig of our Yataholay Indian Snake Oil, she now has a Cherokee grandmother with black braids down to here. *(She indicates her waist. MOTHER MOON FACE then enters with two large placards.)* Ladies and gentlemen, welcome to our Plastic Pow Wow Workshop. *(She indicates first placard.)*

MOTHER M.F.: A package deal. Two days, three nights plus a coupon worth $100 toward the purchase of . . .

PRINCESS P.W.: Yataholay Indian Snake Oil! *(She indicates second placard.)* Three meals a day . . .

MOTHER M.F.: For breakfast, nuts, berries in season gathered at dawn; for lunch, corn soup and

ALL: FRY BREAD!!!

MOTHER M.F.: And for dinner, anything you can catch, with a choice of vegetable; corn, beans, squash and

ALL: FRY BREAD!!!

MOTHER M.F.: And all the springwater you can drink.

PRINCESS P.W.: And all for the low, low price of $3,000 for the weekend. And now, Princess Minnie Hall Runner will walk among you and bring back our first client.

(As MINNIE H.R. is walking through the audience, PRINCESS P.W. holds up the photocopy of the face of an Indian man and the photocopy of the face of an Indian woman.)

PRINCESS P.W.: If you are a man, you will look like this *(indicating man)*. If you are a woman, you will look like this *(indicating woman)*.

(MINNIE H.R. has found someone and brings him up onstage. He is very blond and very fair-skinned.)

PRINCESS P.W.: *(to client)* What is your name?

(He tells her. PRINCESS P.W., MOTHER M.F., and MINNIE H.R. chat him up for a while. As this is going on, ETHEL C.C. is preparing the stage for the transformation ceremony. She places three bath mats across the stage. The stage right one is by itself. The center stage one is placed with a plant spritzer and toilet bowl plunger, the stage left one is placed with a paper medicine bag and the photocopy of the man.)

MOTHER M.F.: Now, (name). We will begin. *(MOTHER M.F. and MINNIE H.R. walk him to the stage right bath mat.)* You will now enter your first space. Bend over, now step forward into the space and stand up. *(He does so.)* Good, good. Now we will perform a spontaneous dance of rejuvenation. *(All perform an Indian dance complete with vocal sound effects.)* OK, (name). That was very good. You are now ready to proceed. Bend over, step backward and stand. Good. Now we will go to our second space.

(They walk to the second space. ETHEL C.C. throws the stage right bath mat off stage left. As the whole process is happening, there are constant comments about the transformation, i.e., higher cheekbones, skin browner. There is also a subplot of MOTHER M.F. having the hots for the client.)

MOTHER M.F.: Good, (name). Now bend over and step forward into your second space. Now you can stand. I will now treat you with essence of sweat lodge. *(MOTHER M.F. picks up the plant spritzer and spritzes him with water.)* Now, Princess Pissy Willow will suck the evil juices out of you.

(PRINCESS P.W. picks up the toilet plunger and sucks the floor stage left, upstage, and stage right of him. She then places the plunger on his behind and makes a sucking noise.)

That was wonderful, (name). Now bend over, step back and we will move on to your third and final space.

(ETHEL C.C. gets rid of center stage props and then moves downstage with the two final large placards. They move to the final space.)

Now, (name). Bend over, step forward and stand up.

PRINCESS P.W.: How are you feeling, (name)? Now a very important decision. You must choose the name of your Indian tribe.

(ETHEL C.C. holds up the placard with the Indian tribes written on it.)

Your choices are: #1 Condaho, #2 Mescalotex, #3 Washamakokie, #4 Rappa Hamburg, #5 Wishee Washee, #6 Gelderfoot, #7 Wanahoho. *(He thinks about it briefly and chooses an Indian tribe. The cast applauds him.)* Now, (name), you are about to make the most important decision of your life, your choice of Indian name. (Ethel C.C. *holds up the placard with the choice of Indian names on it.)* Your choices are: #1 Long Gone Lillie, #2 Cross to the Other Side, #3 Old Dead Eye Dick, #4 Old Drop by the Wayside, #5 End of the Trail, #6 Down the River, #7 Old Rocking Chair, #8 Two Dogs Fucking. (Ethel C.C. *has been vigorously pointing to the last one.)* This is not a decision to be taken lightly. Think about it. *(Everyone is now trying to get him to choose the last name. He finally chooses.)* Now, (Indian name) of the (Indian tribe). You may bend over step back and leave the final space. *(Everyone is congratulating him, shaking his hand, kissing him on the cheek. ETHEL C.C. clears the final props.)* Now, (Indian name) of the (Indian tribe), may you go in peace. On your journey, you must take this medicine bag and you must wear this in front of your face for the rest of your life.

(PRINCESS P.W. gives him the photocopy of the Indian man. MOTHER M.F. escorts him off the stage. They all line up and wave good-bye as he goes back to his seat. The lights fade. ETHEL C.C. and MOTHER M.F. exit. GLORIA and LISA stand stage left.)

LISA AND GLORIA: *(singing)*
> Out of my lodge at eventide
> Among the sobbing pines
> Footsteps echo by my side
> My Indian brave, Pale Moon
> Speak to thy love forsaken
> Thy spirit mantle throw

(MURIEL enters, doing hand signs to the words of the song.)

> Ere thou the great white dawn awaken
> And to the East thou swingest low, swingest low.

(HORTENSIA enters from between them.)

HORTENSIA: MEXICAN, MEXICAN, MEXICAN! A surge of heat would rise through my body and my face would begin to burn. All those Mexicans playing Indian parts. She ain't no Indian, she's Mexican. She speaks all that Spanish stuff. I wanted to say something, but I just stood there, my face getting redder and redder, looking out into space. Mexican, Mexican, Mexican. I am an Indian woman. I speak Spanish and I am learning Nahuatl. Before the invaders, there were no borders. My grandmother married a man whose people came from Spain, and when they came to visit, they would lock her in the back room, so they wouldn't have to look at her. Mexican, Mexican, Mexican. And there is no going back to anywhere. I'll stay here with this Indian face.

MURIEL: She looked at me and smiled and said, "I'm an Indian, too."

LISA: Sellout. Am I? White man lost in make-believe at the powwow. Craftsman, woodcarver. I like him but . . .

GLORIA: Thank-you, thank-you, thank-you. For discovering me, for recognizing me, for saving me. Thank-you for giving me the opportunity to exist. For knowing more about me than I do. Thank-you for giving me spirituality. Thank-you.

MURIEL: TOO!!

LISA: Leave me alone. Don't take your fantasies out on me. Have the decency to have your fantasies in private.

GLORIA: For only through your eyes am I remembered.

MURIEL: Sellout, sellout, sellout.

GLORIA: I am no more.

LISA: Inside, outside, I always say, if I hold my breath, they'll go away.

GLORIA: Remember me, earth mother, princess, handsome brave, warrior.

LISA: Or think of something nice to say.

MURIEL: That's nice. I smile. My rubbery lips stretch over my teeth. My eyes go blank. My shoulders go up. Sellout, sellout, sellout, sellout.

GLORIA: Thank me, thank me, thank me. My spirit, my body, my wisdom. You feed on me, create on me, enjoy my remains. Thank me, thank me, thank me.

(Thunder and lightning begin. They walk around in a circle, MURIEL with the thunder sheet, GLORIA with the rattle, LISA with the bone and HORTENSIA with the conch. All exit. Lights bump up. WINNETOU enters.)

WINNETOU: THE DEATH OF WINNETOU! *(singing)*
They'll be coming round the mountain when they come. Toot, toot.
They'll be coming round the mountain when they come. Toot, toot.
They'll be shooting Winnetou when they come. Bang, bang.
They'll be shooting Winnetou when they come. Bang, bang.

(She falls to the ground.)

Winnetou is dying.

GUNTHER: Winnetou is dying.

HORDES #2: *(offstage)* Dying, dying, dying.

HORDES #1: *(offstage)* Dead.

GUNTHER: Where has my brother been hit?

WINNETOU: Right here, *(pointing to heart)*.

GUNTHER: Here Winnetou lies, an Indian and a great man. He who once had strength now creeps about in corners like a mangy cur.

WINNETOU: Mangy cur?

GUNTHER: The Indian did not become great because he was not permitted to. Here lies the Indian, a sick and dying race. *(HORDES #1 and HORDES #2 enter.)*

HORDES #1: Who died and left you, Indian?

HORDES #2: Hey, Mr Shatterhand, knock, knock. *(GUNTHER looks confused. WINNETOU prompts him.)*

GUNTHER: Who's there?

HORDES #2: Winnetou.
GUNTHER: Winnetou who?
HORDES #2: Winnetou, lose a few.

(Blackout. All laugh in the dark. The movie comes on. HORTENSIA stands in the movie.)

HORTENSIA: He went down to the land to bring back the bones.

(Lights begin to come up.)

MURIEL: On his days off, he went to his patch of land. He planted corn, cilantro, string beans, carrots, rhubarb.
LISA: Father would sit at the window and look out at the sky. A mist would cover his eyes and the child knew he had left.
GLORIA: *(singing)*
I wish I had wings of an angel.
Over these prison walls I would fly.

(She continues to hum the tune.)

LISA: Daddy, don't go. Daddy, take me.
GLORIA: Someday.
MURIEL: Someday.
LISA: The father would say, "One of these days, I'm going to go back home."
HORTENSIA: One day his walk got slower and slower. He went out in the backyard, sat down and died.

(They all repeat "sat down and died" as GLORIA speaks.)

GLORIA: See me. I'm talking, loving, hating, drinking too much, creating, performing; my stories, my songs, my dances, my ideas. Now, I telling you, step back, move aside, sit down, hold your breath, save your own culture. Discover your own spirituality.
ALL: *(in chorus)* Now I telling you. Watch me. I'm alive. I'm not defeated. I begin. Now I telling you.

(They continue in an overlapping chorus as they exit. HORTENSIA is last, blowing the conch. Lights fade out. The movie plays to the end of the reel.)

THE END

Works Held in the NAWPA Collection

Following is a complete list of works held in the Native American Women Playwrights Archive. A more extensive list of works by these authors, as well as plays by authors whose work is not currently included in the archive and published works by other Native authors, can be found on the NAWPA Web site at www.staff.lib.muo hio.edu/nawpa.

Annette Arkeketa (Otoe-Missouria Tribe of Oklahoma and Muscogee Creek). *Hokti.* Ts. *Hokti* has been performed by the Tulsa Indian Actors' Workshop, Tulsa, Oklahoma; and the Thunderbird Theatre, Haskell Indian Nations University, Lawrence, Kansas.

Annette Arkeketa (Otoe-Missouria Tribe of Oklahoma and Muscogee Creek). *Ghost Dance: A Play.* Ts. In the summer of 1999, the actors from the Tulsa Indian Actors' Workshop (TIAW) read *Ghost Dance.* Elizabeth Theobald conducted TIAW's 2000–2001 workshop and directed the production by TIAW in its 2001–2002 production schedule.

Shirley Cheechoo (Cree). *Your Dream Was Mine* (with Greta Cheechoo). Ts. 1994.

Marie Clements (Metis). *Age of Iron.* Ts.

Marie Clements (Metis). *The Girl Who Swam Forever.* Ts. Revised draft, January 3, 1997.

Marie Clements (Metis). *Now Look What You Made Me Do.* Ts.

Marie Clements (Metis). *Urban Tattoo,* Ts. Working draft. Produced by Native Voices in New York, August 1996; and at the Women in View Festival, Vancouver, British Columbia, February 26 and March 1, 1998.

Coatlicue Theatre Company: Hortensia Colorado (Chichimec) and Elvira Colorado (Chichimec). *Open Wounds on Tlalteucli.* Ts.

Coatlicue Theatre Company: Hortensia Colorado (Chichimec) and Elvira Colorado (Chichimec). *Open Wounds on Tlalteucli.* New World Theatre, Amherst, Massachusetts, October 1994. Video recording.

Martha Kreipe de Montaño (Prairie Band Potawatomi). *Harvest Ceremony: Beyond the Thanksgiving Myth.* Ts. Revised 1997 (with Jennifer Fell Hayes).

Diane Glancy (Cherokee). *The Best Fancy Dancer the Pushmataha Pow Wow's Ever Seen.* Ts.

Diane Glancy (Cherokee). *Halfact.* Ts.

Diane Glancy (Cherokee). *Jump Kiss: Seven "Plates."* Ts.

Diane Glancy (Cherokee). *The Lesser Wars: Twelve "Sorties."* Ts.

Diane Glancy (Cherokee). *Mother of Mosquitos.* Ts.

Diane Glancy (Cherokee). *One Horse.* Ts.

Diane Glancy (Cherokee). *The Truth Teller: Four "Seasons."* Ts.

Diane Glancy (Cherokee). *Segwohi.* Ts.

Diane Glancy (Cherokee). *Stone Heart: Everyone Loves a Journey West.* Ts. 2005. World premier, February 17 through March 13, 2006, Native Voices at the Autry (Autry National Center, Los Angles), directed by Randy Reinholz, with Thirza Defoe as Sacajawea.

Diane Glancy (Cherokee). *The Sum of Winter: A Fractional Play.* Ts. 2005. Eight plays of from three to twenty-four pages each that can be presented in various combinations.

Diane Glancy (Cherokee). *The Woman Who Was a Red Deer Dressed for a Deer Dance.* Ts.

LeAnne Howe (Choctaw). *Big Pow Wow* (Roxy Gordon, coauthor). Ts.

LeAnne Howe (Choctaw). *Indian Radio Days* (Roxy Gordon, coauthor). Ts. "Theatrical radio show."

Ione (Lenape/African/French). *Njinga the Queen King (Njinga-Muchino a Muhaito): The Return of the Warrior, a Play with Music and Pageantry.* Ts. 1995.

Ione (Lenape/African/French). *Njinga the Queen King: The Return of the Warrior.* Excerpts from Brooklyn Academy of Music Next Wave Festival, Kingston, New York, Pauline Oliveros Foundation, 1993. Videocassette.

Victoria Nalani Kneubuhl (Hawai'an/Samoan). *The Annexation Debate.* Ts. 1998.

Victoria Nalani Kneubuhl (Hawai'an/Samoan). *The Conversion of Ka'ahumanu.* Ts. 1988.

Victoria Nalani Kneubuhl (Hawai'an/Samoan). *Emmalehua.* Ts. 1995. Produced by Kumu Kahua Theatre, 1996.

Victoria Nalani Kneubuhl (Hawai'an/Samoan). *Fanny and Belle.* Ts. 1998.

Victoria Nalani Kneubuhl (Hawai'an/Samoan). *January 1893.* Ts. 1993.

Victoria Nalani Kneubuhl (Hawai'an/Samoan). *Ka'iulani: A Cantata for the Theatre* (with Dennis Carroll, Robert Nelson, and Ryan Page). Ts. 1987.

Victoria Nalani Kneubuhl (Hawai'an/Samoan). *Ka Wai Ola (The Living Water).* Ts. 1998.

Victoria Nalani Kneubuhl (Hawai'an/Samoan). *Ola Na Iwi (The Bones Live).* Ts. 1994.

Victoria Nalani Kneubuhl (Hawai'an/Samoan). *Paniolo Spurs.* Ts. 1994.

Victoria Nalani Kneubuhl (Hawai'an/Samoan). *Rudyard Kipling's Just So Stories.* Ts. The stories adapted are "How the Camel Got His Hump," "How the Elephant Got His Trunk," "How the Rhinoceros Got His Skin," "The Beginning of Armadillos," "The Sing Song of Old Man Kangaroo," and "The First Letter."

Victoria Nalani Kneubuhl (Hawai'an/Samoan). *The Story of Susanna.* Ts. 1996.

Victoria Nalani Kneubuhl (Hawai'an/Samoan). *Tofa Samoa.* Ts. 1991.

Victoria Nalani Kneubuhl (Hawai'an/Samoan). *Trial of a Queen: 1895 Military Tribunal.* Ts.

Jules Arita Koostachin (Cree). *Asivak's Creation Story.* Ts.

Jules Arita Koostachin (Cree). *Asivak's Creation Story.* Ts. Cree-language version.

Vera Manuel (Shuswap-Kootenai). *Strength of Indian Women.* Ts. 1996.

Monique Mojica (Kuna/Rappahannock). *Birdwoman and the Suffragettes: A Story of Sacajawea*. Radio play. Audiotape from Canadian Broadcasting Corporation production.

Monique Mojica (Kuna/Rappahannock). *ETHNOSTRESS*. Ts. Performance essay.

Monique Mojica (Kuna/Rappahannock). *Princess Pocahontas and the Blue Spots: Two Plays*. Ts. 1991.

Denise Mosley (Cherokee). *Letters*. Ts. 1996.

JudyLee Oliva (Chickasaw). *Angel's Light*. Ts.

JudyLee Oliva (Chickasaw). *Call of the River*. Ts.

JudyLee Oliva (Chickasaw). *The Crow on the Cradle*. Ts.

JudyLee Oliva (Chickasaw). *Face in the Mirror*. Ts.

JudyLee Oliva (Chickasaw). *The Fire and the Rose*. Ts.

JudyLee Oliva (Chickasaw). *Mark of the Feather*. Ts.

JudyLee Oliva (Chickasaw). *On the Showroom Floor*. Ts.

JudyLee Oliva (Chickasaw). *Park View Café, a.k.a.* Ts.

JudyLee Oliva (Chickasaw). *Pasture*. Ts.

JudyLee Oliva (Chickasaw). *Spirit Line*. Ts.

JudyLee Oliva (Chickasaw). *Te Ata (Based on Life of Chickasaw Indian Performer, Te Ata Fisher)*. Ts. "Five Civilized Tribes Best Musical Drama Prize," 2000.

Marcie R. Rendon (White Earth Anishinabe). *Bring the Children Home*. Ts. Produced by Child's Play Theater in collaboration with Pillsbury Theater, Minneapolis, MN, September 1996.

Marcie R. Rendon (White Earth Anishinabe). *Odem Mukwa'*. Ts. In progress: synopsis and outline.

Marcie R. Rendon (White Earth Anishinabe). *Songcatcher: Frances Densmore*. Ts.

Janet Rogers (Mohawk/Tuscarora). *Pauline and Emily: Two Women*. Ts. 2000.

Spiderwoman Theater: Lisa Mayo, Gloria Miguel, Muriel Miguel (Kuna/Rappahannock). Spiderwoman Theater Papers. In 1996, the members of Spiderwoman Theater donated their papers to the Native American Women Playwrights Archive, and these materials are being processed and cataloged. The papers make up two archival boxes of correspondence, photos (personal and performance), programs, posters, flyers, publicity materials, clippings from reviews (some original, some photocopies), partial scripts, and memorabilia. Included are two audiotapes of lectures given at the University of Illinois (1996); a commercial videotape of *Sun, Moon, Feather;* a videotape of a live performance of *Sun, Moon, Feather* at Miami University, February 25, 1997, followed by the awarding of an honorary Doctor of Fine Arts to each of the three Spiderwoman sisters; and a videotape of *Winnetou's Snake Oil Show at Wigwam City,* performed at Miami University, March 1999.

Elizabeth Theobald (Cherokee). *The Circle of Thanks*. Ts. Based on a children's book by Joseph Bruchac. Adapted for the stage by Elizabeth Theobald. Performed November 3–5, 10–12, 17–19, 1999, Mashantucket Pequot Museum and Research Center, Mashantucket, Connecticut.